Gregg Medical Shorthand Dictionary

Edward E. Byers, Ed.D.
Editor in Chief
Business, Management, and Office Education
Gregg Division
McGraw-Hill Book Company
New York, New York

Shorthand written by **Jerome P. Edelman**

Gregg Division McGraw-Hill Book Company
New York/St. Louis/Dallas/San Francisco/Auckland/Düsseldorf/Johannesburg/
Kula Lumpur/London/Mexico/Montreal/New Delhi/Panama/Paris/São Paulo/
Singapore/Sydney/Tokyo/Toronto/

Gregg Medical Shorthand Dictionary

For Secretaries, Stenographers, Typists, and Students

Designer Frank Medina
Assistant Shorthand
   Production Supervisor Jerome P. Edelman
Editor Evelyn Belov
Compositor Intergraphic Technology, Inc.
Printer R. R. Donnelley & Sons Company

Library of Congress Cataloging in Publication Data

Byers, Edward Elmer.
  Gregg medical shorthand dictionary for secretaries, stenographers, typists, and students.

  1. Medical shorthand—Dictionaries. I. Edelman, Jerome P. II. Title. [DNLM: 1. Dictionaries, Medical. 2. Shorthand—Dictionaries. W13 B993g]
Z56.3.M4B9   653′.18′03   75-19197
ISBN 0-07-009504-3

Gregg Medical Shorthand Dictionary

Copyright © 1976 by McGraw-Hill, Inc. All Rights Reserved. Printed in the United States of America. No part of this publication may be reproduced, stored in a retrieval system, or transmitted, in any form or by any means, electronic, mechanical, photocopying, recording, or otherwise, without the prior written permission of the publisher.

    2 3 4 5 6 7 8 9 0 1 2 DODO 7 8 4 3 2 1 0 9 8 7

ISBN 0-07-009504-3

Preface

The *Gregg Medical Shorthand Dictionary* is intended for anyone who writes medical shorthand outlines and who transcribes and processes medical records and correspondence. It is a convenient reference that presents alphabetically the recommended shorthand outlines for a comprehensive list of currently used medical words. It is also a dictionary in that it presents the preferred spelling of medical words and their derivatives as well as their recommended syllabication. A bold accent mark (′) indicates the primary accent of each word and, when needed, a light accent mark (′) indicates a secondary accent. Definitions of words are provided in a style that is brief, clear, and to the point.

Selection of Words. The chief aim was to make the selection of medical words as broad and as complete as possible. A vast number of current medical records and publications were studied for content and vocabulary. The result was a list of more than 4,500 medical words. Such care was taken in compiling this list that it contains all that is relevant in specialized lists many times its size. Unlike other dictionaries, this compact reference omits infrequently used or archaic words. In addition to the basic vocabulary, some words were included which shorthand students have occasion to use during their training.

Shorthand Outlines. Consistency, rather than brevity of outline, was the guiding principle in the construction of the shorthand outlines in the *Gregg Medical Shorthand Dictionary*. The fastest shorthand outline, for all but the most expert writers, is the outline that can be constructed with the least mental effort and that is written consistently and analogically.

The fluency of a shorthand outline is judged by the speed with which it may be constructed by the mind and then supplied by the mind to the hand. For this reason, principles governing shortcuts and outline abbreviations are employed only for words used with such extreme frequency that the writer will recall the shortened outlines as quickly as though they were written in full. Trying to remember a long list of seldom-used medical shorthand abbreviations and shortcuts can be a burden that will almost invariably result in decreasing the writer's speed rather than increasing it.

Authority. In all instances possible, the spelling, accent, syllabication, and meaning of the medical words in this reference have been checked to ensure their agreement with *Dorland's Illustrated Medical Dictionary*,

Twenty-fourth Edition. The spelling, accent, syllabication, and meaning of words not shown in that dictionary have been checked for agreement with *Webster's Seventh New Collegiate Dictionary*, 1971 printing (published by G. & C. Merriam Company, Springfield, Massachusetts) and with *Webster's Third New International Dictionary*.

Reference Section. In addition to the list of medical words and their shorthand outlines, there is a selection of helpful reference matter for those who process medical records and related correspondence. A comprehensive list of medical combining forms is presented as an aid in determining the meaning and spelling of medical words. A list of medical abbreviations and acronyms that can serve as space savers when medical forms are being processed is also presented. However, because several systems of medical abbreviations are currently used, subject to the individual physician's (or institution's) choice, abbreviations and symbols used in medical records must be checked carefully. The drug quick reference contains the names of the generic and brand-name drugs specified in over 66 percent of all new prescriptions and refills.

This reference book, by providing medical shorthand writers with facile and fluent shorthand outlines, becomes a key to the improved use of the language of medicine.

Edward E. Byers

Contents

Alphabetical Shorthand Section   1
Reference Section:
    Combining Forms   323
    Drug Quick Reference   335
    Abbreviations   339

Shorthand

ALPHABETICAL Section

A

abasia ah·ba′zhe·ah	Inability to walk due to defect of coordination.	
abatement ah·bat′ment	Decrease in severity of pain or symptom.	
abdomen ab·do′men	Cavity of body between thorax and pelvis.	
abdominal ab·dom′i·nal	Pertaining to the abdomen.	
abduce ab·dus′	To draw away; abduct.	
abduction ab·duk′shun	Withdrawal of part from axis of body; turning outward.	
abductor ab·duk′tor	Muscle which on contraction draws part away from axis of body.	
aberrant ab·er′ant	Deviation from normal course.	
aberration ab′er·a′shun	Deviation from usual course or condition.	
abeyance ah·ba′ans	Suspension of function or action.	
abiotrophy ab′e·ot′ro·fe	Trophic failure; loss of vitality of cells.	
abirritant ab·ir′i·tant	Diminishing or relieving irritation; soothing.	
ablution ab·lu′shun	Act of washing or bathing.	
abnormal ab·nor′mal	Not normal; contrary to usual structure, position, or condition.	

SHORTHAND DICTIONARY   1

abnormality ab′nor·mal′i·te		Quality or fact of being abnormal; malformation.
abort ah·bort′		To check the usual course of disease. To miscarry.
abortion ah·bor′shun		Premature expulsion from uterus of the product of conception.
abrade ah·brad′		To rub away the external covering or layer of a part.
abrasion ah·bra′zhun		A rubbing or scraping off of skin by unusual processes.
abrasive ah·bra′siv		Causing abrasion.
abscess ab′ses		Localized collection of pus in a cavity.
abscission ab·sish′un		Removal by cutting.
absence ab′sens		Temporary loss of consciousness, as in an epileptic attack.
absolute ab′so·lut		Free from limitations.
absorbent ab·sor′bent		Sucking up or taking up by suction.
absorption ab·sorp′shun		Taking up of fluids by skin, mucous surfaces, or absorbent vessels.
abstinence ab′sti·nens		Refraining from use of food, stimulants, or sexual intercourse.

abstract ab′strakt	Powder made from a drug and brought to twice its original strength. Summary of a book or paper.
abutment ah·but′ment	Supporting structure to sustain lateral or horizontal pressure.
acanthosis ak′an·tho′sis	Thickening of prickle cell layer of skin.
accelerator ak·sel′er·a′tor	Agent or apparatus used to increase rate at which some reaction occurs.
accessory ak·ses′o·re	Supplementary.
accident ak′si·dent	Unforeseen occurrence.
acclimation ak′li·ma′shun	Process of becoming accustomed to new conditions and climate.
accommodation ah·kom′o·da′shun	Adjustment, especially of the eye for various distances.
accouchement ah·koosh·mon′	Delivery in childbed; labor.
acetate as′e·tat	Any salt of acetic acid.
acetic ah·se′tik	Pertaining to vinegar or its acid.
acetone as′e·ton	Colorless liquid; found in small amounts in normal urine, in larger amounts in diabetic urine.
acetonuria as′e·to·nu′re·ah	Excess of acetone bodies in urine.

	acetophenetidin as′e·to·fe·net′i·din	Drug to reduce fever and pain.
	ache ak	Continuous, fixed pain.
	Achilles Ah·kil′ez	Bursa or tendon at the back of the heel.
	achlorhydria ah′klor·hi′dre·ah	Absence of hydrochloric acid from gastric secretions.
	acholic ah·kol′ik	Free from bile.
	achromachia ah′kro·mak′e·ah	Grayness or whiteness of hair.
	achromatic ak′ro·mat′ik	Producing no discoloration.
	achromatosis ah·kro′mah·to′sis	Deficiency of pigmentation in tissues.
	acidify ah·sid′i·fi	To render acid.
	acidity ah·sid′i·te	Quality of being acid or sour.
	acidophilic as′i·do·fil′ik	Cellular or tissue components that readily stain with acid dyes.
	acidosis as′i·do′sis	Pathologic condition resulting from accumulation of acid in body; acid-base imbalance.
	acinus as′e·nus	Small saclike dilatation, particularly in various glands.
	aclasis ak′lah·sis	Pathologic continuity of structure.

acme ak′me	Crisis or critical stage of a disease.
acne ak′ne	Disease of sebaceous glands due to inflammation.
acomia ah·ko′me·ah	Baldness; defect of hair.
acquired ah·kwird′	Not genetic; produced by influences outside organism.
acrasia ah·kra′ze·ah	Lack of self-control; intemperance.
acrid ak′rid	Pungent; producing irritation.
acrisia ah·kri′se·ah	Uncertainty in the nature or character of a disease.
acrodermatitis ak′ro·der′mah·ti′- tis	Inflammation of skin of hands or feet.
acromastitis ak′ro·mas·ti′tis	Inflammation of the nipple.
acromegaly ak′ro·meg′ah·le	Condition characterized by increased size of nose, jaws, fingers, and toes.
acronyx ak′ro·niks	An ingrowing nail.
acrophobia ak′ro·fo′be·ah	Fear of high places.
ACTH	Abbreviation for adrenocorticotropic hormone. Protein hormone that stimulates the adrenal cortex.

actinogram ak·tin′o·gram	Roentgenogram. A film produced by means of roentgen rays.
acuity ah·ku′i·te	Acuteness or sharpness of vision.
acupuncture ak′u·pungk′tur	Insertion of long fine needles into tissues to relieve pain.
acus a′kus	Needle or needlelike process.
acute ah·kut′	Sharp; poignant; having a short and severe course.
acyesis ah′si·e′sis	Sterility in women.
adamantine ad′ah·man′tin	Pertaining to enamel of teeth.
adaptation ad′ap·ta′shun	Power of eye to adjust to variations in intensity of light.
addict ad′ikt	Someone who habitually or obsessively uses a drug or alcohol.
addiction ah·dik′shun	Compulsion to maintain the habitual use of drugs or of alcohol.
adduct ah·dukt′	To draw toward median line of body or neighboring part.
adenalgia ad′e·nal′je·ah	Pain in a gland.
adenic ah·de′nik	Pertaining to or resembling a gland.
adenitis ad′e·ni′tis	Inflammation of a gland.

	adenocarcinoma ad′e·no·kar′si·no′- mah	Cancer of glandular tissue.
	adenoid ad′e·noid	Glandular; of glandlike structure.
	adenoidectomy ad′e·noid·ek′to- me	Excision of pharyngeal tonsil (adenoids).
	adenoma ad′e·no′mah	Epithelial tumor, usually benign.
	adenomatous ad′e·nom′ah·tus	Pertaining to adenoma or to glandular hyperplasia.
	adenomyosis ad′e·no·mi·o′sis	Benign overgrowth of endometrium into uterine musculature.
	adenopathy ad′e·nop′ah·the	Any disease of the glands, particularly the lymphatic glands.
	adenotomy ad′e·not′o·me	Incision or dissection of glands.
	adenotonsillectomy ad′e·no·ton′sil- lek′to·me	Removal of tonsils and adenoids.
	adhere ad·her′	To cling together; to become fastened.
	adhesion ad·he′zhun	Property of remaining in close approximation.
	adhesive ad·he′siv	Substance causing close adherence of adjoining surfaces.
	adiadochokinesia ah·di′ah·do′ko·ki- ne′se·ah	Inability to perform rapidly alternating movements.

| | adipose
ad′i·pos | Fatty or fatlike; fat. |
| | adiposis
ad′i·po′sis | Obesity or corpulence. |
| | adjustment
ad·just′ment | Rearrangement of physical parts or revision of mental attitudes. |
| | adjuvant
ad′ju·vant | Assisting or aiding. |
| | admission
ad·mish′un | Action of being received into a hospital or clinic. |
| | adnexa
ad·nek′sah | Appendages or adjunct parts. |
| | adolescence
ad′o·les′ens | Period of life beginning with appearance of secondary sex characteristics. |
| | adrenal
ad·re′nal | Situated near the kidney; an adrenal gland. |
| | adrenalectomy
ad·re′nal·ek′-
to·me | Excision of the adrenal glands. |
| | Adrenalin
Ad·ren′ah·lin | Trademark for preparation of epinephrine. |
| | adsorbent
ad·sor′bent | Substance which takes up another substance. |
| | adsorption
ad·sorp′shun | Attachment of a substance such as a gas or liquid onto a surface. |
| | adulterant
ah·dul′ter·ant′ | Substance used as an addition to another substance. |

	adventitia ad′ven·tish′e·ah	Outer covering or coat of an artery or organ.
	adventitious ad′ven·tish′us	Accidental or acquired; out of normal place.
	advitant ad′vi·tant	Vitamin.
	aerated a′er·at′ed	Charged with air.
	aerobic a·er·o′bik	Growing only in presence of molecular oxygen.
	aerophagy a′er·of′ah·je	Spasmodic; swallowing of air.
	aerophobia a′er·o·fo′be·ah	Abnormal dread of fresh or bad air.
	aerosol a′er·o·sol′	Solution which can be finely atomized and dispersed as a mist.
	afebrile ah·feb′ril	Without symptoms of fever.
	affectation af′ek·ta′shun	Artificiality of manner or behavior.
	affection ah·fek′shun	Mental element common to states of emotion or feeling. Morbid condition or diseased state.
	afferent af′er·ent	Carrying toward some point of reference or conducting toward a center.
	affinity ah·fin′i·te	Inherent likeness or relationship.

afterbirth af′ter·berth′	Placenta and membranes cast from uterus following birth of child.	
agar ag′ar	Bulk laxative; nutrient media for bacterial cultures.	
agglutination ah·gloo′ti·na′shun	Joining together or uniting.	
aggregate ag′re·gat	To crowd or cluster together.	
aggression ah·gresh′un	A forceful action.	
agitation aj′e·ta′shun	Exceeding restlessness with physical motion or mental disturbance.	
agony ag′o·ne	Severe pain or extreme suffering.	
agraffe ah·graf′	Clamplike instrument for keeping edges of wound together.	
ague a′gu	Malarial fever; chill.	
ailment al′ment	Any disease or affection of body.	
akinesia ak′i·ne′se·ah	Loss of voluntary movements.	
alar a′lar	Pertaining to the armpit; axillary.	
alba al′bah	White; used as an adjective in anatomical names.	
albumin al·bu′min	A protein soluble in water and coagulable by heat.	

	albuminuria al′bu·mi·nu′re·ah	Presence in urine of serum albumin or serum globulin.	
	alcohol al′ko·hol	Liquid used internally as cardiac stimulant and locally as antiseptic and astringent.	
	alcoholism al′ko·hol′izm	Drinking of alcoholic beverages in excess.	
	aleukemia ah′lu·ke′me·ah	Absence or deficiency of leukocytes in the blood.	
	aleukemic ah′lu·ke′mik	Marked by deficiency of leukocytes in blood.	
	algesia al·je′ze·ah	Sensitivity to pain.	
	alible al′i·bl	Nutritive; assimilable as food.	
	alienation al′yen·a′shun	Mental derangement.	
	alignment ah·lin′ment	The act of arranging in a line. Bringing natural teeth into normal articulation.	
	alimentary al′e·men′tar·e	Pertaining to the nutritive process.	
	alimentation al′e·men·ta′shun	Act of nourishing with food.	
	aliquot al′e·kwot	Part of number which will divide it without a remainder.	
	alkali al′kah·li	Compounds which form soluble soaps with fatty acids, turn red litmus blue, and form soluble carbonates.	

	alkaline al′kah·lin	Having the reactions of an alkali.
	alkalosis al′kah·lo′sis	Pathologic condition characterized by increase in pH.
	allergen al′er·jen	Substance capable of inducing allergy.
	allergic ah·ler′jik	Pertaining to, caused by, affected with, allergy.
	allergist al′er·jist	Physician specializing in diagnosis and treatment of allergies.
	allergy al′er·je	Hypersensitivity to a particular allergen.
	alopecia al′o·pe′she·ah	Disease in which hair falls out.
	alpha al′fah	First letter of the Greek alphabet, used with a chemical name to indicate first of a series of compounds.
	alter awl′ter	To castrate.
	alternating awl′ter·nat′ing	Occurring in regular succession; alternately direct and reversed.
	alveolar al·ve′o·lar	Pertaining to an alveolus, a small saclike dilatation or cavity.
	alveolectomy al′ve·o·lek′to·me	Surgical preparation of jaw for prosthesis.
	alveoloplasty al·ve′o·lo·plas′te	Surgical improvement of shape of alveolar process.
	alveolus al·ve′o·lus	A cavity, depression, or pit; a tooth socket.

alveus al′ve·us	Trough or canal.	
alvus al′vus	Abdomen with its contained viscera.	
amatory am′ah·to′re	Pertaining to love or sexual desire.	
amaurosis am′aw·ro′sis	Absolute blindness.	
ambidextrous am′be·dek′strus	Characterized by ability to use either hand for manual tasks.	
ambient am′be·ent	Surrounding; encompassing; prevailing.	
ambivalence am·biv′ah·lens	Simultaneous existence of opposite attitudes toward same object.	
amblyopia am′ble·o′pe·ah	Dimness of vision without organic lesion of eye.	
ambulance am′bu·lans	Vehicle for conveying sick and wounded.	
ambulant am′bu·lant	Walking or able to walk.	
ameba ah·me′bah	Colorless, jellylike one-celled organism.	
amelioration ah·mel′yo·ra′shun	Improvement in condition of a patient.	
amenorrhea ah·men′o·re′ah	Absence or abnormal stoppage of menstruation.	
amentia ah·men′she·ah	Mental deficiency.	

ametropia am′e·tro′pe·ah	Imperfection in refractive powers of eye.
amitosis am′i·to′sis	Direct cell division.
ammonia ah·mo′ne·ah	Colorless alkaline gas.
ammonium ah·mo′ne·um	Stimulant to heart and respiration.
amnesia am·ne′se·ah	Lack or loss of memory.
amnion am′ne·on	Innermost of fetal membranes forming fluid-filled sac for protection of embryo.
Amoeba Ah·me′bah	Protozoa of the subphylum *Sarcodina*.
amor a′mor	Love.
amotio ah·mo′she·o	A removing.
amphoric am·for′ik	Breath sound.
amphoteric am·fo·ter′ik	Having characteristics which affect both red and blue litmus.
amplitude am′ple·tud	Fullness; extent or range.
ampule am′pul	Small glass container capable of being sealed.
ampulla am·pul′ah	Dilated part of a canal or duct.

amputation am′pu·ta′shun	Removal of a limb or other appendage of body.	
amputee am′pu·te′	Person who has one or more limbs amputated.	
amygdaloid ah·mig′dah·loid	Like a tonsil or an almond.	
amyl am′il	The univalent radical.	
amylaceous am′i·la′she·us	Starchy; containing starch.	
amylase am′i·las	Enzyme which hydrolyzes starch to sugar.	
amyloid am′i·loid	Resembling starch.	
amyotrophy ah′mi·ot′ro·fe	Atrophy of muscle tissue.	
Amytal Am′i·tal	Trademark for amobarbital. Sedative and hypnotic; preliminary to surgical anesthesia.	
anabolism ah·nab′o·lizm	Synthetic or constructive metabolism.	
anacidity an′ah·sid′i·te	Lack of normal acidity.	
anaerobic an′a·er·o′bik	Pertaining to an atmosphere devoid of oxygen.	
anaerosis an′a·er·o′sis	Interruption of respiratory function.	
anal a′nal	Pertaining to the anus.	

analeptic an'ah·lep'tik	A drug which acts as a stimulant of the central nervous system; for example, caffeine.
analgesia an'al·je'ze·ah	Insensibility to pain.
analgesic an'al·je'zik	An agent for relieving pain.
analogous ah·nal'o·gus	Resembling or similar in some respects.
analysis ah·nal'i·sis	Separation into component parts or elements; pl. *analyses*.
anamnesis an'am·ne'sis	Faculty of memory.
anaphia an·a'fe·ah	Lack or loss of sense of touch.
anaphoria an'ah·fo're·ah	Tendency for visual axes of both eyes to divert above horizontal plane.
anaphylaxis an'ah·fi·lak'sis	Exaggerated reaction to foreign protein or other substances.
anasarca an'ah·sar'kah	Generalized accumulation of fluid in tissues.
anastomosis ah·nas'to·mo'sis	A surgical or pathologic formation between two normally separate spaces or organs.
anatomy ah·nat'o·me	Science of the structure of body and relation of its parts.
anchorage ang'ker·ij	Surgical fixation; fixation of fillings or artificial crowns or bridges.

androgen an′dro·jen	Hormone which induces development of male sex characteristics.
anemia ah·ne′me·ah	A deficiency in quantity or quality of blood.
anesthesia an′es·the′ze·ah	Full or partial loss of feeling or sensation.
anesthetic an′es·thet′ik	Drug or agent used to abolish sensation of pain.
anesthetize ah·nes′the·tiz	To put under influence of an anesthetic.
aneurysm an′u·rizm	A sac filled with blood formed by dilatation in the wall of an artery or vein.
angiectasis an′je·ek′tah·sis	Dilatation of a blood vessel.
angiitis an′je·i′tis	Inflammation of a blood or lymph vessel.
angina an′ji·nah	Spasmodic choking or suffocative pain; often used to describe the causative disease.
angioblast an′je·o·blast	Tissue from which blood cells and vessels arise.
angiodermatitis an′je·o·der·mah-ti′tis	Inflammation of vessels of skin.
angiofibroma an′je·o·fi·bro′mah	Skin disease characterized by eruption of red papules.
angiokinesis an′je·o·ki·ne′sis	Blood vessel activity.

	angioma an'je·o'mah	Tumor of blood vessels.
	angiomalacia an'je·o·mah·la'- she·ah	Softening of the walls of blood vessels.
	angiomatous an'je·om'ah·tus	Of the nature of a tumor whose cells form blood or lymph vessels.
	angiorrhexis an'je·o·rek'sis	Rupturing of a blood vessel.
	angulus ang'gu·lus	An angle of a particular body structure or part.
	anima an'e·mah	The soul. Active principle of a drug.
	anion an'i·on	Ion with a negative charge.
	ankle ang'kl	Part of leg just above foot.
	ankyloglossia ang'ki·lo·glos'e·ah	Tonguetie.
	ankylosis ang'ki·lo'sis	Stiffness or fixation of a joint.
	anlage ahn'lah·geh *or* an'laj	A rudiment. The earliest embryonic cells or tissue from which an organ or part develops.
	annular an'u·lar	Shaped like a ring.
	annulus an'u·lus	Ringlike anatomical structure; also spelled *anulus*.
	anococcygeal a'no·kok·sij'e·al	Pertaining to the anus and coccyx.

anomaly ah·nom′ah·le	Marked deviation from normal standard.
anoplasty a′no·plas′te	Plastic or restorative operation on the anus.
anorectic an′o·rek′tik	Without appetite for food. Substance causing that condition.
anorexia an′o·rek′se·ah	Loss or lack of appetite for food.
anoxia an·ok′se·ah	Absence or lack of oxygen in body tissues.
ansa an′sah	A looplike structure; pl. *ansae*.
antacid ant·as′id	Substance that neutralizes acidity.
antalgic ant·al′jik	Pain reliever.
antalkaline ant·al′kah·lin′	Agent that neutralizes alkalinity.
antasthenic ant′as·then′ik	Agent for restoring the strength.
antatrophic ant′ah·trof′ik	Correcting or opposing the progress of atrophy.
antecubital an′te·ku′bi·tal	Situated in front of the elbow.
antefebrile an′te·feb′ril	Before onset of fever.
ante mortem an′te mor′tem	Before death.

	antenatal an′te·na′tal	Occurring prior to birth.	
	Antergan Ant″er·gan	Trademark for an antihistamine compound.	
	anterior an·te′re·or	Situated in front of or in forward part of belly surface of body.	
	anteroposterior an′ter·o·pos·te′-re·or	From front to back; from anterior to posterior surface.	
	anteverted an′te·vert′ed	Tipped or bent forward.	
	anthrax an′thraks	Carbuncle or other infection caused by anthrax bacillus.	
	antibiotics an′ti·bi·ot′iks	Drugs which destroy bacteria.	
	antibody an′ti·bod′e	Substance formed by body in response to infection.	
	anticoagulant an′ti·ko·ag′u·lant	Any substance which delays coagulation of blood.	
	anticonvulsive an′ti·kon·vul′siv	Preventing or relieving convulsions.	
	antidote an′ti·dot	Remedy for counteracting a poison.	
	antifebrile an′ti·feb′ril	Substance for diminishing fever.	
	antigen an′ti·jen	Any substance introduced into body which stimulates production of antibodies.	
	antiglobulin an′ti·glob′u·lin	An antibody to soluble antigen which precipitates globulin.	

antihistamines an′ti·his′tah·minz	Drugs which counteract action of histamines.
antimicrobial an′ti·mi·kro′be·al	Destroying microorganisms.
antimony an′ti·mo′ne	An arterial and cardiac depressant.
antiotomy an′ti·ot′o·me	Excision of the tonsils.
antipyretic an′ti·pi·ret′ik	Agent for relieving or reducing fever.
antipyrine an′ti·pi′rin	Antipyretic, antirheumatic, and analgesic.
antiseptic an′ti·sep′tic	Prevents decay or putrefaction.
antispasmodic an′ti·spaz·mod′ik	Capable of relieving spasms.
antitoxin an′ti·tok′sin	Antibody to toxin of a microorganism.
antrum an′trum	Cavity or hollow space in a bone.
anulus an′u·lus	Ringlike anatomical structure.
anuresis an·u·re′sis	Retention of urine in bladder.
anuria ah·nu′re·ah	Failure of kidneys to secrete urine.
anus a′nus	Distal or terminal orifice of alimentary canal.

anvil an′vil	The middle one of the chain of ossicles in the middle ear, so termed for its resemblance to an anvil.
anxiety ang·zi′e·te	Feeling of apprehension, uncertainty, and fear.
aorta a·or′tah	Main trunk from which systemic arterial system proceeds.
aortarctia a′or·tark′she·ah	Constriction of the aorta.
aortectasia a′or·tek·ta′ze·ah	Dilatation of the aorta.
aortic a·or′tik	Of or pertaining to the aorta.
aortitis a′or·ti′tis	Inflammation of the aorta.
aortography a′or·tog′rah·fe	Roentgenography of the aorta.
apathy ap′ah·the	Lack of feeling or emotion; indifference.
apepsia ah·pep′se·ah	Cessation or failure of digestive functions.
aperient ah·pe′re·ent	Mildly cathartic.
apertura ap′er·tu′rah	General term used in anatomical nomenclature to designate an opening.
aperture ap′er·chur	An opening or orifice.
apex a′peks	Summit; the point of a conical structure.

aphakia	Congenital absence of lens of eye.
ah·fa′ke·ah	
aphakic	Having no lens in the eye.
ah·fa′kik	
aphasia	Loss or impairment of capacity to use words as symbols of ideas.
ah·fa′ze·ah	
aphonia	Loss of voice.
ah·fo′ne·ah	
aphtha	Small ulcer; thrush.
af′thah	
apical	Pertaining to or located at the apex.
ap′e·kal	
apices	Plural of apex.
ap′i·sez	
apicolysis	Operation of collapsing upper portion of lung.
a′pe·kol′i·sis	
aplasia	Failure of an organ or part to develop normally.
ah·pla′se·ah	
aplastic	No tendency to develop new tissue.
ah·plas′tik	
apnea	Transient suspension of respiration; asphyxia.
ap·ne′ah	
apomorphine	Morphine derivative to induce vomiting and sleep; an expectorant.
ap′o·mor′fin	
aponeurosis	Flat, tendinous sheet to which muscle is attached with part that it moves.
ap′o·nu·ro′sis	
apoplexy	Stroke marked by coma followed by paralysis.
ap′o·plek′se	

aposia ah·po′ze·ah	Absence of thirst.
apparatus ap′ah·ra′tus	Arrangement of parts acting together in some special function.
appendage ah·pen′dij	Thing or part added.
appendectomy ap′en·dek′to·me	Surgical removal of the appendix.
appendicitis ah·pen′di·si′tis	Inflammation of the appendix.
appendix ah·pen′diks	Supplementary part attached to main structure; appendix vermiformis.
appetite ap′e·tit	Natural and recurring desire, especially for food.
appliance ah·pli′ans	A device used for performing or for facilitating the performance of a particular function. In dentistry, a device used in mouth to produce or prevent movement of teeth.
apprehension ap′re·hen′shun	Anticipatory fear.
approximate ah·prok′si·mat′	To bring close together.
apraxia ah·prak′se·ah	Inability to carry out purposeful movements.
aptitude ap′ti·tud	Natural ability and skill in certain lines of endeavor.
aqua ah′kwah	Water; pl. *aquae*.

aqueduct ak'we·dukt	Passage or channel for passage of fluid in the body structure.
aqueous a'kwe·us	Watery; prepared with water.
arachnoid ah·rak'noid	Resembling a spider's web.
Aralen Ar'ah·len	Trademark for a preparation of chloroquine.
arbor ar'bor	Treelike structure or part; pl. *arbores*.
arc ark	Any part of circumference of a circle.
arch arch	Structure with a curved or bowlike outline.
arcus ar'kus	Structure having curved or bowlike outline; also arch.
area a're·ah	Specific plane surface or portion of an organ.
areola ah·re'o·lah	Minute space or interstice in a tissue; circular area surrounding a central point.
arrest ah·rest'	Stoppage; act of stopping.
arrhenomimetic ah·re'no·mi·met'ik	Phenomena in female resembling those in male.
arrhythmia ah·rith'me·ah	Absence of normal rhythm of heart beat.
arsenic ar'se·nik	Medicinal and poisonous element.

arsphenamine ars·fen′ah·min	Powder used in treatment of syphilis and yaws infections.
arteria ar·te′re·ah	Anatomical term for any vessel carrying blood away from the heart; pl. *arteriae*.
arterial ar·te′re·al	Pertaining to an artery or to the arteries.
arteriogram ar·te′re·o·gram	Tracing of the arterial pulse.
arteriography ar′te·re·og′rah·fe	Description of arteries; recording of arterial pulse.
arteriola ar·te′re·o′lah	Minute arterial branch; also arteriole.
arteriopathy ar′te·re·op′ah·the	Any arterial disease.
arteriorrhagia ar·te′re·o′ra′je·ah	Arterial hemorrhage.
arteriorrhaphy ar·te′re·or′ah·fe	Suture of an artery.
arteriorrhexis ar·te′re·o·rek′sis	Rupture of an artery.
arteriosclerosis ar·te′re·o·skle·ro′-sis	Thickening of the artery walls.
arteriosclerotic ar·te′re·o·skle-rot′ik	Pertaining to, or affected with, arteriosclerosis.
arteritis ar′te·ri′tis	Inflammation of an artery.
artery ar′ter·e	Vessel through which blood passes away from the heart.

arthralgia ar·thral′je·ah	Joint pain.
arthritis ar·thri′tis	Inflammation of a joint.
arthrocele ar′thro·sel	A swollen joint.
arthrodesis ar·throd′e·sis	Surgical fixation of joint.
arthrolysis ar·throl′i·sis	Operative loosening of adhesions in ankylosed joint.
arthropathy ar·throp′ah·the	Any joint disease.
arthrophyma ar′thro·fi′mah	The swelling of a joint.
arthrosis ar·thro′sis	Any disease of the joints.
articulate ar·tik′u·lat	Divided into or united by joints. Adjustment of teeth.
articulatio ar·tic′u·la′she·o	Used in anatomical nomenclature to designate place of junction between two bones.
articulation ar·tik·u·la′shun	Place of union or junction between two or more bones of skeleton.
ascites ah·si′tez	Abnormal effusions of fluid into abdominal cavity.
aseptic ah·sep′tik	Free from infection.

asphyxia as·fik′se·ah	Suffocation.
aspirate as′pi·rat	To draw by suction.
aspiration as′pi·ra′shun	Act of breathing or drawing in.
aspirator as′pi·ra′tor	Apparatus for removing fluids or gases from a cavity by suction.
aspirin as′pi·rin	Acetylsalicylic acid.
assimilation ah·sim′e·la′shun	Transformation of food into living tissue.
association ah·so′se·a′shun	Coordination of functions of similar parts.
asthenia as·the′ne·ah	Weakness; loss of strength and energy.
asthenic as·then′ik	Characterized by weakness or feebleness.
asthma az′mah	Disease with wheezing, cough, and sense of constriction.
asthmatic az·mat′ik	Pertaining to or affected with asthma.
astigmatism ah·stig′mah·tizm	Faulty vision from irregularity in curvature of refractive surfaces of eye.
astringent as·trin′jent	Causing contraction and arresting discharges.
asymmetry a·sim′e·tre	Not equally proportioned.

asymptomatic ah′simp·to·mat′ik	Showing or causing no symptoms.
asynergy ah·sin′er·je	Lack of coordination among parts or organs.
ataxia ah·tak′se·ah	Loss of muscular coordination.
atelectasis at′e·lek′tah·sis	Imperfect expansion of lung; collapse of lung.
athetosis ath′e·to′sis	Continuous movement of fingers and toes.
atlas at′las	First cervical vertebra; ringlike.
atonic ah·ton′ik	Lacking normal tone or strength.
atraumatic a′traw·mat′ik	Not inflicting or causing damage or injury.
atresia ah·tre′ze·ah	Absence or closure of a normal body opening.
atrium a′tre·um	A chamber affording entrance to another organ; pl. *atria*.
atrophoderma at′ro·fo·der′mah	Atrophy of skin or any part of it.
atrophy at′ro·fe	Wasting away of cell, tissue, organ, or part due to defect or nutritional failure.
atropine at′ro·pin	Alkaloid used to relax muscles of organs, increase heart rate, dilate pupils.
attachment ah·tach′ment	State of being fixed or attached.

	attendant ah·ten′dant	Nonprofessional person attached to hospital.
	attenuate ah·ten′u·at	To render thin or less virulent.
	attitude at′i·tud	Posture or position of the body.
	attrition ah·trish′un	Physiologic wearing away of a substance or structure (such as teeth).
	atypical a·tip′e·kal	Irregular; not conformable.
	audiometer aw′de·om′e·ter	Instrument to test the power of hearing.
	auditory aw′di·to·re	Pertaining to sense of hearing.
	aura aw′rah	Sensation preceding a paroxysmal attack.
	aural aw′ral	Pertaining to the ear.
	Aureomycin Aw′re·o·mi′sin	Trademark for specific antibiotic substance.
	auricle aw′re·kl	The pinna or flap of ear. Applied also to ear-shaped appendage of either atrium of the heart.
	auris aw′ris	The ear.
	aurist aw′rist	A hearing specialist.
	auscultation aws′kul·ta′shun	Act of listening for sounds within body.

	autoclave aw′to·klav	Apparatus for effecting sterilization by steam under pressure.
	autokinesis aw′to·ki·ne′sis	Voluntary motion.
	automatic aw′to·mat′ic	Spontaneous or involuntary.
	autonomic aw′to·nom′ic	Self-controlling; functionally independent.
	autopsy aw′top·se	Examination of the body after death.
	avitaminosis a·vi′tah·mi·no′sis	Condition due to deficiency of vitamins in diet.
	avulsion ah·vul′shun	The tearing away of a structure or part.
	axilla ak·sil′ah	Small hollow beneath arm; armpit; pl. *axillae*.
	axillary ak′si·lar′e	Pertaining to armpit.
	axis ak′sis	A line about which a revolving body turns.
	axon ak′son	Axis of body; the spine.

B

	Babinski Bah·bin′ske	Nineteenth-century French physician remembered for many important developments bearing his name: Babinski's law, reflex, sign, syndrome.

bacillus bah·sil′us	Any rod-shaped bacterium; pl. *bacilli*.
bacitracin bas′i·tra′sin	Antibiotic active against gram-positive organisms.
backache bak′ak	Pain in lower lumbar region of back.
bacterial bak·te′re·al	Pertaining to or caused by bacteria.
bactericidal bak′ter·i·si′dal	An agent or measure that destroys bacteria.
bacterium bak·te′re·um	Any rod-shaped microorganism; pl. *bacteria*.
balanitis bal′ah·ni′tis	Inflammation of glans penis.
balm bahm	Healing or soothing medicine.
bandage ban′dij	Strip or piece of gauze for wrapping or applying over a body part.
barbital bar′be·tal	A central nervous system depressant.
barbiturate bar·bit′u·rat	A salt of barbituric acid.
barium ba′re·um	Metallic element belonging to the alkaline earths.
barren bar′en	Sterile; unfruitful.
barrier bar′e·er	An obstruction.

basal ba′sal	Pertaining to or situated near a base; fundamental.
basilar bas′i·lar	Pertaining to a base or basal part.
basis ba′sis	Lower, basic, or fundamental part of a structure or an organ.
basophil ba′so·fil	Structural cell; polymorpho-nuclear granulocyte.
basophilic ba·so·fil′ik	Staining readily with basic dyes.
bastard bas′tard	Person born out of wedlock.
bedpan bed′pan	Vessel for receiving urinary and fecal discharges.
behavior be·hav′yor	Manner in which an individual acts or performs.
belching belch′ing	The eructation of gas.
belladonna bel′ah·don′ah	Preparation used to relieve gastrointestinal spasm.
belly bel′e	Abdomen; fleshy, contractile portion of a muscle.
Benadryl Ben′ah·dril	Trademark for an antihistamine preparation.
benign be·nin′	Not malignant, not recurrent.
Benzedrine Ben′ze·dren	Trademark for preparations of amphetamine whose vapors shrink nasal mucosa.

benzidine ben′zi·din	Compound used as a test for blood.	
benzocaine ben′zo·kan	Ointment used for relief of itching hemorrhoids and dermatoses.	
bicarbonate bi·kar′bo·nat	Salt having two equivalents of carbonic acid to one of a basic substance.	
biceps bi′seps	Muscle having two heads.	
bicuspid bi·kus′pid	Having two cusps or points; premolar tooth.	
bifocal bi·fo′kal	Having two foci; compound spectacle for both near and distant vision.	
bifurcate bi·fur′kat	To divide into two like a fork.	
bifurcation bi′fur·ka′shun	Division into two branches.	
bilateral bi·lat′er·al	Having two sides.	
bile bil	Fluid secreted by liver and poured into intestine to absorb fats.	
biliary bil′e·a·re	Pertaining to bile, bile ducts, or gallbladder.	
bilious bil′yus	Characterized by bile or excess of bile.	
bilirubin bil′e·roo′bin	A red bile pigment.	

binary bi′na·re		Made up of two equal parts or elements.
binder bind′er		Support for abdomen or breasts following childbirth.
biology bi·ol′o·je		Science of life and living organisms.
biopsy bi′op·se		Removal and examination of tissue for diagnosis.
birthmark berth′mark		A circumscribed new growth of congenital origin.
bisection bi·sek′shun		Cutting into two parts.
bisexual bi·seks′u·al		Having gonads of both sexes.
bismuth biz′muth		Metal whose salts are used in inflammatory diseases of stomach and intestines.
bladder blad′er		Sac that holds the urine.
bland bland		Mild or soothing.
blastocyte blas′to·sit		Embryonic cell that has not yet become differentiated.
blastoma blas·to′mah		A true tumor.
bleb bleb		A skin blister filled with fluid.
bleeder bled′er		One who bleeds freely.

SHORTHAND DICTIONARY 35

	blepharitis blef'ah·ri'tis	Inflammation of eyelid.
	blepharoplasty blef'ah·ro·plas'te	Plastic surgery for repair of eyelid.
	blepharoplegia blef'ah·ro·ple'- je·ah	Paralysis of the eyelid.
	blepharotomy blef'ah·rot'o·me	Incision of the eyelid.
	blindness blind'nes	Lack or loss of ability to see.
	blister blis'ter	Localized collection of fluid in epidermis causing an elevation.
	blood blud	Fluid carrying nutriment and oxygen to body cells.
	body bod'e	Trunk or animal frame with its organs. Cadaver or corpse.
	boil boil	Furuncle.
	bolus bo'lus	Rounded mass of food ready to be swallowed.
	borborygmus bor'bo·rig'mus	Rumbling noises from flatus (gas) propelled through intestines.
	boss bos	A rounded swelling on surface of a bone.
	botulism bot'u·lizm	Food poisoning from improperly canned or preserved foods.

| bougie | Slender cylinder for introduction into urethra, rectum, or other orifice. |
| boo·zhe′ | |

bouillon
boo′yon′ — A broth or soup from flesh of animals. A biological culture medium.

bowel
bow′el — The intestine.

bowleg
bo′leg — Outward curve of one or both legs at or below knee; genu varum.

brachial
bra′ke·al — Of or pertaining to arm.

brachialgia
bra′ke·al′je·ah — Pain in the arm or arms.

brachiotomy
bra′ke·ot′o·me — Surgical cutting or removal of arm.

brachium
bra′ke·um — The arm, especially above the elbow.

bradycardia
brad′e·kar′de·ah — Abnormal slowness of heartbeat to 60 or less.

breast
brest — Anterior aspect of chest and glandular structure it bears.

breathing
breth′ing — Act of moving air in and out of the lungs; respiration.

bridge
brij — Dental prosthesis replacing one or more missing teeth.

bromide
bro′mid — A cardiac and cerebral depressant.

Bromsulphalein Brom·sul′fah·lin	Trademark for preparation used to determine functional capacity of liver.
bronchial brong′ke·al	Pertaining to the bronchi or bronchia.
bronchiectasis brong′ke·ek′tah·sis	Dilatation of the bronchial tubes.
bronchiolitis brong′ke·o·li′tis	Bronchopneumonia. Inflammation of lungs.
bronchitis brong·ki′tis	Inflammation of the bronchial tubes.
bronchium brong′ke·um	One subdivision of a bronchus.
bronchocele brong′ko·sel	Dilatation of a bronchus. Goiter.
bronchocephalitis brong′ko·sef′ah·li′tis	Whooping cough.
bronchography brong·kog′rah·fe	Roentgenography of lung.
bronchopneumonia brong′ko·nu·mo′ne·ah	Inflammation of the lungs and bronchioles.
bronchopulmonary brong′ko·pul′mo·ner′e	Pertaining to lungs and their air passages.
bronchoscope brong′ko·skop	Instrument for inspecting interior of bronchi.
bronchoscopy brong·kos′ko·pe	Examination of bronchi by means of the bronchoscope.

bronchus bronɡ′kus	One of the larger air passages within the lungs; pl. *bronchi*.
bruit brwe	Abnormal sound heard in auscultation.
bubo bu′bo	Inflammatory swelling of a lymphatic gland.
buccal buk′al	Pertaining to the cheek.
bulbar bul′bar	Pertaining to a bulb.
bulbus bul′bus	A rounded mass or enlargement.
bulla bul′ah	Blister filled with watery fluid.
burn burn	Lesion caused by the contact of heat.
bursa bur′sah	Small fluid-filled sac situated in tissues where friction would otherwise develop.
bursitis bur·si′tis	Inflammation of a bursa.
buttocks but′oks	Two fleshy masses formed by the gluteal muscles.

C

cachectic kah·kek′tik	Marked by a wasted appearance.
cachexia kah·kek′se·ah	State of ill health characterized by malnutrition.

cadaver kah·dav′er	A dead body preserved for anatomical study.
caduceus kah·du′se·us	A symbol of medical profession; emblem of Marine Corps, U.S. Army.
caffeine kaf′e·in	A central nervous system stimulant.
calcaneus kal·ka′ne·us	Heel bone; largest tarsal bone.
calcareous kal·ka′re·us	Chalky; having appearance of lime.
calcification kal′se·fi·ka′shun	Condition characterized by deposits of lime salts in tissue.
calcium kal′si·um	Yellow metal, the basic element of lime called coagulation factor IV.
calculous kal′ku·lus	A stone (n). Affected with calculi (adj).
calculus kal′ku·lus	Abnormal concretion of organic and mineral substances; pl. *calculi*.
calf kaf	Fleshy mass formed by muscle at base of leg below knee.
caliculus kah·lik′u·lus	A small cup or cup-shaped structure.
caligo kah·li′go	Dimness of vision.
calisthenics kal′is·then′iks	Light gymnastics for promoting strength.
calix ka′liks	Cup-shaped organ or cavity.

callosity kah·los′i·te	A callus; circumscribed thickening of skin.
callous kal′us	Hard; calluslike.
callus kal′us	Circumscribed thickening of skin surface due to friction or pressure.
calor ka′lor	Heat; one of cardinal signs of inflammation.
caloric kah·lo′rik	Pertaining to heat.
calorie kal′o·re	Unit of heat.
calorimeter kal′o·rim′e·ter	Instrument used to determine heat change in an individual.
calva kal′va	Bald scalp of head.
calvaria kal·va′re·ah	Skull cap or upper part of skull. (Also *calvarium*.)
calvitium kal·vish′e·um	Baldness.
calx kalks	Lime or chalk. The heel.
camphor kam′for	Compound used locally as an antipruritic.
canalization kan′al·i·za′shun	Formation of canals or channels in tissues.
cancellous kan′se·lus	Of a spongy or latticelike structure.

	cancellus kan·sel′us	Latticelike bony structure; pl. *cancelli*.
	cancer kan′ser	Any malignant cellular tumor.
	cancerous kan′ser·us	Of the nature of or pertaining to cancer.
	canine ka′nin	Pertaining to a canine tooth.
	cannula kan′u·lah	Tube for insertion into body.
	capillary kap′i·lar′e	Resembling a hair. Minute vessel that connects arterioles and venules.
	capitulum kah·pit′u·lum	A little head or small eminence on a bone.
	capsula kap′su·lah	Cartilaginous, fatty, or fibrous structure enveloping another structure, organ, or part.
	capsule kap′sul	Membranous sheet surrounding a structure. A soluble container for enclosing a dose of medicine.
	caput ka′put	Superior extremity of body containing brain, organs of special sense, and first organs of digestive system.
	carbohydrate kar′bo·hi′drat	Organic substance containing carbon, hydrogen, and oxygen.
	carbon kar′bon	Element found in charcoal and graphite.
	carbonate kar′bon·at	Any salt of carbonic acid.

carbuncle kar′bung·kl		Inflammation of subcutaneous tissue discharging pus.
carcinoid kar′si·noid		Circumscribed tumor in small intestine, stomach, or colon.
carcinoma kar′si·no′mah		Malignant new growth.
carcinosarcoma kar′si·no·sar·ko′- mah		Mixed tumor combining elements of carcinoma and sarcoma.
carcinosis kar′si·no′sis		Widespread cancer throughout body.
cardiac kar′de·ak		Pertaining to the heart.
cardinal kar′di·nal		Of primary importance.
cardioclasis kar′de·ok′lah·sis		Rupture of the heart.
cardiogenic kar′de·o·jen′ik		Originating in the heart. Caused by a condition affecting the heart.
cardiogram kar′de·o·gram		A tracing of heart movements by means of the cardiograph.
cardiograph kar′de·o·graf		Instrument that records the heart's movements.
cardiology kar·de·ol′o·je		Study of heart and its functions.
cardiolysis kar′de·ol′i·sis		Operation freeing pericardial adhesions from surrounding tissues.
cardiomegaly kar′de·o·meg′ah·le		Cardiac hypertrophy.

cardiopathy kar′de·op′ah·the	Any disease or disorder of heart.
cardioplegia kar′de·o·ple′je·ah	Interruption of contraction of myocardium.
cardiorrhaphy kar′de·or′ah·fe	Operation of suturing the heart muscle.
cardiotomy kar′de·ot′o·me	Surgical incision of heart.
cardiovascular kar′de·o·vas′ku·lar	Pertaining to heart and blood vessels.
carditis kar·di′tis	Inflammation of heart.
caries ka′re·ez	Decay or death of bone or teeth.
carious ka′re·us	Affected with caries.
carminative kar·min′ah·tiv	Medicine which relieves flatulence.
carotid kah·rot′id	Relating to principal artery of neck.
carpal kar′pal	Of or pertaining to carpus or wrist.
carpopedal kar′po·pe′dal	Affecting wrist and feet or fingers and toes.
carpus kar′pus	Wrist, consisting of eight short bones.
carrier kar′e·er	Individual who harbors organisms of disease in his body.
cartilage kar′ti·lij	Connective tissue, forming most of developing skeleton.

cartilaginous kar′ti·laj′i·nus	Consisting of or of the nature of cartilage.
caruncle kar′ung·kl	Small fleshy eminence. (Also *caruncula*.)
caseation ka′se·a′shun	Conversion of tissue into cheeselike material.
caseous ka′se·us	Cheeselike in appearance.
cast kast	Rigid bandage to immobilize an injured part. A positive copy of a body part, such as teeth, made by pouring plaster into an impression or mold.
castration kas·tra′shun	Removal of the testes or ovaries.
catabatic kat·ah·bat′ik	Stage of decline of a disease.
catabolism kah·tab′o·lizm	Destructive metabolism.
catagen kat′ah·jen	Transitional phase of the hair cycle.
catalepsy kat′ah·lep′se	Rigidity of muscles so that patient remains in position placed.
catalyst kat′ah·list	Substance which alters rate of or promotes chemical reaction.
catamenia kat′ah·me′ne·ah	The menses; menstruation.
cataract kat′ah·rakt	Opacity of the crystalline eye lens or its capsule.

catastaltic kat′ah·stal′tik	Inhibitory; restraining.
catatonic kat′ah·ton′ik	Pertaining to a form of schizophrenic behavior; phases of stupor or excitement.
catgut kat′gut	Cord used as ligature and in drainage.
catharsis kah·thar′sis	A cleansing or purgation.
cathartic kah·thar′tik	Medicine to quicken evacuations of the bowels.
catheter kath′e·ter	Tubular surgical instrument for withdrawing fluids from a cavity of body.
catheterization kath′e·ter·i·za′- shun	The employment or passage of a catheter.
catheterize kath′e·ter·iz	To introduce a catheter within a body cavity.
cation kat′i·on	Ion with a positive charge.
cauda kaw′dah	A tail or taillike appendage.
caudal kaw′dal	Pertaining to a tail; hind part of body; posterior.
causative kawz′ah·tiv	Effective as a cause or agent.
caustic kaws′tik	Burning or corrosive.
cauterization kaw′ter·i·za′shun	Application of a cautery or caustic.

⌒	cautery kaw′ter·e	Application of hot iron or electric current to kill tissue.	
	cavernous kav′er·nus	Having hollow spaces.	
	cavitation kav′e·ta′shun	Formation of cavities.	
	cavity kav′i·te	Hollow place or space within body. In dentistry, the area of destruction caused by caries.	
	cecal se′kal	Ending in a blind passage. Blind spot in field of vision.	
	cecum se′kum	Intestinal pouch. Any blind pouch or cul-de-sac.	
	celiac se′le·ak	Pertaining to the abdominal cavity.	
	celiectomy se′le·ek′to·me	Surgical removal of any abdominal organ.	
	celiotomy se′le·ot′o·me	Surgical incision into abdominal cavity.	
	cellula sel′u·lah	A small cell.	
	cellular sel′u·lar	Pertaining to or made up of cells.	
	cellulitis sel′u·li′tis	Inflammation of cellular tissue.	
	cellulose sel′u·los	A carbohydrate.	
	cement se·ment′	Adhesive filling material; substance producing union between two surfaces.	

cementicle se·men′ti·kel	Globular mass of dentin in region of tooth root.
centigrade sen′ti·grad	Having one hundred degrees or grades.
centigram sen′ti·gram	One hundredth part of gram.
centiliter sen′ti·le′ter	One hundredth part of liter.
centimeter sen′ti·me′ter	One hundredth part of a meter.
centrifuge sen′tri·fuj	An apparatus for freeing solids from liquids by rotation.
centriole sen′tri·ol	Minute body, rod, or granule within centrosome division center.
centrum sen′trum	Anatomical or other center.
cephalad sef′ah·lad	Toward the head.
cephalalgia sef′ah·lal′je·ah	Headache.
cephaledema sef′al·e·de′mah	Edema of the head.
cephalic se·fal′ik	Pertaining to the head or toward head.
cephalopathy sef′ah·lop′ah·the	Any disease of the head.
cera se′rah	Wax.

	cerebellum ser′e·bel′um	Part of brain concerned in the coordination of movements.
	cerebral ser′e·bral	Pertaining to the main portion of brain.
	cerebromeningitis ser′e·bro·men′in·ji′tis	Inflammation of brain and its membranes.
	cerebropsychosis ser′e·bro′si·ko′sis	Any mental disorder due to disease of cerebrum.
	cerebroscope se·re′bro·skop	Ophthalmoscope for diagnosing brain disease.
	cerebrospinal ser′e·bro·spi′nal	Pertaining to brain and spinal cord.
	cerebrovascular ser′e·bro·vas′ku·lar	Pertaining to blood vessels of brain.
	cerebrum ser′e·brum	Main portion of brain.
	cerumen se·roo′men	Waxlike secretion of the ear.
	cervical ser′vi·kal	Pertaining to neck or any cervix.
	cervicitis ser′vi·si′tis	Inflammation of cervix uteri.
	cervix ser′viks	Constricted portion of an organ; neck.
	cesarean se·sa′re·an	Delivery of fetus through abdominal incision.
	chalazion kah·la′ze·on	A sty; small tumor of eyelid.

	chamber cham'ber	Enclosed space or antrum.
	chancre shang'ker	Primary ulcer or lesion of syphilis.
	chancroid shang'kroid	Nonsyphilitic venereal sore.
	characteristic kar'ak·ter·is'tik	Character; typical of an individual or an entity.
	charlatan shar'lah·tan	A "quack"; pretender to knowledge.
	cheilophagia ki'lo·fa'je·ah	Biting of the lips.
	cheilosis ki·lo'sis	Fissuring and dry scaling of lips and mouth.
	chemistry kem'is·tre	Science which treats of elements and atomic relations of matter.
	chemobiotic ke'mo·bi·ot'ik	Combination of chemotherapeutic agent and antibiotic.
	chemoprophylaxis ke'mo·pro'fi-lak'sis	Prevention of specific disease by use of chemical agent.
	chemoreceptor ke'mo·re·sep'tor	A receptor (such as sense organs) adapted to react to chemical stimulus.
	chemosurgery ke'mo·sur'jer·e	Destruction of tissue by chemical agents.
	chemotaxis ke'mo·tak'sis	Response of organisms to chemical stimuli.
	chemotherapy ke'mo·ther'ah·pe	Treatment of disease by chemical agents.

chest chest	The thorax.
chickenpox chik′en·poks	An acute, communicable disease.
chilblain chil′blan	Itching and painful erythema on fingers, toes, or ears.
chill chil	Shivering; involuntary contractions of voluntary muscles.
chiropractor ki′ro·prak′tor	Practitioner of therapeutics by manipulation, especially of spinal column, of human body.
chloramphenicol klo′ram·fen′i·kol	An antibiotic effective against certain gram-negative organisms.
chloride klo′rid	Salt of hydrochloric acid.
chlormerodrin klor·mer′o·drin	A diuretic agent.
chloroform klo′ro·form	Agent used to induce general anesthesia.
Chloromycetin Klo′ro·mi·se′tin	Trademark for antibiotic substance used against gram-negative organisms.
chloroquine klo′ro·kwin	Antimalarial agent.
chlorothiazide klo′ro·thi′ah·zid	A diuretic agent.
chlorpromazine klor·pro′mah·zen	Tranquilizer and antiemetic.
cholangiography ko·lan′je·og′rah·fe	Roentgenography of biliary ducts.

cholecyst ko′le·sist	The gallbladder.	
cholecystectomy ko′le·sis·tek′to·me	Surgical removal of gallbladder.	
cholecystitis ko′le·sis·ti′tis	Inflammation of gallbladder.	
cholecystogram ko′le·sis′to·gram	Roentgenogram of gallbladder.	
cholecystography ko′le·sis·tog′rah·fe	X-ray examination of the gallbladder.	
choledochostomy ko′led·o·kos′to-me	Surgical formation of opening into common bile duct.	
cholelithiasis ko′le·li·thi′ah·sis	Presence or formation of gallstones.	
cholera kol′er·ah	Acute infectious disease.	
cholestasis ko′le·sta′sis	Stoppage or suppression of the flow of bile.	
cholesterol ko·les′ter·ol	Fatlike substance found in all animal fats and oils.	
cholinesterase ko′lin·es′ter·as	Enzyme found in blood and various other tissues.	
choluria ko·lu′re·ah	Presence of bile in the urine.	
chondroma kon·dro′mah	Hyperplastic growth of cartilage tissue.	
chorda kor′dah	Any cord or sinew.	

	chorditis kor·di′tis	Inflammation of a vocal or a spermatic cord.	
	chorea ko·re′ah	Involuntary muscular twitching; St. Vitus' dance.	
	chorion ko′re·on	Outermost of the fetal membranes.	
	choroid ko′roid	Vascular tunic of the eye.	
	choroiditis ko′roid·i′tis	Inflammation of the choroid.	
	chromatic kro·mat′ik	Pertaining to color.	
	chromatin kro′mah·tin	Protoplasmic substance in the nuclei of cells which is stainable.	
	chromoblast kro′mo·blast	Pigment cell.	
	chromosome kro′mo·som	Bodies in nucleins of cell mitosis, which carry hereditary genes.	
	chronic kron′ik	Long continued; recurring; not acute.	
	chyle kile	Milky fluid formed in small intestine during digestion.	
	chylopoiesis ki′lo·poi·e′sis	Production of chyle.	
	chylosis ki·lo′sis	Conversion of food into chyle and absorption into tissues.	
	chyme kime	Fluid containing partly digested food.	

SHORTHAND DICTIONARY

	cicatrix sik·a′triks (or sik′a·triks)	New tissue formed in healing of a wound.
	cilia sil′e·ah	Eyelashes.
	cilium sil′e·um	An eyelid or its outer edge.
	circulation ser′ku·la′shun	Movement of blood through heart and blood vessels.
	circumference ser·kum′fer·ens	Outer limit or margin of a rounded body.
	circumferential ser′kum·fer·en′shal	Pertaining to forming a circumference.
	circumscribed ser′kum·skribd	Bounded or limited.
	cirrhosis sir·ro′sis	A disease of the liver.
	cirsectomy ser·sek′to·me	Excision of portion of varicose vein.
	cisterna sis·ter′nah	Closed space containing lymph or other body fluid. (Also *cistern*.)
	clamp klamp	An instrument for holding and compressing vessels during surgery.
	claudication klaw′di·ka′shun	Condition marked by limping; lameness.
	claustrophobia klaws′tro·fo′be·ah	Fear of being confined in a small space.
	clavicle klav′i·kl	Bone articulating with sternum and scapula; collarbone.

clavus kla′vus	Corn or horny tubercle of the skin.
cleavage klev′ij	Segmentation of fertilized ovum.
cleoid kle′oid	Dental instrument shaped like a claw for excavating cavities.
climacteric kli′mak·ter′ik	Termination of the reproductive period in the female, accompanying the normal lessening of sexual activity in the male.
climax kli′maks	Period of greatest intensity—crisis, orgasm.
clinic klin′ik	Examination of patients before a class of students. The place where patients are examined and treated.
clinical klin′e·k′l	Referring to the course of a disease.
clivus kli′vus	Bony surface in posterior cranial fossa.
clonic klon′ik	Of the nature of a clonus.
clonus klo′nus	Spasm in which rigidity and relaxation occur alternately.
closure klo′zher	Act of shutting or of bringing together two parts.
clot klot	Semisolidified mass, as of blood or lymph.
clouding klowd′ing	Loss of clarity.

SHORTHAND DICTIONARY

clubbing klub′ing	Deformed fingers or toes, with knotty ends.	
coagulant ko·ag′u·lant	Any agent that accelerates the clotting of blood.	
coagulate ko·ag′u·lat	To cause to clot; solidify.	
coagulation ko·ag′u·la′shun	Process of clot formation.	
coagulose ko·ag′u·los	Enzyme which accelerates formation of blood clots.	
coagulum ko·ag′u·lum	A clot or curd.	
coalescence ko·ah·les′ens	To fuse or grow together.	
coaptation ko′ap·ta′shun	Fitting together of separated or broken parts.	
coarctation ko′ark·ta′shun	Straightening or pressing together; contraction.	
cocaine ko′kan	A local anesthetic, narcotic, and mydriatic.	
coccus kok′us	Spherical bacterial cell; pl. *cocci*.	
coccygeal kok·sij′e·al	Of or pertaining to the coccyx.	
coccyx kok′siks	Last bone of vertebral column, union of four small vertebrae.	
cochlea kok′le·ah	Anything of a spiral form; essential organ of hearing.	
cochleare kok′le·a′re	Spoon or spoonful.	

codeine ko'den	Opium derivative used as an analgesic and antitussive.	
coefficient ko'e·fish'ent	Ratio between two different factors.	
cohesion ko·he'zhun	Force which causes particles to unite.	
coldsore kold'sor	Herpes simplex of lip.	
colectomy ko·lek'to·me	Excision of portion of the colon or of the whole colon.	
colic kol'ik	Pertaining to colon. Acute abdominal pain.	
colitis ko·li'tis	Inflammation of colon.	
collagen kol'ah·jen	Nonelastic, connective-tissue fibers.	
collagenous kol·laj'e·nus	Pertaining to collagen; forming or producing collagen.	
collapse ko·laps'	State of extreme prostration and depression.	
collateral ko·lat'er·al	Secondary or accessory.	
colliculus ko·lik'u·lus	Small elevation or mound.	
collodion ko·lo'de·on	Clear syrupy liquid which dries to tenacious film.	
colloid kol'oid	Glutinous or resembling glue.	
collum kol'lum	Portion of body connecting head and trunk; neck.	

colocentesis ko′lo·sen·te′sis	Surgical perforation of colon.
coloclysis ko·lok′li·sis	Irrigation of colon.
colon ko′lon	Part of large intestine extending from cecum to rectum.
colostomy ko·los′to·me	Surgical creation of an opening of colon to surface of body.
colostrum ko·los′trum	Thin milky fluid secreted by mammary gland.
colpectasia kol·pek·ta′se·ah	Dilatation or distension of the vagina.
colpectomy kol·pek′to·me	Excision of the vagina.
colpitis kol·pi′tis	Inflammation of the vagina.
colpocleisis kol′po·kli′sis	Operation for closing the vaginal canal.
colpocystitis kol′po·sis·ti′tis	Inflammation of vagina and bladder.
colpocytogram kol′po·si′to·gram	Tabulation of cell types in smear taken from mucous membrane of vagina.
colporrhaphy kol·por′ah·fe	Narrowing vagina by operation of suturing vaginal wall.
colporrhexis kol′po·rek′sis	Tearing or rupture of vaginal wall.
colposcope kol′po·skop	Instrument for examining vagina.

colpotomy kol·pot′o·me		Incision into the vagina.
columella kol′u·mel′ah		A little column.
column kol′um		Pillarlike structure or part. (Also *columna*.)
coma ko′mah		State of profound unconsciousness.
comatose ko′mah·tos		Referring to a state of coma.
combustion kom·bust′yun		Rapid oxidation with emission of heat.
comedo ko·me′do		A blackhead.
comminuted kom′i·nut′ed		Broken or crushed into small pieces.
commissura kom′i·su′rah		Site of union of corresponding parts. (Also *commissure*.)
commitment ko·mit′ment		Legal consignment of a mental patient to an institution.
communicable ko·mu′ni·kah·b′l		Capable of transmission from one person to another.
compensation kom′pen·sa′shun		Making up of a deficiency of structure or function.
compensatory kom·pen′sah·to′re		Making good a defect or loss.
complaint kom·plant′		A disease or disorder; presenting symptom.
complex kom′pleks		Complicated; not simple.

complexion kom·plek'shun	Color and appearance of skin of face.
complication kom'pli·ka'shun	Disease concurrent with another disease.
component kom·po'nent	Constituent element or part.
compound kom'pownd	Made of two or more parts or ingredients.
compress kom'pres	A pad applied to make pressure on a particular part.
compulsive kom·pul'siv	Pertaining to an irresistible impulse to perform an act.
concentrate kon'sen·trat	To gather together at one point. To increase strength by diminishing bulk.
concentration kon'sen·tra'shun	Increase in strength by evaporation.
conception kon·sep'shun	Fecundation of the ovum.
concha kong'kah	Structure or part resembling a shell in shape.
concoction kon·kok'shun	Mixture of medicinal substances prepared with heat.
concomitant kon·kom'i·tant	Accompanying; accessory.
concretion kon·kre'shun	Calculus; a stone.
concussion kon·kush'un	Injury of a soft structure such as the brain as a result of a blow.

	condom kon′dum	Cover for the penis worn to prevent impregnation or infection.
	conduction kon·duk′shun	Transfer of sound waves, heat, or nerve influences.
	condyle kon′dil	Rounded projection on a bone. (Also *condylus*.)
	configuration kon·fig′u·ra′shun	General form of a body.
	conflict kon′flikt	Painful state of consciousness due to clash of opposing trends.
	confluent kon′floo·ent	A joining; becoming merged.
	confusion kon·fu′zhun	Disturbance of understanding; bewilderment.
	congenital kon·jen′i·tal	Existing at, and usually before, birth.
	congested kon·jest′ed	Overloaded, as with blood.
	congestion kon·jest′yun	Abnormal amount of blood in a part.
	congestive kon·jes′tiv	Pertaining to or resulting in congestion.
	conglomerate kon·glom′er·at	Heaped together in one mass.
	conical kon′e·kal	Cone-shaped.
	conjugal kon′ju·gal	Pertaining to marriage.

	conjugata kon′ju·ga′tah	Diameter of pelvic inlet.
	conjugate kon′ju·gat	Yoked or coupled; simultaneous.
	conjunctiva kon′junk·ti′vah	Membrane that covers the eyeball and lines the eyelid.
	conjunctivitis kon·junk′ti·vi′tis	Inflammation of conjunctiva.
	conscious kon′shus	Capable of responding to sensory stimuli.
	consciousness kon′shus·nes	Responsiveness of mind to impressions of senses.
	consensual kon·sen′shu·al	Excited by reflex stimulation.
	consolidation kon·sol′i·da′shun	To become solid, as does a lung in pneumonia.
	consonation kon′so·na′shun	Presence of consonating rales.
	constant kon′stant	Not failing; remaining unaltered.
	constipation kon′sti·pa′shun	Infrequent or difficult evacuation of feces.
	constitution kon′sti·tu′shun	Makeup or functional habit of body.
	constriction kon·strik′shun	Narrowing; a sense of tightness.
	constrictor kon·strik′tor	That which constricts, such as a muscle.
	consultant kon·sul′tant	Physician who acts in an advisory capacity.

consultation kon'sul·ta'shun	Deliberation of two or more physicians in a case.	
consumption kom·sump'shun	Wasting away of the body.	
contagious kon·ta'jus	Capable of transmission from one person to another.	
contamination kon·tam'i·na'shun	Soiling or making inferior by contact or mixture.	
contiguous kon·tig'u·us	In contact; adjacent.	
continence kon'ti·nens	Ability to refrain from yielding to desire; self-restraint regarding sexual indulgence or defecation or urination.	
continuous kon·tin'u·us	Not interrupted.	
contour kon'toor	Normal outline or configuration of body or a part.	
contraception kon'trah·sep'shun	Prevention of conception or impregnation.	
contraction kon·trak'shun	A shortening or shrinkage; muscle tension.	
contracture kon·trak'tur	High resistance to passive stretch of a muscle.	
contralateral kon'trah·lat'er·al	Situated on opposite side.	
contrusion kon·troo'zhun	Condition in which teeth are crowded and pushed together.	
contusion kon·tu'zhun	A bruise.	

conus ko′nus	A cone; cone-shaped.	
convalescence kon′vah·les′ens	Stage of recovery after an illness or operation.	
convection kon·vek′shun	Transmission or conveying of heat.	
convergence kon·ver′jens	Inclination toward a common point.	
conversion kon·ver′zhun	Transformation of emotions into physical manifestations.	
convulsion kon·vul′shun	Violent involuntary contraction of the voluntary muscles.	
convulsive kon·vul′siv	Pertaining to violent involuntary contraction.	
coordination ko·or′di·na′shun	Harmonious working together of muscles or groups of muscles.	
copremia kop·re′me·ah	Blood poisoning from retention of fecal matter in blood.	
coprolith kop′ro·lith	Hard mass of fecal matter.	
copulation kop′u·la′shun	Sexual union of male and female; coitus.	
coreometer ko′re·om′e·ter	Apparatus used in measuring the pupil; pupillometer.	
coreoplasty ko′re·o·plas′te	Plastic operation on the iris.	
corn korn	Horny induration and thickening of skin; a clavus.	

	cornea kor′ne·ah	Transparent structure forming anterior part of fibrous tunic of eye.	
	corneal kor′ne·al	Pertaining to the cornea.	
	cornu kor′nu	Hornlike projection; pl. *cornua*.	
	corona ko·ro′nah	A crown; crownlike eminence.	
	coronal ko·ro′nal	Pertaining to a crown of the head or to any corona.	
	coronary kor′o·na·re	Of or pertaining to vessels or ligaments that encircle an organ.	
	corpse korps	A dead body.	
	corpulency kor′pu·len′se	Undue fatness or obesity.	
	corpus kor′pus	A body; main part of a structure.	
	corpuscle kor′pus·l	A small mass or body.	
	correction ko·rek′shun	A setting right.	
	cortex kor′teks	Outer layer of an organ; pl. *cortices*.	
	cortical kor′te·kal	Relating to the cortex.	
	corticocerebral kor′te·ko·ser′e-bral	Pertaining to cerebral cortex.	

corticospinal kor′te·ko·spi′nal	Pertaining to cortex of brain and spinal cord.
corticotropin kor′ti·ko·tro′pin	Hormone (ACTH) to stimulate adrenal cortical activity.
cortisone kor′ti·son	Drug used to treat diseases and arthritis.
coryza ko·ri′zah	Head cold; acute catarrhal condition.
cosmetic koz·met′ik	Beautifying. A beautifying substance or preparation.
costa kos′tah	A rib; pl. *costae*.
costal kos′tal	Referring to a rib or ribs.
costophrenic kos′to·fren′ik	Pertaining to ribs and diaphragm.
cough kawf	Sudden noisy expulsion of air from lungs.
counterirritant kown′ter·ir′i·tant	Agent producing superficial irritation.
counteropening kown′ter·o′pening	A second incision made opposite another.
coxa kok′sah	The hip or hip joint.
crackle krak′l	A small sharp sound.
cramp kramp	Painful spasmodic muscular contraction.

	cranial kra′ne·al	Pertaining to cranium or to the anterior or superior end of body.
	craniofacial kra′ne·o·fa′shal	Pertaining to cranium and face.
	craniopuncture kra′ne·o·punk′tur	Puncture of brain for cranial disease exploration.
	craniotomy kra′ne·ot′o·me	Any operation on cranium.
	cranium kra′ne·um	Skeleton of the head.
	creatinine kre·at′i·nin	A normal constituent of blood and urine.
	creosol kre′o·sol	Antiseptic.
	crepitant krep′i·tant	Rattling or crackling.
	crepitation krep′i·ta′shun	Grating sound heard when ends of fractured bone rub together.
	crepitus krep′i·tus	Discharge of flatus from bowels.
	crescent kres′ent	Shaped like a new moon.
	crest krest	Projection or ridge; crista.
	cretin kre′tin	Person with arrested physical and mental development.
	cretinism kre′tin·izm	Congenital disease marked by lack of physical and mental development.

	cribriform krib′ri·form	Perforated like a sieve.
	cricoid kri′koid	Ring-shaped.
	crinis kri′nis	Hair.
	crisis kri′sis	Turning point of a disease for better or worse.
	crista kris′tah	Projection or ridge; crest.
	croup kroop	Condition characterized by resonant barking cough, hoarseness, and stridor.
	crown krown	Topmost part of organ; upper part of tooth.
	crucial kroo′shal	Shaped like a cross. Severe, decisive.
	crus krus	Leg from knee to foot.
	crust krust	A scab; crusta.
	crutch kruch	Device fitted under arm used for supporting weight of body.
	crypt kript	Minute tubelike depression opening on a free surface.
	cryptic krip′tik	Buried or hidden; larval.
	cryptorchidism krip·tor′ki·dizm	Developmental defect in which testes fail to descend into scrotum.

crystal kris′tal	Naturally produced angular solid of definite form.	
cubital ku′bi·tal	Referring to the forearm or ulna.	
cubitus ku′bi·tus	Bend of the arm; joint between arm and forearm.	
cuboid ku′boid	The cuboid bone; resembling a cube.	
cuboidal ku·boi′dal	Resembling a cube.	
cul-de-sac kul′de·sahk′	A narrow cavity open only at one end; cecum.	
culdoscopy kul·dos′ko·pe	Visual examination of female pelvic viscera.	
culture kul′tur	Propagation of microorganisms or of living tissue cells in special media.	
cumulus ku′mu·lus	A little mound.	
cuneiform ku·ne′i·form	Shaped like a wedge; any one of three bones in foot and one in wrist.	
curare koo·rah′re	Toxic extract used in pharmacological research and in anesthesia. (Also *curari*.)	
curative kur′ah·tiv	Tending to overcome disease and promote recovery.	
curet ku·ret′	Instrument for removing growths from cavity walls. (Also *curette*.)	

curettage ku′reh·tahzh′	The operation of scraping the walls of a cavity.
current kur′ent	Stream of electricity which moves along a conductor.
curvature kur′vah·tur	Deviation from a rectilinear direction.
cusp kusp	A tapering projection, especially segment of cardiac valve or rounded surface on a tooth.
cuspid kus′pid	Having one cusp or point. A canine tooth.
cuspis kus′pis	Tapering projection of cardiac valve; cusp of a tooth.
cutaneous ku·ta′ne·us	Pertaining to the skin.
cuticle ku′te·kl	Outer layer of skin, epidermis.
cutis ku′tis	Outer covering of the body consisting of epidermis and corium.
cutitis ku·ti′tis	Inflammation of the skin.
cyanosis si′ah·no′sis	Bluish tinge of the skin due to lack of oxygen in the blood.
cyanotic si·ah·not′ik	Pertaining to cyanosis.
cycle si′kl	Succession of observable phenomena recurring regularly.
cyclopropane si′klo·pro′pan	A general anesthetic by inhalation.

cyst sist	Any sac, normal or abnormal, especially one containing a liquid material.
cystalgia sis·tal′je·ah	Pain in the urinary bladder.
cystic sis′tik	Pertaining to the urinary bladder, gallbladder, or a cyst.
cystitis sis·ti′tis	Inflammation of the urinary bladder.
cystocarcinoma sis′to·kar′si·no′-mah	Carcinoma associated with cysts.
cystocele sis′to·sel	Hernial protrusion of urinary bladder through vaginal wall.
cystogram sis′to·gram	An X-ray picture of the bladder.
cystoid sis′toid	Resembling a cyst.
cystolithiasis sis′to·li·thi′ah·sis	Development of stones in the bladder.
cystoma sis′to·mah	Tumor containing cysts of neoplastic origin.
cystometrogram sis·to·met′ro·gram	Tracing recorded by cystometrograph.
cystometry sis·tom′e·tre	Study of bladder efficiency by testing its pressure and capacity.
cystoneuralgia sis′to·nu·ral′je·ah	Neuralgia of the bladder.
cystopexy sis′to·pek′se	Surgical fixation of bladder to abdominal wall.

	cystorrhaphy sis·tor'ah·fe	Suturing of the bladder.
	cystoscope sis'to·skop'	Endoscope for examination of urinary tract.
	cystoscopy sis·tos'ko·pe	Visual examination of bladder interior with cystoscope.
	cystostomy sis·tos'to·me	Formation of an opening into bladder.
	cystotomy sis·tot'o·me	Surgical incision into the bladder.
	cytoblast si'to·blast	Nucleus or vital part of a cell; mitochondrium.
	cytology si·tol'o·je	Scientific study of cells, their origin, structure, and function.
	cytopenia si'to·pe'ne·ah	Deficiency of cellular elements of the blood.
	cytoplasm si'to·plazm'	Protoplasm of a cell other than that of the nucleus.
	cytosis si·to'sis	Condition of the nucleus of a leukocyte.

D

	dacryocyst dak're·o·sist	Tear sac; lacrimal sac.
	dacryocystocele dak're·o·sis'to·sel	Hernial protrusion of lacrimal sac. (Also *dacryocele*.)
	dacryoma dak're·o'mah	Tumor of the tear gland.
	dacryostenosis dak're·o·ste·no'sis	Stricture or narrowing of a lacrimal sac.

dactylitis dak′ti·li′tis		Inflammation of a finger or toe.
dactylogram dak·til′o·gram		A fingerprint.
dactylospasm dak′ti·lo·spazm		Spasm of a finger or toe.
dandruff dan′druf		Scaly material desquamated from scalp.
deafness def′nes		Lack or loss, complete or partial, of hearing.
deaminase de·am′i·nas		Enzyme causing removal of amino group from organic compounds.
debilitant de·bil′i·tant		Causing debility or loss of strength.
debility de·bil′i·te		Weak; without strength.
debridement da·bred·maw′		Cleaning a wound by removing devitalized tissue and other foreign matter.
debris de·bre′		Accumulated fragments; in dentistry, soft foreign matter loosely attached to tooth surface.
decagram dek′ah·gram		Ten grams.
decalcification de′kal·si·fi·ka′·shun		Loss of calcium salts from bone or tooth.
decaliter dek′ah·le′ter		Ten liters.

SHORTHAND DICTIONARY 73

	decalvant de·kal′vant	Removing or destroying hair.
	decameter dek′ah·me′ter	Ten meters.
	decibel des′i·bel	Unit of hearing or audition. (Abbreviated *db*.)
	decidua de·sid′u·ah	Mucous lining of uterus thrown off after parturition.
	deciduous de·sid′u·us	Not permanent. Teeth of first dentition.
	decigram des′i·gram	One-tenth of a gram.
	deciliter des′i·le′ter	One-tenth of a liter.
	decimeter des′i·me′ter	One-tenth of a meter.
	decompensation de′kom·pen·sa′- shun	Failure of heart to maintain adequate circulation.
	decongestant de′kon·jes′tant	Tending to reduce congestion or swelling.
	decontamination de′kon·tam·i·na′- shun	Freeing of person or object of contaminating gas or radioactive material.
	decrepitation de·krep′i·ta′shun	Crackling noise.
	decubation de′ku·ba′shun	Period in course of infectious disease from the disappearance of symptoms to recovery and the end of infectious period.

	decubitus de·ku′bi·tus	Act or position of lying down.
	decussate de·kus′at	To cross or intersect in form of letter X.
	decussation de′kus·sa′shun	A crossing over. (Also *decussatio*.)
	defecation def′e·ka′shun	Evacuation of fecal matter from rectum.
	defect de′fekt	Imperfection; failure; absence.
	deferent def′er·ent	Conveying anything away from a center; deferens.
	deficiency de·fish′en·se	A lack or defect.
	deformity de·for′mi·te	Distortion of any part resulting in disfigurement.
	degenerate de·jen′er·at	Person of perverted mental or physical constitution. To change from a higher to a lower type or form.
	degeneration de·jen′er·a′shun	Deterioration to a lower form.
	deglutition deg′loo·tish′un	Act of swallowing.
	dehiscence de·his′ens	Act or process of splitting.
	dehydrate de·hi′drat	To remove water from.
	dehydration de′hi·dra′shun	Loss of water from tissues.

delactation de′lac·ta′shun	Cessation of lactation. Weaning.
deleterious del′e·te′re·us	Injurious; harmful.
delirium de·lir′i·um	Mental disturbance marked by hallucinations.
delivery de·liv′er·e	Expulsion or extraction of a child at birth.
deltoid del′toid	Of a triangular outline.
delusion de·lu′zhun	False belief which cannot be corrected by reason.
demarcation de′mar·ka′shun	Setting limits or determining boundaries.
demented de·ment′ed	Deprived of reason; mentally deteriorated.
dementia de·men′she·ah	General designation for mental deterioration.
Demerol Dem′er·ol	Trademark for meperidine; analgesic, spasmolytic, and sedative drug.
demilune dem′e·lun	Half moon or crescent; crescent shaped.
demineralization de·min′er·al·i·za′shun	Loss or decrease of mineral or inorganic salts in the body.
demulcent de·mul′sent	Soothing; bland; allaying irritation.
denatured de·na′turd	Having its nature changed. Rendered unfit for human consumption.

dendritic den·drit′ik		Having branches like a tree.
denervation de′ner·va′shun		Cutting off nerve supply of a part or an organ.
density den′si·te		Quality of being compact or dense.
dental den′tal		Pertaining to teeth.
denticle den′ti·kl		Small toothlike process.
dentifrice den′ti·fris		Preparation with which to clean and polish teeth.
dentin den′tin		Chief substance or tissue of teeth. (Also *dentine*.)
dentistry den′tis·tre		Department of healing arts concerned with teeth, oral cavity, and associated structures.
dentulous den′tu·lus		Possessing natural teeth.
denture den′tur		Entire set of natural or artificial teeth.
denudation den′u·da′shun		Removal of a covering or protective layer.
deodorant de·o′der·ant		Agent which neutralizes unpleasant odors.
dependence de·pend′ens		Psychophysical state of addict in which drugs are required to prevent abstinence symptoms.
depilatory de·pil′ah·to·re		Agent used to remove or destroy hair.

SHORTHAND DICTIONARY 77

depolarization de·po′lar·i·za′shun	Alteration of polarized semipermeable membranes.
depressant de·pres′ant	Agent reducing functional activity and vital energies.
depressed de·prest′	Carried below normal level; depression.
depressive de·pres′iv	Causing depression.
depressor de·pres′or	That which depresses, as a muscle, agent, or instrument.
derangement de·ranj′ment	Mental disorder.
derma der′mah	The skin; corium.
dermal der′mal	Pertaining to the skin.
dermatitis der′mah·ti′tis	Inflammation of the skin.
dermatocyst der′mah·to·sist	Cyst of the skin.
dermatologist der′mah·tol′o·jist	A skin specialist.
dermatology der′mah·tol′o·je	The diagnosis and treatment of diseases of the skin.
dermatolysis der′mah·tol′i·sis	Relaxed and hypertrophied state of the skin.
dermatomycosis der′mah·to·mi·ko′sis	Superficial infection of the skin.

dermatophobia der'mah·to·fo'-be·ah	Morbid dread of having cutaneous lesion.
dermatoplasty der'mah·to·plas'te	Surgical replacement of destroyed skin.
dermatosis der'mah·to'sis	Any skin disease.
dermis der'mis	Layer of skin between epidermis and subcutaneous tissue.
dermoid der'moid	Resembling skin. A dermoid cyst.
descensus de·sen'sus	Process of descending or falling.
desensitize de·sen'si·tiz	Deprive of sensation. Remove antibody from sensitized cells to prevent allergy.
desiccant des'i·kant	Promoting dryness.
desiccate des'i·kat	To render thoroughly dry.
desmoid des'moid	Fibrous or fibroid.
desquamation des'kwah·ma'shun	Shedding of skin in scales or sheets.
detachment de·tach'ment	Separation of usually attached areas.
detergent de·ter'jent	Purifying or cleansing agent.
deterioration de·ter'e·o·ra'shun	Condition of becoming worse.

determination de·ter′mi·na′shun	Establishment of exact nature of entity or event.
detoxification de·tok′si·fi·ka′- shun	Reduction of toxic properties of a poison.
detrition de·trish′un	Wearing away, as of teeth, by friction.
detritus de·tri′tus	Broken down tissue or material.
devascularization de·vas′ku·lar·i- za′shun	Interruption of the circulation of blood to a part.
development de·vel′op·ment	Growth.
deviant de′ve·ant	Varying from a determinable standard.
deviation de′ve·a′shun	Turning away from regular standard or cause.
devitalize de·vi′tal·iz	To deprive of vitality or life.
devorative dev′o·ra′tiv	Intended to be swallowed without chewing.
dextral deks′tral	Right as opposed to left. A right-handed person.
dextrose deks′tros	Preparation used intravenously as a nutrient.
dextroverted deks′tro·vert′ed	Turned to the right.
diabetes di′ah·be′tez	A metabolic disorder characterized by the body's inability to utilize carbohydrates.

diabetic di′ah·bet′ik	Pertaining to or affected with diabetes.
diabetogenic di′ah·bet′o·jen′ik	Disease or drug that causes diabetes.
diaclasis di·ak′lah·sis	A fracture, especially one made for a surgical purpose.
diagnosis di′ag·no′sis	The art of distinguishing one disease from another.
diagnostic di′ag·nos′tik	Pertaining to or subserving diagnosis.
diameter di·am′e·ter	Straight line passing through center of a circle.
diaphoresis di′ah·fo·re′sis	Perspiration, especially profuse perspiration.
diaphoretic di′ah·fo·ret′ik	Pertaining to or promoting profuse perspiration.
diaphragm di′ah·fram	Partition separating the abdominal from the thoracic cavity. A contraceptive device.
diaphragmatic di′ah·frag·mat′ik	Pertaining to diaphragm.
diaphysis di·af′i·sis	Shaft of a long bone between extremities.
diarrhea di′ah·re′ah	Frequent loose bowel evacuation.
diarthrosis di′ar·thro′sis	Freely movable joint.
diastasis di·as′tah·sis	Simple separation of normally joined parts.

diastole di·as′to·le	Rhythmic period of relaxation of the heart ventricle.	
diastolic di′ah·stol′ik	Of or pertaining to diastole.	
diathermy di′ah·ther′me	Generation of heat in body tissues by electric current.	
diathesis di·ath′e·sis	Predisposition to disease.	
Dicumarol Di·koo′mah·rol	A collective trademark for a coumarin derivative; anticoagulant, preventing venous thrombosis.	
didymus did′i·mus	A testis.	
diet di′et	Allowance of food and drink from day to day.	
dietary di′e·ta′re	Regular or systematic scheme of diet.	
diethylstilbestrol di·eth′il·stil·bes′-trol	Estrogenic compound used in treating menopausal symptoms. (Called also *stilbestrol.*)	
differential dif′er·en′shal	Pertaining to a difference.	
differentiation dif′er·en′she·a′-shun	Distinguishing of one thing or disease from another.	
diffuse dif·fus′	Not limited or localized.	
diffusion di·fu′zhen	Process of becoming widely spread.	

digestant di·jes′tant	Assisting or stimulating digestion.
digestion di·jest′yun	Act or process of converting food into assimilable form.
digestive di·jes′tiv	Pertaining to digestion. A digestant.
digit dij′it	A finger or toe.
digital dij′i·tal	Performed with a finger.
digitalis dij′i·tal′is	Cardiotonic agent.
digitalization dij′i·tal·i·za′shun	Administration of digitalis until desired effect is produced.
digitoxin dij′i·tok′sin	Drug used in treatment of congestive heart failure.
digitus dij′i·tus	Finger or toe.
dihydrostreptomycin di·hi′dro·strep·to·mi′sin	Antibiotic.
Dilantin Di·lan′tin	Trademark for anticonvulsant preparations.
dilatation dil·ah·ta′shun	Dilated or stretched beyond normal dimensions.
dilation di·la′shun	Process of enlarging or dilating.
dilator di·la′tor	Appliance used to enlarge an orifice or canal.

SHORTHAND DICTIONARY   83

Dilaudid Di·law'did	Trademark for a narcotic analgesic.
dilution di·lu'shun	Process or state of being rendered less potent. An attenuated medicine.
dimension di·men'shun	Measurement of an organ or body part.
diminution dim'i·nu'shun	Reduction in size or degree.
dimple dim'pl	Slight depression.
diopter di·op'ter	Refractive power of a lens with focal distance of one meter.
dioxide di·ok'sid	Molecule having two atoms of oxygen.
diphasic di·fa'zik	Occurring in two phases or stages.
diphtheria dif·the're·ah	Acute infectious disease.
diphtheroid dif'ther·oid	Resembling diphtheria.
diplococcus dip'lo·kok'us	A spherical bacterium.
diplopia di·plo'pe·ah	Double vision.
dipsomania dip'so·ma'ne·ah	Uncontrollable desire for alcoholic beverages.
discharge dis·charj'	To set free or liberate.

discission dis·sizh'un	Cutting in two or division.
discoid dis'koid	Shaped like a disk; medicated tablet.
discoloration dis·kul'er·a'shun	Change in or loss of natural color.
discrete dis·kret'	Separate; distinct; not joined together.
discus dis'kus	Circular or rounded flat plate or organ. (Also *disc* or *disk*.)
disease di·sez'	A reversal from state of health.
disinfectant dis'in·fek'tant	An agent which kills bacteria.
disintegration dis'in·te·gra'shun	Decay or breaking up.
disk disk	Circular or rounded flat plate or organ. (Also *disc*.)
dislocation dis'lo·ka'shun	Displacement of an organ or bone.
disorder dis·or'der	Derangement or abnormality of function.
disorientation dis·o're·en·ta'shun	Loss of one's bearings; state of mental confusion.
dispensary dis·pen'sah·re	A place where drugs and medical services are provided, usually for the indigent.
dispersion dis·per'shun	Act of scattering or separating.

	displacement dis·plas′ment	Removal from normal position.
	disposition dis′po·zish′un	Tendency toward certain diseases.
	disproportion dis′pro·por′shun	Lack of proper relationship between two elements.
	disruptive dis·rup′tiv	Bursting apart; rending.
	dissect dis·sekt′	To cut apart or separate; especially applied to anatomical study made of a cadaver.
	dissection dis·sek′shun	The act of dissecting tissue.
	disseminated dis·sem′i·nat′ed	Scattered; distributed over an area.
	dissociation dis·so′she·a′shun	Act of separating or state of being separated.
	distal dis′tal	Near the end of extremity; away from the center.
	distention dis·ten′shun	Distended or enlarged.
	distillation dis·til·la′shun	Vaporization.
	distortion dis·tor′shun	Twisted out of the normal shape or position.
	distraction dis·trak′shun	Diversion of attention from main portion of experience.
	distress dis·tres′	Physical or mental anguish or suffering.

diuresis di′u·re′sis	Increased excretion of urine.	
diuretic di′u·ret′ik	Agent that promotes secretion of urine.	
diurnal di·er′nal	Taking place during the day.	
divergent di·ver′jent	Extending in different directions.	
diverticulitis di′ver·tik·u·li′tis	Inflammation of a diverticulum.	
diverticulosis di′ver·tik′u·lo′sis	Presence of diverticula, particularly intestinal.	
diverticulum di′ver·tik′u·lum	A pouch or sac opening off a main cavity or tube.	
division di·vizh′un	Act of separating into two or more parts.	
dizziness diz′i·nes	Sensation of unsteadiness; disturbed sense of relationship to space.	
DNA	Abbreviation for deoxyribonucleic acid, which is found in all living cells.	
doctor dok′tor	Practitioner of medicine or surgery.	
dolor do′lor	Pain; sign of inflammation.	
dominance dom′i·nans	Supremacy; superior manifestation.	
donor do′nor	Organism or person which supplies living material for use in another body.	

dormant dor′mant	Sleeping; inactive; quiescent.	
dorsal dor′sal	Pertaining to the back or to any dorsum.	
dorsiflexion dor′si·flek′shun	Backward bending, as of the hand or foot.	
dorsum dor′sum	Vertebral aspect of body; the back; posterior.	
dosage do′sij	The determination and regulation of a quantity administered at one time.	
dotage do′tij	Feebleness of mind in old age; senility.	
douche doosh	Stream of water or gas directed against a part or into a cavity.	
drainage dran′ij	Withdrawal of fluids and discharges from wound.	
dram dram	Unit of weight.	
Dramamine Dram′ah·men	Trademark for preparation used as antihistaminic in motion sickness.	
dressing dres′ing	Material applied for protection of a wound.	
droplet drop′let	A diminutive drop, such as make up the particles of moisture expelled from mouth when coughing or talking.	
dropsy drop′se	Abnormal accumulation of fluid in cavity or tissues of body.	

drowsy drau′ze	Ready to fall asleep.	
duct dukt	A passage with well-defined walls, especially one for the passage of body excretions and secretions.	
ductless dukt′les	Having no excretory duct.	
ductule dukt′ul	A very small duct.	
ductulus duk′tu·lus	A minute duct.	
ductus duk′tus	A passage with well-defined walls.	
dullness dul′nes	Lack of normal resonance on percussion.	
duodenal du′o·de′nal	Of or situated in duodenum.	
duodenitis du′od·e·ni′tis	Inflammation of duodenum.	
duodenostomy du′od·e·nos′to·me	Surgical formation of permanent opening into duodenum.	
duodenum du′o·de′num	First or proximal portion of small intestine.	
dura du′rah	Abbreviated term for dura mater, outermost membrane covering brain and spinal cord.	
dwarfism dwarf′izm	Abnormal underdevelopment of body.	
dynamometer di′nah·mom′e·ter	Instrument for measuring muscular contraction.	

	dysarthria dis·ar′thre·ah	Imperfect articulation in speech.
	dyscrasia dis·kra′ze·ah	A morbid condition, especially one involving an imbalance of component elements.
	dysentery dis′en·ter′e	Inflammation of intestines.
	dysesthesia dis′es·the′ze·ah	Impairment of sensation, especially the sense of touch.
	dysfunction dis·funk′shun	Abnormal functioning of an organ.
	dysmenorrhea dis′men·o·re′ah	Painful menstruation.
	dysmetria dis·me′tre·ah	Inability to measure, and therefore to control, movements in muscular acts.
	dysopia dis·o′pe·ah	Painful or faulty eyesight.
	dyspepsia dis·pep′se·ah	Impairment of power or function of digestion.
	dysphagia dis·fa′je·ah	Painful or difficult swallowing.
	dysphasia dis·fa′ze·ah	Impairment of the faculty of speech.
	dysphonia dis·fo′ne·ah	Difficulty in producing vocal sounds.
	dysphoria dis·fo′re·ah	Feeling of disquiet or restlessness.
	dysplasia dis·pla′se·ah	Abnormal development or growth.

	dyspnea disp′ne·ah	Difficult breathing.
	dystrophy dis′tro·fe	A disorder arising from faulty nutrition.
	dysuria dis·u′re·ah	Painful urination.

E

	ear er′	Organ of hearing.
	earache er′ak	Pain in the ear.
	earwax er′waks	Waxlike secretion found within the external meatus of the ear.
	ebriety e·bri′e·te	Drunkenness.
	eccentric ek·sen′trik	Situated away from a center or median line.
	ecchymosis ek′i·mo′sis	Black-and-blue spot; extravasation of blood under skin.
	ecdemic ek·dem′ik	Not endemic; disease caused by factor originating far from place disease is observed.
	eclampsia ek·lamp′se·ah	Convulsions and coma during pregnancy.
	ectasia ek·ta′ze·ah	A stretching out; dilatation; distention.
	ecthyma ek·thi′mah	Pustular eruption.

ectoderm ek′to·derm	The outermost layer of skin; ectoblast.
ectodermal ek′to·der′mal	Pertaining to ectoderm.
ectopia ek·to′pe·ah	Displacement or malposition of an organ.
ectopic ek·top′ik	Pertaining to abnormal position of organ or part.
ectoplasm ek′to·plazm	Outermost layer of the cytoplasm of the cell.
ectropion ek·tro′pe·on	Turning outward of an edge or margin, such as eyelid.
eczema ek′ze·mah	Inflammatory skin disease with lesions.
eczematoid ek·zem′ah·toid	Resembling eczema.
eczematous ek·zem′ah·tus	Affected with or of the nature of eczema.
edema e·de′mah	Swelling due to accumulation of fluid in the tissue spaces; dropsy.
edematous e·dem′ah·tus	Characterized by edema.
edentulous e·den′tu·lus	Without teeth.
eduction e·duk′shun	Restoration to normal state of an anesthetized patient.
effect e·fekt′	Result produced by an action.

| | efferent
ef′er·ent | Carrying blood or nerve impulses outward, away from a center. |
|---|---|---|
| | effusion
ef·fu′zhen | Escape of fluid into a part or tissue. |
| | ejaculation
e·jak′u·la′shun | Expulsion of the semen. |
| | elastic
e·las′tik | Susceptible of being stretched and then assuming original shape. |
| | Elastoplast
E·las′to·plast | Trademark for an elastic bandage. |
| | elation
e·la′shun | Emotional excitement marked by speeding up of mental and bodily activity. |
| | elbow
el′bo | Joint connecting arm and forearm. |
| | electrocardiogram
e·lek′tro·kar′de·o-gram | Graphic tracing of upward and downward deflections of auricular and ventricular activity. |
| | electrocardiograph
e·lek′tro·kar′de·o-graf | Instrument for tracing contractions of heart muscle. |
| | electrocautery
e·lek′tro·kaw′ter·e | Apparatus for cauterizing tissue. |
| | electrode
e·lek′trod | Medium used between electric conductor and body of a patient. |
| | electroencephalo-gram
e·lek′tro·en·sef′ah-lo·gram | Graphic recording of electric currents developed in the brain. |

electroencephalograph e·lek′tro·en·sef′- ah·lo·graf	Instrument for recording electric currents developed in the brain.
electrolysis e·lek·trol′i·sis	Destruction of tissue or growths by passage of electric current.
electrolyte e·lek′tro·lit	Solution that conducts electricity by means of its ions.
electrolytic e·lek′tro·lit′ik	Pertaining to or characterized by electrolysis.
electron e·lek′tron	Unit or "atom" of negative electricity.
electrophoresis e·lek′tro·fo·re′sis	Movement of charged particles in a liquid on media, under the influence of an electric field.
electroshock e·lek′tro·shok	Shock produced by application of electric current to brain.
element el′e·ment	Any one of primary parts or constituents of a thing.
elephantiasis el′e·fan·ti′ah·sis	Chronic enlargement of subcutaneous tissues.
elevation el′e·va′shun	Raised area or point of greater height.
elevator el′e·va′tor	Instrument for lifting a depressed part or for removing tissue.
elixir e·lik′ser	Sweetened liquid containing active medicinal agents.
ellipsis e·lip′sis	Omission of words or ideas by a patient during psychoanalysis.

	emaciation e·ma′se·a′shun	Excessive leanness.
	emanation em·ah·na′shun	That which is given off or emitted from a substance.
	embalming em·bahm′ing	Treatment of dead body with preservatives and antiseptics.
	embed em·bed′	Fixation of tissue specimen in a firm medium during cutting of thin sections.
	embolism em′bo·lizm	Clot in an artery or vein.
	embolus em′bo·lus	A clot or plug lodging in blood vessel, obstructing circulation; pl. *emboli*.
	embrasure em·bra′zhur	Space between the sloping proximal surfaces of the teeth.
	embryo em′bre·o	Fetus during the first two months after conception. The early or developing stage of any organism.
	emergency e·mer′jen·se	Unlooked for or sudden occasion; an accident.
	emesis em′e·sis	Vomiting.
	emetic e·met′ik	An agent that causes vomiting.
	eminence em′i·nens	Prominence or projection such as a bone.
	emmenagogue e·men′ah·gog	Agent or measure inducing menstruation.

emollient e·mol′e·ent	Agent which is soothing to the skin or mucous membrane.
emphysema em′fi·se′mah	Condition in which there is overdistention of air spaces in lungs.
emphysematous em′fi·sem′ah·tus	Pertaining to or affected with emphysema.
empiric em·pir′ik	Based solely on experience.
Empirin Em′pi·rin	Trademark for tablets containing acetylsalicylic acid, acetophenetidin, and caffeine.
empyema em′pi·e′mah	Presence of pus in a cavity of the body.
emulsion e·mul′shun	One liquid distributed in small globules throughout body of a second liquid.
enamel en·am′el	Hard, white substance that covers dentin of crown of teeth.
encephalalgia en·sef′a·lal′je·ah	Pain in the head.
encephalitis en′sef·ah·li′tis	Inflammation of the brain. Sleeping sickness.
encephalogram en·sef′ah·lo·gram	Roentgenogram of the head.
encephaloma en′sef·ah·lo′mah	Hernia of the brain.
encephalomalacia en·sef′ah·lo·mah-la′she·ah	Morbid softness of the brain.

	encephalomyelitis en·sef'ah·lo·mi'e- li'tis	Inflammation of both brain and spinal cord.
	encephalon en·sef'ah·lon	Mass of nerve tissue contained within the cranium.
	encephalopathy en·sef'ah·lop'ah- the	Any degenerative disease of the brain.
	endemic en·dem'ik	Present at all times but occurring in only small numbers of cases.
	endocarditis en'do·kar·di'tis	Inflammation of the endocardium.
	endocardium en'do·kar'de·um	Endothelial lining membrane of heart.
	endocrine en'do·krin	Ductless glands which pass secretions into the blood or lymph.
	endocrinology en'do·kri·nol'o·je	Study of the glands of internal secretion and their role in body physiology.
	endocrinopathy en'do·kri·nop'- ah·the	Disease of any of the glands of internal secretion.
	endocrinous en·dok'ri·nus	Of or pertaining to an internal secretion.
	endodermal en'do·der'mal	Pertaining to the endoderm (entoderm), the innermost of the three primary germ layers lining the gut.

endodontics en'do·don'tiks		Dentistry concerned with prevention, diagnosis, and treatment of diseases and injuries affecting tooth pulp.
endodontium en'do·don'she·um		Dental pulp.
endolymph en'do·limf		Fluid contained in membranous labyrinth of the ear.
endometrium en·do·me'tre·um		Mucous membrane lining uterus.
endopelvic en'do·pel'vik		Within the pelvis.
endoplast en'do·plast		Nucleus of a cell.
endoscope en'do·skop		Instrument for examining interior of a hollow organ such as the bladder.
endoscopy en'dos'ko·pe		Inspection of cavity of body with endoscope.
endothelium en'do·the'le·um		Simple squamous epithelium lining the cavities of the heart and of the blood and lymph vessels.
endotracheal en'do·tra'ke·al		Within or through the trachea.
enema en'e·mah		Rectal injection for therapeutic, diagnostic, or nutritive purposes.
energy en'er·je		Capacity for doing work; power to produce motion.
enervation en'er·va'shun		Lack of nervous energy. Removal of a nerve.

engorgement en·gorj′ment		Local congestion; hyperemia.
Enovid E′no·vid		Trademark for an oral contraceptive.
enteralgia en′ter·al′je·ah		Pain in the intestine.
enterectomy en′ter·ek′to·me		Excision of a part of intestine.
enteritis en′ter·i′tis		Inflammation of intestine.
enterobiliary en′ter·o·bil′e·er·e		Pertaining to intestine and bile passages.
enterocele en′ter·o·sel		Intestinal hernia.
enterocleisis en′ter·o·kli′sis		Closure of a wound in the intestines. Occlusion of the lumen of the intestine.
enteroclysis en′ter·ok′li·sis		Injection of a nutrient or medicinal liquid into the intestines.
enterococcus en′ter·o·kok′us		Any streptococcus of the human intestine.
enterocolitis en′ter·o·ko·li′tis		Inflammation involving both small intestine and colon.
enteroptosis en′ter·op·to′sis		Downward displacement of the intestine in the abdominal cavity.
enterorrhaphy en′ter·or′ah·fe		Suturing a gap or wound of the intestine.
enterospasm en′ter·o·spazm		Spasm of the intestine.

enterostaxis en′ter·o·stak′sis	Oozing of blood through intestinal mucous membrane.
enterostomy en′ter·os′to·me	Creation of an artificial opening to intestine.
enterotomy en′ter·ot′o·me	Incision of intestine.
entoderm en′to·derm	Innermost of three primary germ layers of embryo.
enucleate e·nu′kle·at	To remove whole and clean; to shell out.
enuresis en′u·re′sis	Involuntary discharge of urine.
environment en·vi′ron·ment	Total of all that make up surroundings of individual.
enzyme en′zim	Organic compound, frequently a protein, a catalyst that activates chemical reactions within the body.
eosin e′o·sin	Dye used to stain tissue sections on slides.
eosinophil e′o·sin′o·fil	Structure or cell capable of being stained by eosin.
eosinophilia e′o·sin′o·fil′e·ah	Abnormal increase in number of eosinophils in blood.
epicondyle ep′i·kon′dil	An eminence upon a bone, above its condyle. (Also *epicondylus*.)
epidemic ep′i·dem′ik	Attacking many people in any region at the same time.
epiderm ep′i·derm	Epidermis.

epidermis ep′i·der′mis	Outermost layer of skin.
epidermoid ep′i·der′moid	Resembling the epidermis.
epidermophytosis ep′i·der′mo·fi·to′sis	Fungal infection of skin or nails.
epididymis ep′i·did′i·mis	Cordlike structure along posterior border of testis.
epigastric ep′i·gas′trik	Pertaining to upper middle region of abdomen.
epigastrium ep′i·gas′tre·um	Upper middle region of abdomen.
epiglottis ep′i·glot′is	Lidlike structure covering entrance to larynx.
epilepsy ep′i·lep′se	Disease of nervous system characterized by seizures and loss of consciousness.
epileptic ep′i·lep′tik	Pertaining to, or affected with, epilepsy.
epinephrine ep′i·nef′rin	Chief hormone of the adrenal medulla. Also produced synthetically; used as a cardiac stimulant and to relax bronchial smooth muscles.
epiphysis e·pif′i·sis	The end of a long bone.
epiploic ep′i·plo′ik	Pertaining to the omentum.
epiploon e·pip′lo·on	Omentum, usually the great omentum.

episiotomy e·piz′e·ot′o·me	Surgical incision of vulvar orifice.
episode ep′i·sod	Noteworthy happening for which the time can be fixed.
epispastic ep′i·spas′tik	Causing a blister or discharge from a superficial lesion.
epistaxis ep′i·stak′sis	Hemorrhage from nose; nosebleed.
epistropheus ep′i·stro′fe·us	Second cervical vertebra.
epithelial ep′i·the′le·al	Pertaining to or composed of epithelium.
epitheliolysis ep′i·the′le·ol′i·sis	Destruction of epithelial cells.
epithelioma ep′i·the′le·o′mah	An epithelial cancer.
epithelium ep′i·the′le·um	Tissue covering internal and external body surfaces.
equilibrium e′kwi·lib′re·um	Balance.
equivalent e·kwiv′ah·lent	Having the same value.
ergonovine er′go·no′vin	Ergot alkaloid used to relieve migraine headache.
ergot er′got	Powerful drug useful in childbirth; an oxytocic.
Ergotrate Er′go·trat	Trademark for preparations of ergonovine.
erosion e·ro′zhun	Eating or gnawing away; ulceration.

erotic e·rot′ik	Pertaining to love or to lust.
eructation e·ruk·ta′shun	Belching.
eruption e·rup′shun	Breaking out, especially skin lesions.
erysipelas er′i·sip′e·las	Contagious, infectious skin disease with redness and swelling.
erysiphake er·is′i·fak	Instrument for removing lens in cataract by suction.
erythema er′i·the′mah	Redness of skin due to congestion of capillaries.
erythematous er′i·them′ah·tus	Of the nature of erythema.
erythremia er′i·thre′me·ah	Abnormal increase in the red blood cells; polycythemia vera.
erythroblast e·rith′ro·blast	Rudimentary red blood cell.
erythrocyte e·rith′ro·sit	Red blood cell.
erythroderma e·rith′ro·der′mah	Abnormal redness of skin.
erythromycin e·rith′ro·mi′sin	A broad-spectrum antibiotic substance.
erythropoiesis e·rith′ro·poi·e′sis	Formation of red blood cells in red bone marrow.
eschar es′kar	Slough produced by a burn or a caustic.

escharotic es·kah·rot′ik		Corrosive.
Escherichia Esh′er·i′ke·a		Genus of gram-negative rod-shaped bacteria in lower bowel of man.
escutcheon es·kuch′an		Distribution pattern of pubic hair.
eserine es′er·in		Physostigmine; an alkaloid made from the Calabar bean.
esophageal e·sof′ah·je′al		Pertaining to or belonging to esophagus.
esophagoptosis e·sof′ah·gop·to′sis		Prolapse of the esophagus.
esophagoscope e·sof′ah·go·skop		Endoscope for examination of esophagus.
esophagospasm e′so·fag′o·spazm		Spasm of the esophagus.
esophagostenosis e·sof′ah·go·ste-no′sis		Stricture or constriction of esophagus.
esophagus e·sof′ah·gus		Passage extending from pharynx to stomach.
esophoria es′o·fo′re·ah		Tendency of one eye to deviate inward.
esotropia es′o·tro′pe·ah		Deviation of visual axis toward other eye.
essence es′ens		That which gives to anything its character or quality.
ester es′ter		Compound formed from alcohol and an acid by the removal of water.

estrogen es′tro·jen	Generic term for estrus-producing compounds.
etat a·tah′	State; condition.
ether e′ther	A volatile liquid, used by inhalation as a general anesthetic.
ethmoid eth′moid	A bone of the base of the skull.
ethmoidal eth·moi′dal	Of or pertaining to the ethmoid bone.
ethyl eth′il	Transparent, colorless liquid used as a solvent and as a flavoring agent.
ethylene eth′i·len	A colorless gas used by inhalation as a general anesthetic.
etiology e′te·ol′o·je	Study of the causation of disease.
eunuch u′nuk	One who has undergone complete loss of testicular function.
euphoria u·fo′re·ah	Sense of well-being; absence of pain or distress.
eupnea yoop·ne′ah	Normal respiration.
eustachian u·sta′ke·an	A canal; tube; valve.
eutocia u·to′se·ah	Normal labor or childbirth.
evacuation e·vak′u·a′shun	Emptying, as of the bowels.

evagination e·vaj′i·na′shun	An outpouching of a layer or part.	
evaporation e·vap′o·ra′shun	Conversion of liquid or solid into vapor.	
eversion e·ver′zhun	Turning outward or inside out.	
Evipal E·vi′pal	Trademark for a preparation of hexobarbital; sedative and hypnotic.	
evisceration e·vis′er·a′shun	Removal of the internal organs; disembowelment.	
exacerbation eks·as′er·ba′shun	Increase in severity of any symptoms of disease.	
examination eks·am′i·na′tion	Inspection or investigation as a means of diagnosing disease.	
excavation eks′kah·va′shun	Act of hollowing out.	
excise ek·siz′	To cut out or off.	
excision ek·sizh′un	A cutting out; surgical removal.	
excitability ek·sit′ah·bil′i·te	Readiness of response to stimulus; irritability.	
excitation ek′si·ta′shun	Act of irritation or stimulation.	
exclusion eks·kloo′zhun	Process of ejecting or extruding. An operation separating a portion of an organ from the rest of it without removing it from the body.	

	excoriation eks·ko′re·a′shun	Superficial loss, as of the skin by scratching.	
	excrement eks′kre·ment	Fecal matter.	
	excrescence eks·kres′ens	Abnormal outgrowth from a surface.	
	excrete eks·kret′	To discharge waste material.	
	excretin eks′kre·tin	Crystalline compound from human feces.	
	excursion eks·kur′zhun	Movements from a normal, or rest, position of a movable part.	
	exenteration eks·en′ter·a′shun	Surgical removal of inner organs.	
	exercise ek′ser·siz	Performance of physical exertion for improvement of health.	
	exeresis eks·er′e·sis	Removal or excision of nerve, vessel, part, or organ.	
	exfoliation eks′fo·le·a′shun	Falling off in scales or layers.	
	exhale eks·hal′	Expel from lungs by breathing.	
	exhaustion eg·zawst′zun	Privation of energy with inability to respond to stimuli.	
	exhibitionism ek′si·bish′un·izm	Display of one's body or parts for purpose of attracting sexual interest.	
	exocardial ek′so·kar′de·al	Outside the heart.	

exocrine ek·so′krin	Secreting outwardly.
exogastritis ek′so·gas·tri′tis	Inflammation of stomach wall.
exophthalmic ek′sof·thal′mik	Characterized by protrusion of the eyeball.
exostosis ek′sos·to′sis	Bony growth projecting outward from bone.
exotropia ek′so·tro′pe·ah	Deviation of visual axis away from that of other eye.
expectation eks′pek·ta′shun	That which may be anticipated or looked forward to.
expectorant eks·pek′to·rant	An agent that promotes spitting mucus from lungs and trachea.
expectoration eks·pek′to·ra′shun	Coughing up and spitting out mucus from lungs or throat.
expiration eks′pi·ra′shun	Breathing out air from lungs. Termination; death.
expiratory eks·pi′rah·to′re	Subserving or pertaining to expiration.
expire ek·spir′	To breathe out. To die.
exploration eks′plo·ra′shun	Act of search, investigation, or examination.
exploratory eks·plo′rah·to′re	Pertaining to research. An exploration.
expression eks·presh′un	Facial aspect or appearance of face. Act of squeezing.
expulsive eks·pul′siv	Driving or forcing out; tending to expel.

	exsanguinate eks·sang'gui·nat	To deprive of blood. Anemic or bloodless.	
	extender eks·ten'der	Something which enlarges or prolongs.	
	extension eks·ten'shun	Act of extending or straightening a limb.	
	extensor eks·ten'sor	A muscle that extends or stretches a limb or part.	
	exterior eks·te're·or	Situated on or near the outside; outer.	
	exteriorize eks·te're·or·iz	To expose an organ or part temporarily and bring it outside the body.	
	exteroceptor eks'ter·o·sep'tor	Sensory nerve terminal which is stimulated by external environment.	
	extirpation ek·ster·pa'shun	Complete removal of an organ or part.	
	extract eks'trakt	Concentrated preparation of a vegetable or animal drug.	
	extraction eks·trak'shun	Process or act of pulling or drawing out.	
	extractor eks·trak'tor	Instrument used in drawing out, pulling, or extracting.	
	extrahepatic eks'trah·he·pat'ik	Situated outside of the liver.	
	extraneous eks·tra'ne·us	Existing or belonging outside the organism.	
	extraocular eks'trah·ok'u·lar	Situated outside the eye.	

extrasystole eks′trah·sis′to·le	Premature contraction of the heart which is independent of the normal rhythm.
extravasation eks·trav′ah·sa′shun	Discharge or escape of a body fluid, as of blood from vessel into tissues.
extravascular eks′trah·vas′ku·lar	Situated outside a vessel.
extraversion eks′trah·ver′zhun	Turning outward or objectifying of personal interests or emotions.
extremity eks·trem′i·te	Distal or terminal portion. Arm or leg.
extrinsic eks·trin′sik	Originating or coming from the outside.
extrovert eks′tro·vert	Person whose interest is turned outward toward external values.
extrusion eks·troo′zhen	Pushing out; repulsion.
extubation eks′tu·ba′shun	The removal of a tube.
exudate eks′u·dat	Material that has escaped from blood vessels and has been deposited in tissues or on tissue surfaces, usually due to inflammation.
exutory eks·u′tor·e	Drawing off.
eyeball i′ball	The globe of the eye.

eyebrow i′brow	Transverse elevation at junction of forehead and upper eyelid. The hairs growing at the junction.
eyeground i′ground	The fundus or base of the eye.
eyelash i′lash	One of the hairs growing at edge of eyelid.
eyelid i′lid	Either of two folds that protect anterior surface of eyeball.
eyestrain i′stran	Fatigue of eye from overuse or from uncorrected defect of focus.

F

face fas	Anterior aspect of head from forehead to chin.
facet fas′et	Small plane surface, usually on a bone.
facial fa′shal	Pertaining to the face.
facies fa′she·ez	Expression of the face.
facilitation fah·sil′i·ta′shun	Promotion of any natural process.
faculty fak′ul·te	Any normal power or function, especially mental.
Fahrenheit Far′en·hit	A scale of temperature describing 180 degrees between freezing point, 32 degrees, and boiling point, 212 degrees.

fallopian fal·lo′pe·an	Parts of the body named for the Italian anatomist Fallopia, e.g., Fallopian tube, ligament.
familial fah·mil′e·al	Affecting members of the same family.
fascia fash′e·ah	Band or sheet of tissue which covers muscles or organs; pl. *fasciae*.
fascial fash′e·al	Relating to membrane covering muscles.
fascicle fas′i·k′l	A small bundle or cluster, especially of nerve or muscle fibers.
fasciculation fah·sik′u·la′shun	Formation of nerve or muscle fibers.
fasciculus fah·sik′u·lus	Bundle of nerve, muscle, or tendon fibers.
fatigability fat′i·gah·bil′i·te	Easily fatigued.
fatigue fah·teg′	Discomfort and decreased efficiency from excessive exertion.
fauces faw′sez	Passage between the mouth and the pharynx.
faucial faw′shal	Pertaining to the fauces.
febrile feb′ril	Characterized by or pertaining to fever.
fecalith fe′kah·lith	An intestinal stone.

feces fe′sez	Excrement from intestines; fecal discharge.	
fecundation fe′kun·da′shun	Impregnation or fertilization.	
feminine fem′i·nin	Pertaining to the female sex.	
femoral fem′or·al	Pertaining to the thigh bone or femur.	
femur fe′mur	The thigh bone; largest, longest, and heaviest bone in body.	
fenestra fe·nes′trah	Windowlike opening.	
fenestration fen′es·tra′shun	Act of perforating.	
fermentation fer′men·ta′shun	Decomposition of complex molecules with enzymes.	
fertile fer′til	Fruitful; not sterile or barren.	
fertilization fer′ti·li·za′shun	Impregnation; union of male and female gametes.	
fetal fe′tal	Pertaining to a fetus.	
fetor fe′tor	Stench; offensive odor.	
fetus fe′tus	Unborn child in uterus after end of second month.	
fever fe′ver	High body temperature; pyrexia.	
fiber fi′ber	Elongated threadlike structure.	

fibril fi′bril	A very small fiber or filament.	
fibrillation fi·bri·la′tion	Contraction of muscles, invisible under skin.	
fibrin fi′brin	Whitish, insoluble protein formed in clotting of blood.	
fibrinogen fi·brin′o·jen	Soluble protein in blood plasma. Coagulation factor I.	
fibroadenoma fi′bro·ad′e·no′mah	Adenoma containing fibrous tissue.	
fibroblast fi′bro·blast	Connective tissue cell.	
fibrocystic fi′bro·sis′tik	Characterized by development of cystic spaces.	
fibrofatty fi′bro·fat′e	Both fibrous and fatty.	
fibroid fi′broid	Having a fibrous structure.	
fibroma fi·bro′mah	Tumor composed of fibrous connective tissue.	
fibroplasia fi′bro·pla′se·ah	Formation of fibrous tissue in healing of wounds.	
fibrose fi′bros	To form fibrous tissue.	
fibrosis fi·bro′sis	Development of fibrous tissue.	
fibrositis fi′bro·si′tis	Inflammatory hyperplasia of white fibrous tissue.	
fibrotic fi·brot′ik	Characterized by fibrosis.	

fibrous fi′brus	Containing fibers.
fibula fib′u·lah	Outer and smaller of two bones of leg.
filament fil′ah·ment	A delicate fiber or thread.
filling fil′ing	Material inserted into prepared tooth cavity.
filtration fil·tra′shun	Passage of a liquid through a filter.
fimbriated fim′bre·at·ed	Fringed.
finger fing′ger	Any one of five digits of hand.
fingerbreadth fing′ger·breth	Unit of length based on breadth of a finger.
fingerprint fing′ger·print	Impression of cutaneous ridges of distal portion of finger.
fission fish′un	Act of splitting.
fissure fish′ur	Any cleft or groove, normal or otherwise. (Also *fissura*.)
fistula fis′tu·lah	Abnormal opening or canal from one body cavity to another or from one body cavity to surface of body.
fistulous fis′tu·lus	Pertaining to a fistula.
fixation fiks·a′shun	Act or operation of holding, suturing, or fastening in a fixed position.

	flaccid flak′sid	Soft, flabby, relaxed, weak.
	flatfoot flat′foot	One or more arches of foot flattened out.
	flatulence flat′u·lens	Distended with gas in stomach.
	flatulent flat′u·lent	Characterized by distention with gas.
	flatus fla′tus	Gas or air in the digestive tract.
	flexion flek′shun	Bending or being bent.
	flexor flek′sor	Any muscle that flexes a joint.
	flexure flek′sher	A bending; a bent portion of a structure or organ.
	flocculent flok′u·lent	Containing downy or flaky particles.
	fluctuant fluk′tu·ant	Showing varying levels; wavelike motion.
	fluctuation fluk′tu·a′shun	A variation; a wavelike impulse or motion.
	fluid floo′id	A liquid or a gas.
	fluorescence floo′o·res′ens	Property of emitting light after exposure to light.
	fluoroscope floo·o′ro·skop	Instrument to examine deep structures by roentgen rays.
	fluoroscopy floo′or·os′ko·pe	Examination by roentgen rays.

flutter flut′er	Quick vibration or pulsation.	
focus fo′kus	Point of convergence of light rays or sound waves; pl. *foci*.	
follicle fol′li·k′l	Small excretory duct or sac.	
follicular fo·lik′u·lar	Pertaining to a follicle.	
folliculitis fo·lik′u·li′tis	Inflammation of a follicle or follicles.	
fomentation fo′men·ta′shun	Application of warm, moist cloths for relief of pain.	
fontanelle fon′tah·nel′	Soft spot between cranial bones of an infant. (Also *fontanel*.)	
foot foot	Terminal organ of leg.	
foramen fo·ra′men	A natural opening or passage; general term for such a passage, especially in a bone.	
forceps for′seps	Instrument for pulling, holding, or extracting.	
forearm for′arm	Part of arm between elbow and wrist.	
forehead for′hed	Part of face above the eyes.	
formative for′mah·tiv	Concerned in origination of an organism, part, or tissue.	
formula for′mu·lah	Specific statement, using numerals and symbols, giving directions for preparing a compound.	

fornicate for′ni·kat	To engage in illicit sexual intercourse.
fornix for′niks	An archlike structure or the vaultlike space it creates.
fossa fos′sah	A hollow or depressed area; pl. *fossae*.
fossula fos′su·lah	Small fossa.
fovea fo′ve·ah	Small pit or depression.
fracture frak′tur	A break, especially of a bone.
fragility frah·jil′i·te	Susceptibility or lack of resistance.
freckle frek′l	Brownish pigmented spot on skin.
fremitus frem′i·tus	Vibration felt on palpating chest wall.
friable fri′ah·b′l	Easily torn or easily crumbled into powder.
frigidity fri·jid′i·te	Coldness, especially sexual indifference.
frontal fron′tal	Pertaining to the anterior part or aspect of an organ or body. Pertaining to the forehead.
frontoparietal fron′to·pah·ri′e·tal	Pertaining to frontal and parietal bones.
frostbite frost′bit	Damage to tissues resulting from exposure to low temperatures.

	frustration frus·tra′shun	Emotional tension resulting from failure to achieve sought satisfaction.
	fugue fug′	A state in which rational behavior is followed by amnesia regarding it.
	fulguration ful′gu·ra′shun	Destruction of tissue by electric sparks.
	fulminate ful′mi·nat	To occur suddenly, with great intensity.
	function funk′shun	Special, normal, or proper action of any part or organ.
	fundus fun′dus	Base or part of a hollow organ farthest removed from its mouth; pl. *fundi*.
	fungus fung′gus	Vegetable organism of low order of development. A growth on body.
	furrow fur′o	A groove or trench.
	furuncle fu′rung·k′l	A boil or cutaneous abscess.
	fusiform fu′si·form	Shaped like a spindle.
	fusion fu′zhun	Act or process of melting. Abnormal coherence of adjacent parts or bodies.

G

	gag gag	Surgical device for holding mouth open; to retch.

	gait gat	Style of walking.
	galactagogue gah·lak′tah·gog	Agent that promotes the flow of milk.
	galactocele gah·lak′to·sel	Cystic enlargement of mammary gland containing milk.
	galactophoritis gah·lak′to·fo·ri′tis	Inflammation of milk ducts.
	galactorrhea gah·lak′to·re′ah	Excessive flow of milk.
	galactosis gal·ak·to′sis	Formation of milk by the lacteal glands.
	galactostasis gal′ak·tos′tah·sis	Cessation of milk secretion.
	galea ga′le·ah	Helmetlike structure.
	gallbladder gawl′bladder	Reservoir for bile on under-surface of liver.
	gallop gal′op	Intensification of normal third or fourth heart sound.
	gallstone gawl′ston	Concretion of cholesterol, bilirubin, and other elements in gallbladder or bile duct.
	galvanometer gal′vah·nom′e·ter	Instrument for measuring current.
	gamete gam′et	Mature male or female reproductive cell.
	ganglioma gang′gle·o′mah	Tumor of a lymphatic ganglion.

ganglion gang′gle·on	Knot of nerve cells outside central nervous system; pl. *ganglia*.
ganglionectomy gang′gle·o·nek′-to·me	Excision of a ganglion.
ganglionitis gang′gle·on·i′tis	Inflammation of a ganglion.
gangrene gang′gren	Death of tissue and putrefaction.
gangrenous gang′gre·nus	Pertaining to or of the nature of gangrene.
gargle gar′g′l	Solution used for rinsing mouth and throat.
gaseous gas′e·us	Of the nature of gas.
gastralgia gas·tral′je·ah	Pain in the stomach.
gastrectasia gas·trek·ta′ze·ah	Dilatation of the stomach.
gastrectomy gas·trek′to·me	Total or partial removal of stomach.
gastric gas′trik	Of or pertaining to stomach.
gastritis gas·tri′tis	Inflammation of stomach.
gastrocele gas′tro·sel	Hernial protrusion of the stomach.
gastrocnemius gas′trok·ne′me·us	Muscle on the posterior aspect of the leg.

gastrodynia gas′tro·din′e·ah		Stomachache.
gastroenteritis gas′tro·en·ter·i′tis		Inflammation of stomach and intestines.
gastroenterologist gas′tro·en·ter·ol′- o·jist		Specialist in diseases of the stomach and intestines.
gastroenterostomy gas′tro·en·ter·os′- to·me		Surgical opening between stomach and small intestine.
gastrointestinal gas′tro·in·tes′- ti·nal		Pertaining to the stomach and intestine.
gastropathy gas·trop′ah·the		Any disease of stomach.
gastrorrhagia gas′tro·ra′je·ah		Hemorrhage from the stomach.
gastrorrhaphy gas·tror′ah·fe		Surgical repair of stomach wound.
gastroscopy gas·tros′ko·pe		Inspection of stomach interior with gastroscope.
gastrostomy gas·tros′to·me		Surgical creation of artificial opening into stomach.
gauge gaj		An instrument for determining the dimensions or caliber of anything.
gauze gawz		Sterile fabric used in surgery.
gavage gah·vahzh′		Feeding by means of the stomach tube.

gelatin jel'ah·tin		Product used as food, and pharmaceutically in manufacture of capsules.
Gelfoam Gel'fom		Trademark for absorbable gelatin sponge.
gene jen		Biologic unit of heredity.
general jen'er·al		Affecting many parts; not local.
generalize jen'er·al·iz		To convert from local to general disease.
genetic je·net'ik		Pertaining to reproduction, birth, or origin; inherited.
genital jen'i·tal		Pertaining to reproduction or its organs.
genitalia jen'i·ta'le·ah		The reproductive organs.
genitourinary jen'i·to·u'ri·nar·e		Pertaining to genital and urinary organs.
genius jen'yus		Distinctive character; superlative ability.
genome je'nom		Complete set of hereditary factors.
genu je'nu		Site of articulation between thigh and leg. The knee.
geriatrics jer'e·at'trics		Branch of medicine which treats all problems peculiar to the aging and the aged.
germ jerm		A pathogenic microorganism.

germicide jer′mi·sid	Agent that destroys pathogenic microorganisms.
gestation jes·ta′shun	Period of intrauterine development; pregnancy.
giantism ji′ant·izm	Abnormal size of cells or nuclei.
gigantism ji′gan·tizm	Abnormal overgrowth in size and stature.
gingiva jin′ji′vah	The mucous membrane which overlies the crowns of teeth; pl. *gingivae*. The gums.
gingival jin′ji·val	Pertaining to the gingivae.
gingivitis jin·ji·vi′tis	Inflammation involving the gingival tissue only.
girdle ger′d′l	Encircling structure or part.
gland gland	Cells or organs that excrete materials. (Also *glandula*.)
glandular glan′du·lar	Pertaining to a gland.
glans glanz	Small rounded mass or gland-like body.
glaucoma glaw·ko′mah	Disease of eye, characterized by elevated intraocular pressure.
glioblastoma gli′o·blas·to′mah	Tumor containing spongioblasts.
glioma gli·o′mah	A tumor composed of tissue representing neuroglia.

～ℓ	gliosis gli·o′sis	Disease condition with presence of gliomas.
～	globule glob′ul	Small spherical mass, globe, or pellet. A blood disk or corpuscle.
～	globulin glob′u·lin	Proteins insoluble in water but soluble in saline solutions.
～	globus glo′bus	A sphere or ball; spherical mass.
～	glomerulus glo·mer′u·lus	A tuft or cluster; pl. *glomeruli*.
～	glomus glo′mus	Small body composed of fine arterioles.
～	glossa glos′ah	Tongue.
～	glossal glos′al	Of or pertaining to the tongue.
～	glossitis glos·si′tis	Inflammation of tongue.
～	glossocele glos′o·sel	Swelling and protrusion of tongue.
～	glossodynia glos′o·din′e·ah	Pain in the tongue.
～	glottis glot′is	Vocal apparatus of larynx.
～	glucagon gloo′kah·gon	Protein secreted by the pancreas in response to hypoglycemia.
～	gluconate gloo′ko·nat	Salt of gluconic acid.

glucose gloo′kos	Syrupy, sweet liquid made by incomplete hydrolysis of starch.
gluteal gloo′te·al	Pertaining to the buttocks.
glutinous gloo′ti·nus	Sticky; adhesive; gluey.
glycemia gli·se′me·ah	Presence of sugar in blood.
glycerin glis′er·in	Colorless, syrupy liquid used as solvent for drugs.
glycogen gli′ko·jen	Carbohydrate stored in the liver and converted, as needed, into glucose.
glycolysis gli·kol′i·sis	Conversion of carbohydrates into sugar.
glycolytic gli′ko·lit′ik	Pertaining to the breaking down of carbohydrates.
glyconeogenesis gli′ko·ne′o·jen′- e·sis	Formation of carbohydrates from protein or fat molecules.
glycopenia gli′ko·pe′ne·ah	Abnormally low blood sugar level.
glycosuria gli′ko·su′re·ah	Presence of sugar in the urine.
gnathodynia nath′o·din′e·ah	Pain in the jaw.
gnathoplasty nath′o·plas′te	Plastic surgery of jaw or cheek.
goiter goi′ter	Enlargement of the thyroid gland, causing a swelling in the neck.

	gonad gon'ad	Ovary or testis; gamete-producing gland.	
	gonococcus gon'o·kok'us	Specific organism which causes gonorrhea.	
	gonorrhea gon'o·re'ah	Contagious inflammation of genital mucous membranes.	
	gouge gowj	Hollow chisel used in cutting and removing bone.	
	gout gowt	Excess of uric acid in blood and decreased excretion of uric acid in urine, accompanied by fever and painful arthritis.	
	grafting graft'ing	Implantation of skin or other tissue from another site or source.	
	grain gran	A unit of weight of the troy, avoirdupois, and apothecaries' systems. A minute particle.	
	gram gram	The basic unit of mass, and of weight, of the metric system.	
	gram-negative gram-neg'ah·tiv	Losing stain by alcohol in Gram's method of staining.	
	gram-positive gram-poz'i·tiv	Retaining stain by alcohol in Gram's method of staining.	
	grand mal grahn mahl	A major epileptic attack.	
	granular gran'u·lar	Made up of granules or grains.	
	granulation gran'u·la'shun	Formation of small, rounded fleshy masses on surface of a wound.	

	granule gran'ul	A minute particle or grain.
	granuloma gran'u·lo'mah	Tumor or neoplasm made up of granulation tissue.
	gravel grav'el	Minute particles of stone passed with the urine.
	gravid grav'id	Pregnant.
	gravida grav'i·dah	A pregnant woman.
	gravity grav'i·te	Weight; tending toward the center of the earth.
	grippe grip	Influenza.
	groin groin	Lowest part of abdominal wall near junction with thigh.
	gustatory gus'tah·to're	Pertaining to the sense of taste.
	gut gut	The intestine or bowel.
	gynecoid jin'e·koid	Womanlike; resembling a woman.
	gynecologic jin'e·ko·loj'ik	Pertaining to or affecting the female reproductive tract.
	gynecology jin'e·kol'o·je	Branch of medicine pertaining to diseases of the reproductive tract of women.
	gyniatrics jin'e·at'riks	Treatment of female diseases.

| gyrus | One of the convolutions on the surface of the cerebrum. |
| ji′rus | |

H

| habit | Fixed practice established by frequent repetition. |
| hab′it | |

| habitus | General appearance; physique. |
| hab′i·tus | |

| halitosis | Offensive breath. |
| hal·i·to′sis | |

| hallucination | A sense perception not founded upon objective reality. |
| hah·lu′si·na′shun | |

| hallucinogenic | Hallucinatory agent. |
| hah·lu′sin·no·jen′ik | |

| hallux | The great toe; first digit of foot. |
| hal′uks | |

| hammer | Hammer-shaped bone of middle ear. An instrument with a head designed for striking blows. |
| ham′er | |

| hamstring | Muscles of the back of the thigh. |
| ham′string | |

| hand | Composed of carpus, metacarpus, and fingers. |
| hand | |

| haploid | Having a single set of chromosomes. |
| hap′loid | |

| harelip | Congenital cleft or defect in upper lip. |
| har′lip | |

| haunch | The hip and buttock. |
| hawnch | |

	hay fever ha fe′ver	Acute conjunctivitis with nasal catarrh, regarded as an allergic condition.
	headache hed′ak	Pain in the head.
	heliopathia he′le·o·path′e·ah	Any pathological disturbance caused by sunlight.
	heliosis he′le·o′sis	Sunstroke.
	helix he′liks	A coiled structure.
	hemacytometer hem′ah·si·tom′-e·ter	Instrument used to count blood corpuscles.
	hemangioma he·man′je·o′mah	Benign tumor filled with blood vessels.
	hematoblast hem′at·to·blast	Cell from which red blood cell is developed.
	hematocele hem′ah·to·sel	Effusion of blood into a cavity.
	hematocrit he·mat′o·krit	Volume percentage of erythrocytes in whole blood.
	hematocyst hem′ah·to·sist	Effusion of blood into bladder or cyst.
	hematology hem′a·tol′o·je	Branch of biology which treats morphology of blood.
	hematoma hem′ah·to′mah	Tumor containing effused blood.
	hematopiesis hem′ah·to·pi′e·sis	Blood pressure.

	hematopoiesis hem'ah·to·poi- e'sis	Process of blood cell formation.
	hematosis hem'ah·to'sis	Formation of blood. Aeration of blood in lungs.
	hematoxylin hem'ah·tok'si·lin	Dye used to stain tissue sections on slides.
	hematuria hem'ah·tu're·ah	Discharge of blood in urine.
	hemianopia hem'e·ah·no'pe·ah	Blindness in half of visual field.
	hemiparesis hem'e·par'e·sis	Muscular weakness on one side of body.
	hemiplegia hem'e·ple'je·ah	Paralysis of one side of body.
	hemocyte he'mo·sit	Any blood corpuscle.
	hemoglobin he'mo·glo'bin	Oxygen-carrying pigment of red blood corpuscles.
	hemogram he'mo·gram	Blood analysis record.
	hemolysis he·mol'i·sis	Liberation of hemoglobin.
	hemolytic he'mo·lit'ik	Pertaining to, characterized by, or producing hemolysis.
	hemophilia he'mo·fil'e·ah	Hereditary hemorrhagic diathesis in males but transmitted by females.
	hemophiliac he'mo·fil'e·ak	Individual with hemophilia.

	hemophobia he′mo·fo′be·ah	Morbid dread of blood.
	hemoptysis he·mop′ti·sis	Expectoration of blood.
	hemorrhage hem′or·ij	Bleeding. Copious escape of blood from the vessels.
	hemorrhoid hem′o·roid	Vascular tumor of rectal mucous membrane; pile.
	hemorrhoidectomy hem′o·roid·ek′- to·me	Excision of hemorrhoids.
	hemostasis he·mos′tah·sis	Arrest of an escape of blood.
	hemostat he′mo·stat	Instrument for compressing a bleeding vessel.
	hemostatic he′mo·stat′ik	An agent that arrests the flow of blood.
	heparin hep′ah·rin	Drug used to prevent or to treat thrombosis.
	hepatic he·pat′ik	Pertaining to the liver.
	hepatitis hep′ah·ti′tis	Inflammation of the liver.
	hepatodynia hep′ah·to·din′e·ah	Pain in the liver.
	hepatoma hep′ah·to′mah	Tumor of the liver.
	hepatomegaly hep′ah·to·meg′ah·le	Enlarged liver.

hepatosplenomegaly hep′ah·to·sple′no- meg′ah·le	Enlargement of liver and spleen.
hereditary he·red′i·ter′e	Condition genetically transmitted from parent to offspring.
hernia her′ne·ah	Protrusion of a loop of organ or tissue through an abnormal opening.
hernioplasty her′ne·o·plas′te	Surgical repair of a hernia.
herniorrhaphy her′ne·or′ah·fe	Suture of a hernia.
heroin her′o·in	Anodyne and sedative.
herpes her′pez	Inflammatory skin disease marked by groups of watery blisters. Herpes simplex.
heterogenic het′er·o·jen′ik	Occurring in the wrong sex.
hexamethonium hek′sah·me·tho′- ne·um	Ganglionic blocking agent for high blood pressure.
hiant hi′ant	Yawning or gaping; opening wide.
hiatus hi·a′tus	An opening; a gap or cleft.
hiccup hik′up	Involuntary spasmodic contraction of diaphragm.
hidroa hid·ro′ah	Skin affection accompanied by sweating.

	hidropoiesis hid′ro·poi·e′sis	The formation of sweat.
	hidrorrhea hid·ro·re′ah	Profuse perspiration.
	hidrosis hid·ro′sis	Secretion and excretion of sweat.
	hilar hi′lar	Pertaining to a hilus.
	hillock hil′ok	A small prominence or elevation.
	hilus hi′lus	Depression in organ where nerves and vessels enter.
	Hinton Hin′ton	Test for syphilis.
	hirsute her′sut	Shaggy; hairiness.
	hirsutism her′sut·izm	Excessive hairiness, especially in women.
	Histadyl His′tah·dil	Trademark for an antihistaminic.
	histamine his′tah·min	An amine occurring in all vegetable and animal tissues. The pharmaceutical preparation reduces sensitivity to allergens.
	histidine his′ti·din	An alpha-amino acid essential for optimal growth in infants.
	histology his·tol′o·je	Science dealing with minute structure of tissues.
	histoma his·to′mah	Any tissue tumor; fibroma.

hives hivz′	Urticaria; skin condition with itching wheals or welts.
hoarseness hors′nes	Rough quality of voice.
homergy hom′er·je	Normal metabolism.
homicide hom′i·sid	Taking the life of another individual.
homogeneous ho′mo·je′ne·us	Of the same kind or quality throughout.
homologous ho·mol′o·gus	Similar in structure, origin, or place, but not function.
homonymous ho·mon′i·mus	Having same sound or name.
homosexual ho′mo·seks′u·al	Individual attracted toward person of the same sex.
hormone hor′mon	A specific chemical produced in the body. Regulatory secretion produced by an endocrine gland.
hospital hos′pit′l	Institution for treatment of sick.
hospitalization hos′pit′l·i·za′shun	Confinement of patient in a hospital.
hostility hos·til′i·te	Antagonism; animosity; anger.
humeroscapular hu′mer·o·skap′- u·lar	Pertaining to humerus and scapula.
humerus hu′mer·us	Bone between the elbow and shoulder; pl. *humeri*.

humor hu′mor	Fluid or semifluid substance.
hyalin hi′ah·lin	A translucent albumoid substance, one of the products of amyloid degeneration.
hyaloid hi′ah·loid	Resembling glass.
hydrated hi′drat·ed	Combined with water.
hydration hi·dra′shun	State of a compound which contains water in chemical combination.
hydremia hi·dre′me·ah	Excess of water in the blood.
hydroa hid·ro′ah	Skin disease marked by red patches with vesicles.
hydrobromide hi′dro·bro′mid	Addition salt of hydrobromic acid.
hydrocele hi′dro·sel	Accumulation of fluid in the scrotum.
hydrocephalus hi′dro·sef′ah·lus	Accumulation of cerebrospinal fluid within the cranial cavity.
hydrochloride hi′dro·klo′rid	An addition salt of hydrochloric acid.
hydrocyst hi′dro·sist	Cyst with watery contents.
hydrogen hi′dro·jen	Lightest element; found in water and in all organic compounds.

hydrolysis hi·drol′i·sis	Breaking down of a compound into fragments by the addition of water.	
hydrolytic hi·dro·lit′ik	Pertaining to hydrolysis.	
hydronephrosis hi′dro·ne·fro′sis	Collection of urine in the pelvis of the kidney.	
hydropathy hi·drop′ah·the	Treatment of disease by use of water.	
hydrophobia hi′dro·fo′be·ah	Fear of water; rabies.	
hydrops hi′drops	Abnormal accumulation of serous fluid in tissues or body cavity.	
hydrosalpinx hi′dro·sal′pinks	Accumulation of fluid in a uterine tube.	
hydrotherapy hi·dro·ther′ah·pe	Use of water in treatment of disease.	
hydrothorax hi′dro·tho′raks	Presence of fluid in the pleural cavity.	
hygiene hi′je·en	Science of health and its preservation.	
hygienist hi′je·en·ist	Specialist in hygiene.	
hygroma hi·gro′mah	Sac, cyst, or bursa distended with fluid.	
hymen hi′men	Mucous membrane that partially occludes the vaginal outlet.	
hymenorrhaphy hi′men·or′ah·fe	Closure of vagina by sutures.	

	hymenotome hi·men′o·tom	Instrument for cutting membranes.
	hyoid hi′oid	Pertaining to hyoid bone.
	hyperacidity hi′per·ah·sid′i·te	Excessive degree of acidity.
	hyperactivity hi′per·ak·tiv′i·te	Abnormally increased activity.
	hyperalgesia hi′per·al·je′ze·ah	Abnormal sensitivity to pain.
	hypercapnia hi′per·kap′ne·ah	Excessive carbon dioxide content in the blood.
	hyperemesis hi′per·em′e·sis	Excessive vomiting.
	hyperemia hi′per·e′me·ah	Excess blood in a body part.
	hyperesthesia hi′per·es·the′ze·ah	Abnormal sensitivity of the skin or of a sensory organ.
	hyperglycemia hi′per·gli′se′me·ah	Increased level of glucose in blood.
	hypergonadism hi′per·go′nad·izm	Excessive growth and precocious sexual development.
	hyperhidrosis hi′per·hi·dro′sis	Excessive perspiration.
	hyperinsulinemia hy′per·in′su·lin·e′- me·ah	Excessive amount of insulin in the blood.
	hyperkalemia hy′per·kah·le′- me·ah	Abnormally high potassium content of the blood.

	hyperkinesia hi′per·ki·ne′ze·ah	Excessive activity or mobility.
	hyperopia hi′per·o′pe·ah	Farsightedness.
	hyperorexia hi′per·o·rek′se·ah	Abnormally increased appetite.
	hyperphagia hi′per·fa′je·ah	Excessive ingestion of food.
	hyperphoria hi′per·fo′re·ah	Upward deviation of the visual axis of an eye when fusion is prevented.
	hyperplasia hi′per·pla′ze·ah	Abnormal overgrowth of tissue due to excessive cell division.
	hyperpnea hi′perp·ne′ah	Abnormally deep and rapid breathing.
	hyperpyrexia hi′per·pi·rek′se·ah	Highly elevated body temperature.
	hyperreflexia hi′per·re·flek′se·ah	Exaggeration of reflexes.
	hyperresonance hi′per·rez′o·nans	An exaggerated resonance of a percussion note.
	hypersensitiveness hi′per·sen′si·tiv′nes	State in which body reacts to foreign agent more strongly than normal.
	hypertension hi′per·ten′shun	Abnormally high blood pressure; excessive tension.
	hypertensive hi′per·ten′siv	Causing increased tension or pressure.
	hyperthermia hi′per·ther′me·ah	Abnormally high body temperature.

	hyperthyroidism hi′per·thi′roid·izm	Excessive activity of thyroid gland.
	hypertonia hi′per·to′ne·ah	Condition of excessive tone, tension, or activity.
	hypertrophy hi·per′tro·fe	Abnormal enlargement of organ or part.
	hyperventilation hi′per·ven′ti·la′-shun	Abnormally rapid and deep respiration.
	hypnosis hip·no′sis	Artificially induced passive state and responsiveness to suggestions.
	hypnotic hip·not′ik	A drug that induces sleep.
	hypoactivity hi′po·ak·tiv′i·te	Abnormally diminished activity.
	hypochromia hi′po·kro′me·ah	Abnormal decrease in hemoglobin content of erythrocytes.
	hypodermic hi·po·der′mik	Administered beneath the skin.
	hypodermoclysis hi′po·der·mok′-li·sis	Subcutaneous injection of large quantities of fluids.
	hypogastric hi′po·gas′trik	Situated below the stomach.
	hypogonadism hi′po·go′nad·izm	Decreased functional activity of gonads resulting in retarded sexual development.
	hypometabolism hi′po·me·tab′o·lizm	Low metabolic rate.

hypoplasia hi′po·pla′ze·ah	Incomplete or defective development.
hypostasis hi·pos′tah·sis	The deposit of sediment.
hypotension hi′po·ten′shun	Low blood pressure.
hypothenar hi·poth′e·nar	Ridge of palm along bases of fingers.
hypothesis hi·poth′e·sis	Supposition assumed as a basis of reasoning.
hypothyroidism hi′po·thi′roid·izm	Deficiency of thyroid activity.
hypotonic hi·po·ton′ik	Below normal strength or tension.
hypoventilation hi′po·ven′ti·la′-shun	Shallow breathing with reduced air entering pulmonary alveoli, resulting in elevation of carbon dioxide tension.
hypoxemia hi′pok·se′me·ah	Deficient oxygenation of the blood.
hysteralgia his′ter·al′je·ah	Pain in the uterus.
hysterectomy his′ter·ek′to·me	Removal of the uterus.
hysteria his·ter′e·ah	Psychoneurosis, with symptoms based on conversion, characterized by uncontrolled acts and emotions.
hysteropexy his′ter·o·pek·se	Fixation of a displaced uterus by surgery.

| | hysteroscope
his′ter·o·skop | Instrument for visual examination of uterine cavity. |

I

	ichor i′kor	A thin, serous fluid from a sore or wound.
	ichthyosis ik′the·o′sis	Dryness, roughness, and scaliness of skin.
	icteric ik·ter′ik	Relating to or affected with jaundice.
	icterus ik′ter·us	Jaundice.
	ictus ik′tus	Stroke, blow, sudden attack.
	idea i·de′ah	Mental impression or conception.
	ideation i′de·a′shun	Mental presentation of objects.
	identification i·den′ti·fi·ka′shun	Mental mechanism of the unconscious by which ego attaches qualities of others to one's own identity.
	idiocy id′e·o·se	Complete congenital imbecility.
	idiopathic id′e·o·path′ik	Of unknown causation.
	idiot id′e·ot	Person without intellect and understanding.
	ileitis il′e·i′tis	Inflammation of ileum.

ileocecal il′e·o·se′kal	Pertaining to ileum and cecum.
ileocolitis il′e·o·ko·li′tis	Inflammation of ileum and colon.
ileorrhaphy il′e·or′ah·fe	Operation of suturing the ileum.
ileostomy il′e·os′to·me	Surgical creation of an opening into ileum.
Iletin Il′e·tin	Trademark for preparations of insulin for injection.
ileum il′e·um	Distal portion of small intestine.
ileus il′e·us	Obstruction of the intestines.
iliac il′e·ak	Pertaining to the ilium.
ilium il′e·um	Superior portion of hip bone.
illusion i·lu′zhun	False or misinterpreted sensory impression.
imbalance im·bal′ans	Lack of balance, especially between muscles.
imbecile im′be·sil	Defective mentally.
imbricated im′bri·kat′ed	Overlapping, like tiles or shingles.
immature im′ah·tur′	Unripe; not fully developed.
immedicable im·med′i·kah·b′l	Beyond hope of cure.

	immersion i·mer′shun	Plunging of a body into a liquid.
	immobilize im·mo′bil·iz	To render incapable of being moved.
	immunity i·mu′ni·te	Security against particular disease or poison.
	immunization im′u·ni·za′shun	Process of rendering subject immune.
	impacted im·pakt′ed	Driven closely in; lodged in position.
	imperforate im·per′fo·rat	Not open; abnormally closed.
	impetigo im′pe·ti′go	Inflammatory skin disease marked by pustules.
	implantation im′plan·ta′shun	Insertion of part or tissue in a new site in body.
	impotence im′po·tens	Lack of power or virility.
	impression im·presh′un	Slight indentation or depression.
	impulse im′puls	Sudden pushing force. Sudden determination to act.
	inanition in′ah·nish′un	Wasting of the body from malnutrition.
	incapacitate in·kah·pas′i·tat	To disable.
	incarcerated in·kar′ser·at′ed	Held fast; constricted.
	incest in′sest	Sexual intercourse between closely related persons.

inch		One-twelfth of a foot.
inch		
incidence	in′si·dens	Rate at which a certain event occurs.
incipient	in·sip′e·ent	Beginning to exist.
incision	in·sizh′un	Cut, or a wound produced by cutting.
incisor	in·si′zer	Tooth adapted for cutting.
incisure	in·si′zhur	Cut, notch, or incision.
incoherent	in′ko·her′ent	Not understandable.
incompatible	in′kom·pat′i·b'l	Not suitable for combination. Mutually repellent.
incompetence	in·kom′pe·tens	Inadequacy or insufficiency.
incontinence	in·kon′ti·nens	Inability to refrain from yielding to normal impulses.
incoordination	in′ko·or′di·na′shun	Failure of muscles to work harmoniously.
increment	in′kre·ment	Addition or increase.
incrustation	in′krus·ta′shun	Formation of crust, scale, or scab.
incubation	in′ku·ba′shun	Period between exposure to disease and appearance of symptoms.

	index in′deks	Second digit of hand; ratio; mold.
	indigestion in′di·jes′chun	Lack or failure of digestion.
	indisposition in′dis·po·zish′un	A slight illness.
	indirect in′di·rekt′	Not immediate or straight.
	indolent in′do·lent	Causing little pain.
	indurated in′du·rat′ed	Hardened; rendered hard.
	induration in′du·ra′shun	State of being hard.
	inebriation in·e′bre·a′shun	Condition of being drunk.
	inertia in·er′she·ah	Sluggishness of motion; inactivity.
	infancy in′fan·se	First 12 to 14 months of life.
	infantilism in·fan′ti·lizm	Condition in which characters of childhood persist in adult life.
	infarct in′farkt	Necrosis of tissue due to local anemia.
	infarction in·fark′shun	Formation of an infarct.
	infection in·fek′shun	Invasion of tissue by pathologic organisms.

	infectious in·fek′shus	Capable of being communicated by infection.
	inferior in·fe′re·or	Situated below or directed downward.
	infertility in′fer·til′i·te	Absence of ability to conceive or to induce conception.
	infestation in·fes·ta′shun	Invasion of body by arthropods.
	infiltration in′fil·tra′shun	Accumulation in a tissue of a substance not normal to it.
	infirmary in·fir′mah·re	Hospital or institution for sick or infirm.
	inflammation in′flah·ma′shun	Tissue response to injury: swelling, pain, redness, heat.
	influenza in′flu·en′zah	An acute, infectious, epidemic disease.
	infracostal in′frah·kos′tal	Below a rib.
	infraction in·frak′shun	Incomplete fracture of a bone.
	infrared in′frah·red′	Noting rays of energy beyond red end of spectrum, between red and radio waves.
	infrasternal in′frah·ster′nal	Below the sternum.
	infundibulum in′fun·dib′u·lum	Funnel-shaped passage.
	infusion in·fu′zhun	Steeping of a substance in water to extract its active principles.

	ingestion in·jes′chun	Taking substance into stomach by mouth.
	inguinal ing′gwi·nal	Pertaining to the groin.
	inhalant in·ha′lant	A drug to be inhaled into body.
	inhalation in′hah·la′shun	Drawing air or other vapor into lungs.
	inhaler in·ha′ler	Apparatus for administering vapor by inhalation.
	inherent in·her′ent	Implanted by nature; innate.
	inheritance in·her′i·tans	Acquiring characters or qualities from parent to offspring.
	inhibition in′hi·bish′un	Arrest or restraint of a process.
	injection in·jek′shun	The act of forcing a liquid into a part or organ.
	injury in′ju·re	Harm or hurt; wound or maim.
	inlay in′la	Filling cemented into tooth.
	innervation in′er·va′shun	Distribution of nerves to an organ or part.
	innocuous i·nok′u·us	Harmless.
	innominate i·nom′i·nat	Unnamed part or organ.

inoculate in·ok′u·lat	To communicate disease by introducing its virus into body. To introduce immune serum to prevent or cure disease.	
insanity in·san′i·te	Mental derangement or disorder.	
insemination in·sem′i·na′shun	Introduction of semen into vagina; impregnation.	
insidious in·sid′e·us	Coming on in stealthy manner.	
insight in′sit	Patient's knowledge his symptoms are abnormal.	
insoluble in·sol′u·b′l	Not susceptible of being dissolved.	
insomnia in·som′ne·ah	Inability to sleep.	
inspiration in′spi·ra′shun	Drawing air into lungs.	
inspiratory in·spi′rah·to′re	Pertaining to act of drawing air into lungs.	
inspissated in·spis′at·ed	Rendered less fluid.	
instep in′step	Dorsal part of arch of foot.	
instinct in′stinkt	Propensity to perform useful or beneficial actions without reason.	
instrumentation in′stroo·men·ta′- shun	Use of instruments.	

insufficiency in′su·fish′en·se	Inability to perform allotted duty.
insufflation in′su·fla′shun	Blowing powder or gas into cavity of body.
insulin in′su·lin	Antidiabetic hormone that regulates carbohydrate metabolism.
intake in·tak′	Substances taken in and utilized by body.
integument in·teg′u·ment	Covering or investment.
intelligence in·tel′i·jens	Ability to comprehend or understand.
intensive in·ten′siv	Increasing force or intensity.
intercarpal in′ter·kar′pal	Between the carpal bones.
intercellular in′ter·sel′u·lar	Situated between cells.
intercostal in′ter·kos′tal	Situated between the ribs.
intercourse in′ter·kors	Mutual exchange. Coitus.
interdigital in′ter·dij′i·tal	Between two adjacent fingers or toes.
interlobar in′ter·lo′bar	Situated between lobes.
interlobular in′ter·lob′u·lar	Situated between lobules.
intermarriage in′ter·mar′ij	Marriage of persons related by blood.

intermediate in′ter·me′de·at		Placed between; intervening.
intermission in′ter·mish′un		An interval; temporary cessation.
intermittent in′ter·mit′ent		Occurring at separated intervals.
intermuscular in′ter·mus′ku·lar		Situated between muscles.
intern in′tern		Graduate of medical school serving and residing in hospital.
internal in·ter′nal		Situated or occurring within.
internist in·ter′nist		Physician specializing in diagnosis and treatment of internal disorders.
interoceptor in′ter·o·sep′tor		Sensory nerve terminal transmitting impulses from viscera.
interphalangeal in′ter·fah·lan′je·al		Situated between two contiguous phalanges.
interrupted in′ter·rupt′ed		Not continuous.
interscapular in′ter·skap′u·lar		Situated between the shoulder blades.
intersex in′ter·seks		Intersexuality.
interspace in′ter·spas		Space between two similar structures.
interstice in·ter′stis		Gap, space, or hole in the structure of an organ or tissue.

SHORTHAND DICTIONARY

interstitial in′ter·stish′al	Occupying the interspaces of a tissue.
intertrigo in′ter·tri′go	Chafed patch of skin, especially on opposed surfaces.
interval in′ter·val	Space between two parts; lapse of time.
intervertebral in′ter·ver′te·bral	Situated between contiguous vertebrae.
intestinal in·tes′ti·nal	Pertaining to the intestine.
intestine in·tes′tin	Portion of alimentary canal.
intima in′ti·mah	Innermost coat of a blood vessel.
intolerance in·tol′er·ans	Lack of capacity to endure light, pain, or drug.
intoxication in·tok′si·ka′shun	Poisoning. Condition due to excessive use of alcohol.
intracapsular in′trah·kap′su·lar	Within a capsule.
intracranial in′trah·kra′ne·al	Situated within the cranium.
intraduodenal in′trah·du′o·de′nal	Within the duodenum.
intramedullary in′trah·med′u·lar′e	Within the spinal cord.
intramural in′trah·mu′ral	Within the wall of an organ.
intramuscular in′trah·mus′ku·lar	Within the substance of a muscle.

intranasal in′trah·na′zal	Within the nose.
intranatal in′trah·na′tal	Occurring during birth.
intraocular in′trah·ok′u·lar	Within the eye.
intraoral in′trah·o′ral	Within the mouth.
intraperitoneal in′trah·per′i·to- ne′al	Within the peritoneal cavity.
intrapleural in′trah·ploor′al	Within the pleura.
intrathecal in′trah·the′kal	Within a sheath.
intrathoracic in′trah·tho·ras′ik	Within the thorax; endothoracic.
intrauterine in′trah·u′ter·in	Within the uterus.
intravascular in′trah·vas′ku·lar	Within the vascular system.
intravenous in′trah·ve′nus	Within the veins.
intraventricular in′trah·ven·trik′- u·lar	Within a ventricle.
intravesical in′trah·ves′e·kal	Situated within the bladder.
intrinsic in·trin′sik	Situated entirely within or pertaining exclusively to a part.

introitus in·tro′i·tus	Entrance to a cavity or space.	
introspection in′tro·spek′shun	Contemplation or observation of one's own thoughts and feelings.	
introversion in′tro·ver′shun	A turning within.	
introvert in′tro·vert	Person whose interests are turned inward upon himself, not to the outside world.	
intubation in′tu·ba′shun	Introduction of a tube into a body canal or cavity.	
intumescence in·tu·mes′ens	A swelling, either normal or abnormal.	
intussusception in′tus·sus·sep′shun	Prolapse of portion of intestine into adjacent portion.	
intussusceptum in′tus·sus·sep′- tum	Segment of intestine which has been pushed into another segment.	
inversion in·ver′zhun	A turning inward, inside out, or other reversal of the normal relation of a part.	
involuntary in·vol′un·ter′e	Not controlled by the will.	
involution in′vo·lu′shun	Turning or rolling inward. Process of decline.	
iodine i′o·din	Constituent of thyroid gland. Germicide.	
ion i′on	Particle bearing a positive or negative electric charge.	

154 GREGG MEDICAL

ipsilateral ip′si·lat′er·al	Situated on the same side.	
iridectomy ir′i·dek′to·me	Cutting out part of the iris.	
iridic i·rid′ik	Pertaining to the iris.	
iridoplegia ir′i·do·ple′je·ah	Paralysis of sphincter of iris.	
iridoptosis ir′i·dop·to′sis	Prolapse of the iris.	
iris i′ris	Circular pigmented membrane behind cornea.	
iritis i·ri′tis	Inflammation of iris.	
irradiation ir·ra′de·a′shun	Exposure to radiation.	
irregularity ir·reg′u·lar′i·te	Quality of not conforming with rule of nature or of not occurring in regular intervals.	
irreversibility ir′re·ver′si·bil′i·te	Quality of being incapable of being reversed.	
irrigate ir′i·gat	Wash out.	
irritability ir′i·tah·bil′i·te	Condition or quality of being excitable.	
irritable ir′i·tah·b′l	Capable of reacting to stimulus.	
irritant ir′i·tant	Agent that produces irritation.	

ischemia is·ke′me·ah	Deficiency of blood in a part.
ischium is′ke·um	Lower dorsal part of the hip bone.
ischuria is·ku′re·ah	Suppression or retention of urine.
islet i′let	Cluster of cells or an isolated piece of tissue.
isolation i′so·la′shun	Process of separation.
isometric i′so·met′rik	Of equal dimensions.
isoniazid i′so·ni′ah·zid	Compound used in treatment of tuberculosis.
isoproterenol i′so·pro′te·re′nol	Cardiac stimulant and antispasmodic.
isotonia i′so·to′ne·ah	Condition of equal tone, tension, or activity.
isotope i′so·top	Element with same atomic number as another but different atomic mass.
isthmus is′mus	Narrow connection between two larger bodies or parts.
Isuprel I′su·prel	Trademark for drug used for imbalances of nervous system.
itching ich′ing	Unpleasant cutaneous sensation provoking scratching.
I.V.	Abbreviation for intravenous.

J

jaundice
jawn'dis
Disease of liver marked by yellowness of skin and sclerae.

jejunostomy
je'joo·nos'to·me
Surgical creation of opening through abdominal wall into jejunum.

jejunum
je·joo'num
Portion of small intestine from duodenum to ileum.

jerk
jerk
Sudden reflex or involuntary movement.

joint
joint
Place of union between two or more bones.

jugular
jug'u·lar
Pertaining to the neck.

junction
junk'shun
Place of meeting of two organs or types of tissue.

juxtaposition
juks'tah·po·zish'un
Adjacent position; apposition.

K

keloid
ke'loid
New growth or tumor of skin.

keratin
ker'ah·tin
Scleroprotein constituent of epidermis, hair, nails.

keratitis
ker'ah·ti'tis
Inflammation of the cornea.

keratoma
ker'ah·to'mah
Growth of horny tissue.

keratosis
ker'ah·to'sis
Any horny growth, such as a wart.

	ketone ke′ton	Any compound containing the carbonyl group.
	ketonuria ke′to·nu′re·ah	Presence of ketone bodies in urine.
	ketosis ke·to′sis	Abnormally elevated concentration of ketone bodies in blood, resulting in acidosis.
	kidney kid′ne	One of two glandular bodies that secrete urine.
	kilogram kil′o·gram	A unit of weight equal to 1,000 grams or 2.2 pounds.
	kiloliter kil′o·le′ter	Unit of capacity equal to 1,000 liters or 264.18 gallons.
	kilometer kil′o·me′ter	Unit of linear measurement equal to 1,000 meters.
	kleptomania klep′to·ma′ne·ah	Uncontrollable impulse to steal.
	kneading ned′ing	Movement in massage consisting of pressing of muscles.
	knee ne	Site of articulation between thigh and leg.
	knife nif	Cutting instrument for dissection.
	knuckle nuk′l	Dorsal aspect of any phalangeal joint.
	kymograph ki′mo·graf	Instrument that measures variations of pressure or movement.
	kyphosis ki·fo′sis	Humpback; exaggerated thoracic curve.

L

labial	la′be·al	Pertaining to a lip or labium.
labile	la′bil	Gliding. Chemically unstable.
labium	la′be·um	A lip; fleshy border or edge; pl. *labia*.
labor	la′bor	Function of expelling product of conception from uterus through vagina.
laboratory	lab′o·rah·to′re	Place equipped for performing experimental or investigative work.
labyrinth	lab′i·rinth	System of intercommunicating cavities or canals.
labyrinthitis	lab′i·rin·thi′tis	Inflammation of labyrinth; inflammation of the inner ear.
lac	lak	Milk.
lacerated	las′er·at′ed	Torn.
laceration	las′er·a′shun	Wound made by tearing.
lacrimal	lak′ri·mal	Pertaining to the tears.
lacrimation	lak′ri·ma′shun	Secretion and discharge of tears.
lactation	lak·ta′shun	Secretion of milk.

lacteal lak′te·al	Intestinal lymphatics that take up chyle, a milky fluid.
lactogenic lak′to·jen′ik	Stimulating the production of milk.
lacuna lah·ku′nah	Small pit or hollow cavity.
lagnosis lag·no′sis	Excessive sexual desire in the male.
lamella lah·mel′ah	Thin plate or leaf, as of bone.
lamina lam′i·nah	Thin flat plate or layer; pl. *laminae*.
laminated lam′i·nat′ed	Made up of thin layers.
laminectomy lam′i·nek′to·me	Excision of posterior arch of a vertebra.
lance lans	To cut or open with a lancet.
lancet lan′set	Small pointed, two-edged surgical knife.
laparectomy lap′ah·rek′to·me	Excision of a portion of abdominal wall.
laparotomy lap·ah·rot′o·me	Surgical incision through abdominal wall.
lapsus lap′sus	Error or slip, considered revealing of unconscious wish.
laryngeal lah·rin′je·al	Pertaining to the larynx.
laryngectomy lar′in·jek′to·me	Removal of the larynx.

	Term	Definition
	laryngitis lar′in·ji′tis	Inflammation of the larynx.
	laryngoplegia lar′ing·go·ple′je·ah	Paralysis of the larynx.
	laryngorrhagia lar′ing·go·ra′je·ah	Hemorrhage from larynx.
	laryngostasis lar′ing·gos′tah·sis	Croup; suffocative breathing.
	laryngopathy lar′ing·gop′ah·the	Any disorder of larynx.
	larynx lar′inks	Sphincter guarding entrance into trachea. Organ of voice.
	laser la′zer	Device producing intense, small beam of monochromatic radiation which can be used as a surgical tool.
	lassitude las′i·tud	Weakness; exhaustion.
	latent la′tent	Concealed; not manifest; dormant.
	lateral lat′er·al	Located away from midline; on the side.
	lateralis lat′er·a′lis	Lateral; structure situated farther from midline of body.
	laterality lat′er·al′i·te	Tendency to use hand, foot, ear, eye of same side.
	latissimus lah·tis′i·mus	Widest.
	latus la′tus	Broad; wide; side; flank.

	Term	Definition
	lavage lah·vahzh′	Washing out of organ, such as stomach or bowel.
	laxative laks′ah·tiv	Agent promoting bowel evacuation.
	layer la′er	Sheetlike substance superimposed one above another.
	lecithin les′i·thin	Crystalline compound found in animal tissues, said to have therapeutic properties of phosphorus.
	leech lech	A small species of worm used for drawing blood.
	leiomyoma li′o·mi·o′mah	Benign tumor composed of muscle fiber.
	lemniscus lem·nis′kus	Band or bundle of fibers in central nervous system.
	lens lenz	Part of refracting mechanism of eye. Glass used to increase visual acuity.
	lenticular len·tik′u·lar	Shaped like a lens.
	lesion le′zhun	Injury, wound, or change in tissue formation.
	lethargy leth′ar·je	Condition of drowsiness of mental origin.
	leukemia lu·ke′me·ah	Disease characterized by proliferation of white blood cells.
	leukocyte lu′ko·sit	Any colorless, amoeboid cell mass. Applied especially to the formed elements of blood.

	leukocytosis lu′ko·si·to′sis	Increase in number of white blood cells in blood.	
	leukoderma lu′ko·der′mah	Abnormal whiteness of the skin appearing in patches.	
	leukopenia lu′ko·pe′ne·ah	Decrease below the normal number of leukocytes in the blood.	
	leukoplakia lu′ko·pla′ke·ah	White, thickened patches on gums, tongue, or cheeks.	
	leukosis lu·ko′sis	Proliferation of leukocyte-forming tissue.	
	levator le·va′tor	A muscle or an instrument which acts to elevate, raise, or lift up an organ or a part.	
	libido li·bi′do	Sexual desire.	
	lichen li′ken	Name applied to many papular skin diseases.	
	lien le′en	Large glandlike but ductless organ.	
	ligament lig′ah·ment	Band of tissue that connects bones or supports viscera.	
	ligate li′gat	To tie or bind with a ligature.	
	ligation li·ga′shun	Application of a ligature.	
	ligature lig′ah·tur	Thread or wire for tying a vessel.	
	limb lim	An arm or a leg with all its component parts.	

	limbus lim′bus	Rim or border of an organ.
	limen li′men	Threshold; beginning point or boundary of a structure.
	liminal lim′i·nal	Barely appreciable to the senses; pertaining to a threshold.
	limitation lim·i·ta′shun	Act of limiting or state of being confined.
	linea lin′e·ah	Stripe; mark; narrow ridge.
	linear lin′e·ar	Resembling a line.
	lingua ling′gwah	Movable, muscular organ on floor of mouth.
	lingula ling′gu·lah	Small tonguelike structure.
	liniment lin′i·ment	Liquid intended for application to skin by gentle friction.
	lipase lip′as	A fat-splitting enzyme occurring in digestive organs.
	lipid lip′id	Any of numerous fats and fatlike materials that together with carbohydrates and proteins constitute the principal structural materials of living cells.
	lipodystrophy lip′o·dis′tro·fe	Any disturbance of fat metabolism.
	lipoid lip′oid	Fatlike; resembles fat.
	lipoma lip·o′mah	A benign fatty tumor.

lipsis lip′sis	Ending; cessation.	
liquefaction lik′we·fak′shun	Changing into a liquid form.	
liquid lik′wid	Substance that flows readily.	
liquor lik′er	A liquid, especially an aqueous solution, not obtained by distillation.	
liter le′ter	Basic unit of capacity in metric system.	
lithiasis lith·i′ah·sis	Formation of calculi and concretions.	
lithotomy lith·ot′o·me	Incision of a duct or organ for removal of stone.	
litmus lit′mus	Blue pigment used as a test for acidity and alkalinity.	
livedo li·ve′do	Discolored spot or patch on skin, commonly due to passive congestion.	
liver liv′er	Large gland in abdomen which produces bile and converts sugars into glycogen.	
lobe lob	Well-defined portion of any organ.	
lobectomy lo·bek′to·me	Excision of a lobe of thyroid, liver, brain, or lung.	
lobotomy lo·bot′o·me	Incision into a lobe. In psychosurgery, surgical incision of all the fibers of the lobe.	

lobule lob'ul		A small lobe.
lobulus lob'u·lus		Term used in anatomical nomenclature to designate a small lobe.
lobus lo'bus		Well defined portion of any organ.
localization lo'kal·i·za'shun		Determination of site or place of a process or lesion.
localized lo'kal·izd		Not general; restricted to a limited region.
lochia lo'ke·ah		Vaginal discharge after childbirth.
lockjaw lok'jaw		Tetanus; trismus.
longitudinal lon'ji·tu'di·nal		Lengthwise; parallel to long axis of body.
loop loop		A turn or curve in a cordlike structure.
lordosis lor·do'sis		Forward curvature of the spine.
lotion lo'shun		Liquid used for washing; a wash.
lues lu'ez		Syphilis.
lumbago lum·ba'go		Backache due to vascular causes.
lumbar lum'ber		Pertaining to or affecting the loins.

lumbosacral lum′bo·sa′kral	Pertaining to loins and sacrum.
lumbus lum′bus	Part of back between thorax and pelvis; loin.
lumen lu′men	The space inside a tube, blood vessel, or duct.
lunacy lu′nah·se	Insanity.
lunate lu′nat	Moon-shaped; one of proximal row of carpal bones.
lung lung	Organ of respiration.
lunula lu′nu·lah	Small crescentic or moon-shaped area.
lupus lu′pus	Destructive type of skin condition.
luteoma lu′te·o′mah	Neoplasm derived from lutein cells of ovary.
luxation luks·a′shun	Dislocation or displacement.
lymph limf	Transparent, yellow liquid circulating in the lymph vessels.
lymphadenitis lim·fad′e·ni′tis	Inflammation of lymph glands.
lymphadenopathy lim·fad′e·nop′- ah·the	Disease of lymph nodes.
lymphangioma lim·fan′je·o′mah	Tumor composed of new-formed lymph spaces.

	lymphangitis lim′fan·ji′tis	Inflammation of lymphatic vessels.
	lymphatic lim·fat′ik	Pertaining to or containing lymph.
	lymphedema lim′fe·de′mah	Swelling of subcutaneous tissues due to excessive lymph fluid.
	lymphoblastoma lim′fo·blas·to′mah	Malignant lymphoma.
	lymphocele lim′fo·sel	Tumor containing lymph.
	lymphocyte lim′fo·sit	White blood corpuscle.
	lymphocytosis lim′fo·si·to′sis	Excess of lymphocytes in blood or in any effusion.
	lymphogranuloma lim′fo·gran′u·lo′- mah	Hodgkin's disease.
	lymphoma lim·fo′mah	Neoplastic disorder of the lymphoid tissue.
	lymphopenia lim·fo·pe′ne·ah	Deficiency in number of lymphocytes in the blood.
	lysin li′sin	Antibody with power of causing dissolution of cells.
	lysis li′sis	Destruction, as of cells by specific lysin.

M

	macrocyst mak′ro·sist	A large cyst.

	macrophage mak′ro·faj	Large mononuclear wandering phagocytic cell.	
	macula mak′u·lah	Discolored spot, stain, or opacity.	
	macular mak′u·lar	Pertaining to maculae.	
	magnesia mag·ne′ze·ah	Magnesium oxide, used as gastric antacid.	
	maim mam	To disable by a wound; dismember by violence.	
	mal mahl	Term for disease, used in combination with more explicit description.	
	mala ma′lah	Cheek or cheek bone.	
	malacia mah·la′she·ah	Morbid softening of part or tissue.	
	maladjustment mal′ad·just′ment	Defective adaptation to environment.	
	malady mal′ah·de	Any illness or disease. (Also *maladie*.)	
	malaise mal·az′	Vague feeling of bodily discomfort.	
	malar ma′lar	Pertaining to cheek or cheek bone.	
	malaria mah·la′re·ah	Infectious febrile disease.	
	malformation mal′for·ma′shun	Deformity, abnormality of shape or structure.	

SHORTHAND DICTIONARY

malignancy mah·lig′nan·se	Tending to progress in virulence. The quality of being malignant.
malignant mah·lig′nant	Becoming progressively worse and resulting in death.
malingerer mah·ling′ger·er	One who feigns illness or injury.
malleable mal′e·ah·b'l	Capable of being beaten or rolled into a thin sheet or plate.
malleolus mal·le′o·lus	Rounded process or protuberance.
malleus mal′e·us	Largest of the auditory ossicles.
malnutrition mal′nu·trish′un	Disorder due to imperfect assimilation of food.
malocclusion mal·o·kloo′zhun	Any deviation from normal occlusion of teeth.
malodorous mal·o′dor·us	Ill-smelling; rank; fetid.
malpractice mal·prak′tis	Unskillful and faulty medical or surgical treatment.
malunion mal·un′yon	Faulty union of fractured bone fragments.
mamma mam′mah	Glandular structure in female that secretes milk.
mammary mam′er·e	Pertaining to the breast or mamma.
mandible man′di·b'l	Bone of lower jaw.
mandibula man·dib′u·lah	Horseshoe-shaped bone forming lower jaw.

	mandibular man·dib′u·lar	Pertaining to lower jaw.	
	maneuver mah·noo′ver	Any skillful procedure.	
	mania ma′ne·ah	Phase of mental disorder marked by excessive excitement.	
	manipulation mah·nip′u·la′shun	Dextrous treatment by the hand.	
	mannerism man′er·izm	Stereotyped movement or habit.	
	mannitol man′i·tol	A sugar used in test of kidney function.	
	manometer mah·nom′e·ter	Instrument for measuring pressure of gases or liquids, such as blood.	
	manus ma′nus	Distal portion of arm or hand.	
	marasmus mah·raz′mus	Progressive wasting and emaciation.	
	margin mar′jin	Edge or border of an organ.	
	marihuana mar′i·hwan′ah	Habit-forming, intoxicating agent. (Also *marijuana*.)	
	marisca mah·ris′kah	A hemorrhoid.	
	marrow mar′o	Soft material that fills cavities of bones.	
	marsupialization mar·su′pe·al·i·za′-shun	Surgical exposure of cyst and creation of a pouch.	

	masculinity mas′ku·lin′i·te	Possession of normal masculine qualities.
	massage mah·sahzh′	Stroking and kneading of body as therapy.
	masseur mah·ser′	Man who performs massage.
	masseuse mah·suhz′	Woman who performs massage.
	mastauxe mas·tawk′se	Enlargement of the breast.
	mastectomy mas·tek′to·me	Removal of the breast.
	mastication mas′ti·ka′shun	The chewing of food.
	mastitis mas·ti′tis	Inflammation of the breast; milk fever.
	mastocarcinoma mas′to·kar′si·no′- mah	Cancer of the breast.
	mastoid mas′toid	Shaped like a nipple. Mastoid process of the temporal bone.
	mastoidectomy mas′toid·ek′to·me	Excision of mastoid cells or process.
	mastoiditis mas′toid·i′tis	Inflammation of mastoid antrum and cells.
	mastopathy mas·top′ah·the	Disease of the mammary gland.
	mastoplasty mas′to·plas′te	Repair of the breast. (Also *mammoplasty*.)

mastosis mas·to'sis	Pathologic changes in the breast.	
masturbation mas'tur·ba'shun	Orgasm by self-manipulation of genitals.	
material mah·te're·al	Substance or matter.	
maternal mah·ter'nal	Pertaining to the mother.	
matrix ma'triks	Formative part of a tooth or a nail. Groundwork on which anything is cast.	
maturation mat'u·ra'shun	Process of coming to full development.	
maxilla mak·sil'ah	Upper jaw.	
maxillary mak'si·ler'e	Pertaining to the maxilla.	
maximal mak'si·mal	The greatest possible.	
measles me'zelz	Contagious eruptive fever due to virus.	
meatus me·a'tus	Opening to some passageway in body.	
Mebaral Meb'ah·ral	Trademark for preparation of mephobarbital, an anticonvulsant.	
mechanism mek'ah·nizm	Machine or machinelike structure.	
meconium me·ko'ne·um	Green material in intestine of full term fetus.	

medial me′de·al	Toward midline or the middle of body or structure.
median me′de·an	Located in middle or midline of a body.
mediastinitis me′de·as′ti·ni′tis	Inflammation of mediastinum.
mediastinum me′de·as·ti′num	Median septum or partition; middle section of thorax.
medical med′i·kal	Pertaining to medicine.
medication med′i·ka′shun	Treatment with a medicine.
medicinal me·dis′i·nal	Having healing qualities.
medicine med′i·sin	Any drug or remedy.
medium me′de·um	Means; substance transmitting impulses.
medulla me·dul′lah	Inmost portion of organ or structure.
megalocardia meg′ah·lo·kar′-de·ah	Abnormally large heart.
megalomania meg′ah·lo·ma′-ne·ah	Delusion of grandeur.
melancholia mel′an·ko′le·ah	Depressed and unhappy emotional state.
melanin mel′ah·nin	Dark amorphous pigment of skin and hair.

	melanoderma mel'ah·no·der'mah	Dark discoloration of the skin.
	melanosis mel'ah·no'sis	Melanism; abnormal pigmentary deposits.
	melena mel'e·nah	Passage of dark and pitchy stools stained with blood.
	melituria mel'i·tu're·ah	Presence of any sugar in urine.
	membrane mem'bran	Thin layer of tissue which covers a surface.
	membranous mem'brah·nus	Pertaining to a membrane.
	memory mem'o·re	Mental faculty by which sensations and ideas are recalled.
	menarche me·nar'ke	The time when menstrual cycle begins.
	meningeal me·nin'je·al	Pertaining to the meninges.
	meninges me·nin'jes	The three membranes that envelop the brain and spinal cord.
	meningioma me·nin'je·o'mah	A hard, slow-growing vascular tumor.
	meningitis men'in·ji'tis	Inflammation of the meninges.
	meningocele me·ning'go·sel	Hernial protrusion of the meninges.
	meningococcus me·ning'go·kok'us	Microorganism causing epidemic cerebrospinal meningitis.

meningocortical me·ning′go·kor′-ti·kal	Affecting meninges and cortex of brain.
meningoencephalitis me·ning′go·en-sef′ah·li′tis	Inflammation of brain and meninges.
meninx me′ninks	Membrane enveloping brain and spinal cord.
meniscus me·nis′kus	A crescent-shaped structure.
menopausal men′o·paw′zal	Pertaining to the menopause.
menopause men′o·pawz	Cessation of menstruation in female.
menorrhagia men′o·ra′je·ah	Excessive uterine bleeding at regular intervals.
menorrhalgia men′o·ral′je·ah	Distress associated with menstruation, such as tension, pelvic vascular congestion, and pain.
menorrhea men′o·re′ah	Normal flow of the menses.
menses men′sez	Monthly flow of blood from genital tract of a woman.
menstrual men′stroo·al	Pertaining to menses.
menstruation men′stroo·a′shun	Monthly female cycle of menses from puberty to menopause.
mental men′tal	Pertaining to the mind.

mentum men′tum	The chin.	
meperidine me·per′i·din	Analgesic; narcotic pain killer.	
mercurial mer·ku′re·al	Pertaining to mercury.	
mercury mer′ku·re	Metallic element; quicksilver.	
Mercuzanthin Mer′ku·zan′thin	Trademark for preparation of mercurophylline; used as a diuretic.	
mesencephalon mes′en·sef′ah·lon	Part of central nervous system known as the midbrain.	
mesenteric mes′en·ter′ik	Pertaining to mesentery.	
mesenteritis mes′en·ter·i′tis	Inflammation of the mesentery.	
mesentery mes′en·ter′e	Peritoneal fold attaching small intestine to dorsal body wall.	
mesial me′ze·al	Situated in middle; median; middle line.	
mesiobuccal me′ze·o·buk′kal	Formed by mesial and buccal surfaces of a tooth.	
mesmerism mes′mer·izm	Method or practice of inducing hypnosis.	
mesocardium mes′o·kar′de·um	Embryonic mesentery connecting heart with body wall and foregut.	
mesocolon mes′o·ko′lon	Process by which colon is attached to abdominal wall.	

mesoderm mes′o·derm	Middle of three primary germ layers of embryo.
mesonasal mes′o·na′zal	Situated in middle of nose.
mesothelium mes′o·the′le·um	Layer of flat cells covering surface of all serous membranes.
metabolism me·tab′o·lizm	The sum of all the physical and chemical processes by which living organized substance is produced and maintained.
metabolite me·tab′o·lit	Product of metabolic change.
metacarpal met′ah·kar′pal	One of the bones of the metacarpus.
metacarpus met′ah·kar′pus	Five bones of hand, each with head, shaft, and base.
metamorphosis met′ah·mor′fo·sis	A change in shape, structure, or function, particularly in transition from one developmental stage to another.
Metamucil Met′ah·mu′sil	Trademark for a preparation of laxative.
metaplasia met′ah·pla′ze·ah	Change of type of cells in a tissue to a form not normal for that tissue.
metastasis me·tas′tah·sis	Transfer of disease from one part of body to another.
metastasize me·tas′tah·siz	To form new foci of disease in distant part.
metatarsal met′ah·tar′sal	Pertaining to part of foot between tarsus and toes.

metatarsus met′ah·tar′sus	Five bones of foot, each with head, shaft, and base.
meteorism me′te·er·izm	Distention of abdomen due to gas.
meter me′ter	Unit of linear measure in metric system; 39.37 inches.
methadone meth′ah·don	A narcotic analgesic.
methenamine meth′en·am′in	A urinary antibacterial.
method meth′ud	Manner of performing any act or operation.
methyl meth′il	The univalent radical CH_3.
metra me′trah	The uterus or womb.
metrectasia me′trek·ta′se·ah	Dilation of unpregnant uterus.
metritis me·tri′tis	Inflammation of the uterus.
metrocele me′tro·sel	Hernia of the uterus.
metrophlebitis me′tro·fle·bi′tis	Inflammation of veins of uterus.
metrorrhagia me′tro·ra′je·ah	Normal uterine bleeding at irregular intervals.
metrorrhea me′tro·re′ah	Abnormal uterine discharge.

	Metycaine Met′i·kan	Trademark for preparations of local or spinal anesthetic; piperocaine.
	microbe mi′krob	Minute living organism capable of causing disease.
	microblast mi′kro·blast	An erythroblast of small size.
	microcardia mi′kro·kar′de·ah	Abnormally small heart.
	micrococcus mi′kro·kok′us	A cell that divides in two directions, or irregularly.
	microcyst mi′kro·sist	A small cyst.
	microgram mi′kro·gram	Unit of weight being one-thousandth of a milligram; Ab., mcg.
	microlithiasis mi′kro·li·thi′ah·sis	Formation of minute concretions in an organ.
	microscope mi′kro·skop	Instrument for obtaining enlarged image of small objects.
	microscopic mi′kro·skop′ic	Of extremely small size.
	micturate mik′tu·rat	Urinate.
	midbrain mid′bran	Mesencephalon.
	midfrontal mid·fron′tal	Middle of the forehead.
	midget mij′et	A normal dwarf; undersized.

midline mid′lin	Line that bisects a figure symmetrically.	
midriff mid′rif	Diaphragm; upper part of abdomen.	
midsection mid·sek′shun	A cut through middle of any organ.	
midtarsal mid·tar′sal	Between two rows of bones of the tarsus.	
midwife mid′wif	Woman who assists in childbirth.	
migraine mi′gran	Periodic sick headache, often one-sided.	
miliaria mil′e·a′re·ah	Cutaneous changes associated with sweat retention.	
milliequivalent mil′le·e·kwiv′ah-lent	Number of grams of a solute contained in one milliliter of solution.	
milligram mil′li·gram	Unit of mass in metric system.	
milliliter mil′li·le′ter	Metric measure of capacity; one cubic centimeter.	
millimeter mil′li·me·ter	Linear metric measure.	
millisecond mil′e·sek′ond	One one-thousandth of a second.	
minim min′im	Liquid measure; about one drop of water.	
minimal min′i·mal	The smallest or least possible.	

minimum min′i·mum	Smallest amount or lowest limit.
miosis mi·o′sis	Excessive contraction of the pupil.
miotic mi·ot′ik	Agent which causes pupil of eye to contract.
miscarriage mis·kar′ij	Expulsion of the fetus before it is viable.
mistura mis·tu′rah	Mixture.
mitochondrion mi′to·kon′dre·on	Granular component of cytoplasm.
mitosis mi·to′sis	Indirect division of a cell.
mitral mi′tral	Shaped like a bishop's headdress.
mixture miks′tur	Combination of different drugs or ingredients.
mnemonic ne·mon′ik	Promoting recollection or memory.
mobilization mo′bi·li·za′shun	Restoring the power of joint motion.
modality mo·dal′i·te	Homeopathic term signifying a condition which modifies drug action.
moist moist	Somewhat wet; damp.
molar mo′lar	Pertaining to a mass; not molecular. Tooth for grinding.

	molecule mol′e·kul	Minute mass of matter.	
	molluscum mol·lus′kum	Name of various skin diseases marked by soft rounded cutaneous tumors.	
	monitor mon′i·tor	Constantly checking a state or condition.	
	monocyte mon′o·sit	A large leukocyte.	
	monomania mon′o·ma′ne·ah	Insanity on a single idea or subject.	
	mononucleosis mon′o·nu′kle·o′sis	Infectious disease with fever and swelling of lymph nodes.	
	mood mood	Mental state or emotion.	
	morbid mor′bid	Diseased state or condition.	
	morbidity mor·bid′i·te	Condition of being diseased.	
	morbilli mor·bil′i	Measles.	
	morbus mor′bus	Disease.	
	moribund mor′i·bund	In a dying condition; near death.	
	morphine mor′fen	Principal alkaloid of opium. A narcotic analgesic.	
	mortality mor·tal′i·te	The death rate. Quality of being mortal.	

	mottling mot′ling	Condition of spotting with patches of color.
	movement moov′ment	Act of moving; motion.
	mucin mu′sin	Chief constituent of mucus.
	mucocutaneous mu′ko·ku·ta′ne·us	Affecting the mucous membrane and skin.
	mucoid mu′koid	Resembling mucus.
	mucopurulent mu′ko·pu′roo·lent	Containing both mucus and pus.
	mucosa mu·ko′sah	A mucous membrane.
	mucosal mu·ko′sal	Pertaining to mucous membrane.
	mucous mu′kus	Relating to or resembling mucus.
	mucus mu′kus	Viscid liquid secreted by mucous membrane.
	multigravida mul′ti·grav′i·dah	Woman pregnant for third or more time.
	multipara mul·tip′ah·rah	Woman who has had two or more pregnancies.
	multiple mul′ti·pl	Manifold; occurring in various parts of body at once.
	multisensitivity mul′ti·sen′si·tiv′- i·te	Condition of being allergic to more than one antigen.

	mumps mumps	Contagious disease marked by inflammation and swelling of parotid gland.
	murmur mur′mur	Gentle blowing sound heard in auscultation.
	muscle mus′el	Organ which by contraction produces movement.
	muscular mus′ku·lar	Pertaining to a muscle.
	muscularis mus′ku·la′ris	Muscular coat of an artery or organ.
	muscularity mus′ku·lar′i·te	Quality of being muscular.
	mute mut	Unable to speak.
	myasthenia mi′as·the′ne·ah	Muscle weakness.
	myatonia mi′ah·to′ne·ah	Lack of muscle tone.
	mycosis mi·ko′sis	Any disease caused by fungus.
	mydriasis mid·ri′ah·sis	Extreme dilatation of pupil.
	mydriatic mid′re·at′ik	Any drug that dilates the pupil.
	myelin mi′e·lin	Fatlike substance forming sheath around nerve fibers.
	myelitis mi′e·li′tis	Inflammation of bone marrow.

SHORTHAND DICTIONARY 185

	myeloblast mi'e·lo·blast	One of the cells of bone marrow.
	myelocyte mi'e·lo·sit	One of the typical cells of red bone marrow.
	myelogram mi'e·lo·gram	Roentgenogram of spinal cord.
	myeloid mi'e·loid	Pertaining to bone marrow or spinal cord.
	myeloma mi'e·lo'mah	Tumor composed of cells found in bone marrow.
	myelon mi'e·lon	The spinal cord.
	myeloplast mi'e·lo·plast	Any leukocyte of bone marrow.
	myelosis mi'e·lo'sis	Proliferation of marrow tissue.
	myocardia mi'o·kar'de·ah	Cardiac insufficiency. Non-inflammatory myocardial disease.
	myocardial mi'o·kar'de·al	Relating to muscular tissue of heart.
	myocarditis mi'o·kar·di'tis	Inflammation of myocardium.
	myocardium mi'o·kar'de·um	The cardiac muscle.
	myoclonus mi·ok'lo·nus	Shocklike contractions of a part of a muscle or of a muscle or group of muscles.
	myodynia mi'o·din'e·ah	Pains in a muscle.

	myodystrophia mi′o·dis·tro′fe·ah	Malnourished muscle.
	myoid mi′oid	Resembling or like a muscle.
	myolysis mi·ol′i·sis	Degeneration of muscle tissue.
	myoma mi·o′mah	Tumor made up of muscular elements.
	myometrium mi·o·me′tre·um	The uterine muscular structure.
	myopathy mi·op′ah·the	Any disease of muscles.
	myopia mi·o′pe·ah	Nearsightedness due to elongated eyeball.
	myoplasty mi′o·plas′te	Plastic surgery on muscle.
	myosin mi′o·sin	Principal protein globin in muscle.
	myositis mi′o·si′tis	Inflammation of a voluntary muscle.
	myospasm mi′o·spazm	Spasm of a muscle.
	myotonia mi′o·to′ne·ah	Muscular irritability and contractility.
	myringomycosis mi′ring′go·mi- ko′sis	Fungus infection of eardrum.
	myringoplasty mi′ring′go·plas′te	Surgical repair of the eardrum.

myringotomy mir'in·got'o·me	Surgical incision of tympanic membrane.
myrinx mi'rinks	Membrana tympani.
myxedema mik'se·de'mah	Hypothyroidism with dry waxy type of swelling of face.
myxocyte mik'so·sit	Characteristic cell of mucous tissue.
myxoma mik·so'mah	Tumor composed of mucous tissue.

N

narcolepsy nar'ko·lep'se	Condition of recurrent attacks of uncontrollable desire for sleep.
narcoma nar·ko'mah	Stuporous state produced by narcotics.
narcosis nar·ko'sis	State of unconsciousness produced by drugs.
narcotic nar·kot'ik	Drug which produces insensibility or stupor.
nares na'rez	External orifices of nose; the nostrils.
naris na'ris	One of the openings of nasal cavity; pl. *nares*.
nasal na'zal	Pertaining to the nose.
nasolacrimal na'zo·lak'ri·mal	Pertaining to nose and tear glands.
natal na'tal	Pertaining to birth.

nausea naw′se·ah	Unpleasant sensation accompanying tendency or inclination to vomit.
nauseate naw′se·at	To affect with nausea.
nauseous naw′se·us	Pertaining to or producing nausea.
navel na′vel	The umbilicus.
nearsighted ner·sit′ed	Myopic.
nebula neb′u·lah	Slight corneal opacity. Cloudiness in urine.
necrosis ne·kro′sis	Death of tissue. Gangrene.
needle ne′d′l	Sharp instrument for sewing or puncture.
negative neg′ah·tiv	Value of less than zero; a lack or absence.
negativism neg′ah·tiv·izm	Propensity to do opposite of what most people would do.
Neisseria nis·se′re·ah	A genus of gram-negative cocci.
Nembutal Nem′bu·tal	Trademark for preparations of pentobarbital; a hypnotic and sedative.
neoarsphenamine ne′o·ars·fen′ah·min	Soluble compound used like arsphenamine.
neomycin ne′o·mi′sin	Antibacterial substance.

	neonate ne′o·nat	Newborn infant.
	neoplasm ne′o·plazm	New and abnormal growth; tumor.
	neostigmine ne′o·stig′min	Cholinergic drug to improve muscle function.
	Neo-synephrine Ne′o-sin·ef′rin	Trademark for preparations of phenylephrine.
	nephrectomy ne·frek′to·me	Surgical excision of a kidney.
	nephritis ne·fri′tis	Inflammation of kidney.
	nephrogenous ne·froj′e·nus	Originating or arising in kidney.
	nephroma ne·fro′mah	Tumor of kidney or kidney tissue.
	nephron nef′ron	Anatomical and functional unit of the kidney.
	nephropexy nef′ro·pek′se	Operation for fixation of floating kidney.
	nephrosclerosis nef′ro·skle·ro′sis	Hardening of the kidney.
	nephrosis ne·fro′sis	Any disease of the kidney.
	nephrostomy ne·fros′to·me	Creation of opening into pelvis of kidney.
	nephrotomy ne·frot′o·me	Incision into a kidney.

nerve nerv	A cordlike structure that conveys impulses between a part of the central nervous system and some other region of the body. (Also *nervus*.)
nervous ner'vus	Pertaining to nerves; unduly excitable.
nervousness ner'vus·nes	Undue excitability or irritability.
network net'werk	Meshlike structure of interlocking fibers.
neural nu'ral	Pertaining to a nerve or to nerves.
neuralgia nu·ral'je·ah	Pain along course of one or more nerves.
neurasthenia nu'ras·the'ne·ah	Nervous prostration or exhaustion with fatigability.
neuritis nu·ri'tis	Inflammation of a nerve.
neuroblast nu'ro·blast	Embryonic cell which develops into a nerve cell or neuron.
neurocoele nu'ro·sel	The neural canal.
neurocyte nu'ro·sit	A nerve cell; neuron.
neurocytoma nu'ro·si·to'mah	Brain tumor consisting of undifferentiated cells of nervous origin.
neurogenic nu'ro·jen'ik	Forming nervous tissue. Originating in the nervous system.

neurolemma nu′ro·lem′mah	Thin membrane enwrapping nerve fiber.
neurologist nu·rol′o·jist	Expert in neurology or in the treatment of nervous disorders.
neurology nu·rol′o·je	Science dealing with nervous system, both normal and in disease.
neuroma nu·ro′mah	Tumor or new growth largely made up of nerve cells and nerve fibers.
neuron nu′ron	Complete nerve cell.
neuropathy nu·rop′ah·the	Degenerative disease of the nervous system.
neuropsychiatry nu′ro·si·ki′ah·tre	Study of nervous and mental diseases.
neurosis nu·ro′sis	Disorder of the psychic or mental constitution.
neurosthenia nu′ro·sthe′ne·ah	Great nervous power and excitement.
neurosurgeon nu′ro·sur′jun	Physician who specializes in neurosurgery.
neurosurgery nu′ro·sur′jer·e	Surgery of nervous system.
neurotic nu·rot′ik	Affected with a neurosis.
neurotoxicity nu′ro·toks·is′i·te	Quality of exerting a poisonous effect on nerve tissue.
neutropenia nu′tro·pe′ne·ah	Decrease in number of neutrophilic leukocytes in the blood.

	neutrophil nu′tro·fil	Stainable by neutral dyes. A cell or structural element, particularly a leukocyte.	
	nevus ne′vus	A mole or birthmark of congenital origin.	
	niacin ni′ah·sin	Nicotinic acid.	
	nicking nik′ing	Localized constrictions in retinal blood vessels.	
	nipple nip′l	Conic organ which gives outlet to milk from breast.	
	nitrite ni′trit	Any salt of nitrous acid. Nitrites act as antispasmodics and lessen arterial tension.	
	nitrogen ni′tro·jen	Colorless, gaseous element found free in air; symbol, N.	
	nitroglycerin ni·tro·glis′er·in	Glyceryl trinitrate. Used as a vasodilator.	
	nitrous ni′trus	Pertaining to nitrogen in its lowest valency.	
	nociceptor no′se·sep′tor	Receptor which responds to injury.	
	nocturia nok·tu′re·ah	Excessive urination at night.	
	nocturnal nok·tur′nal	Pertaining to night.	
	node nod	A swelling or protuberance.	
	nodose no′dos	Characterized by nodes or projections.	

SHORTHAND DICTIONARY

nodule nod'ul	A small node or boss detectable by touch.
nodus no'dus	A knot; small mass of tissue.
nonopaque non'o·pak'	Not opaque to roentgen ray.
normal nor'mal	Agreeing with the regular and established type.
normoblast nor'mo·blast	Nucleated red blood cell of medium size.
normocyte nor'mo·sit	Erythrocyte that is normal in size, shape, and color.
nosology no·sol'o·je	Science of the classification of diseases.
nostril nos'tril	One of the external orifices of the nose.
nostrum nos'trum	A patent remedy.
notch noch	Indentation or depression.
novobiocin no'vo·bi'o·sin	Antibacterial substance produced by growth of streptomyces.
Novocain No'vo·kan	Trademark for preparations of procaine hydrochloride; local anesthetic.
noxious nok'shus	Harmful; poisonous or deleterious.
nucha nu'kah	Back, nape, or scruff of neck.

nucleated nu′kle·at′ed	Possessing a nucleus or nuclei.
nucleoid nu′kle·oid	Resembling a nucleus.
nucleolus nu·kle′o·lus	Small spherical body within the cell nucleus.
nucleoprotein nu′kle·o·pro′te·in	A substance composed of a simple basic protein combined with a nucleic acid.
nucleus nu′kle·us	The differentiated central protoplasm of a cell.
nulliparous nul·lip′ah·rus	A woman who has never given birth to a viable infant.
numbness num′nes	Deficiency of sensation.
nummular num′u·lar	Coin shaped; made up of round flat disks.
Nupercaine Nu′per·kan	Trademark for preparation of dibucaine, a local anesthetic.
nurse nurs	Person who takes care of the sick or enfeebled.
nutrient nu′tre·ent	Nourishing; affording nutriment.
nutritional nu·trish′un·al	Relating to or affecting the assimilation of food.
nyctalopia nik′tah·lo′pe·ah	Night blindness. Failure of vision at night or in a dim light, with good vision only on bright days.
nylon ni′lon	Synthetic used as suture material.

	nystagmus nis·tag′mus	Rapid, involuntary movement of eyeball.
	nystatin nis′tah·tin	An antibiotic substance used to treat certain infections.

O

	obese o·bes′	Excessively fat.
	obesity o·bes′i·te	Excessive accumulation of fat in the body.
	objective ob·jek′tiv	Perceptible to the external senses.
	oblique ob·lek′	Slanting; inclined.
	obliteration ob·lit′er·a′shun	Complete removal by disease or surgery.
	obsession ob·sesh′un	Morbid preoccupation with an idea or emotion.

	obsessive-
	  compulsive
	ob·ses′iv-kom-
	  pul′siv
		Marked by compulsion to repetitively perform certain acts.

	obstetric ob·stet′rik	Pertaining to pregnancy, labor, and puerperium.
	obstetrician ob′ste·trish′un	One who practices obstetrics.
	obstetrics ob·stet′riks	Surgery dealing with pregnancy and labor.
	obstipation ob′sti·pa′shun	Obstinate constipation.

obstruction ob·struk′shun	A blocking or clogging.	
obtuse ob·tus′	Blunt; dull. Having a dull intellect.	
occipital ok·sip′i·tal	Pertaining to the back part of head.	
occiput ok′si·put	Back part of the head.	
occlude o·klood′	To fit close together; to close tight.	
occlusion o·kloo′zhun	A closure or state of being closed.	
occult o·kult′	Obscure; concealed from observation.	
ocular ok′u·lar	Pertaining to the eye.	
oculist ok′u·list	Ophthalmologist; eye specialist.	
oculomotor ok′u·lo·mo′tor	Pertaining to eye movements.	
oculonasal ok′u·lo·na′zal	Pertaining to eye and nose.	
odontoid o·don′toid	Toothlike; resembling a tooth.	
odontolith o·don′to·lith	Tartar on teeth; dental calculus.	
odontology o′don·tol′o·je	The sum of knowledge regarding the teeth.	
odontoma o·don·to′mah	An exostosis, or bony growth, on a tooth.	

odontoscope o·don'to·skop	Dental mirror for examining teeth.	
odor o'dor	An emanation perceived by the sense of smell.	
ointment oint'ment	Semisolid preparation used externally for protective and emollient effect.	
olecranon o·lek'rah·non	Bony prominence which forms the tip of the elbow.	
olfaction ol·fak'shun	Act of smelling; sense of smell.	
olfactometer ol'fak·tom'e·ter	Instrument for testing the power of smell.	
olfactory ol·fak'to·re	Pertaining to the sense of smell.	
oligocythemia ol'i·go·si·the'-me·ah	Deficiency in number of red cells in blood.	
oliguria ol'i·gu're·ah	Diminished urine output in relation to fluid intake.	
omentum o·men'tum	Fold of peritoneum extending from the stomach to adjacent organs in the abdominal cavity.	
omohyoid o'mo·hi'oid	Pertaining to shoulder and hyoid bone.	
oncology ong·kol'o·je	Study of tumors.	
onychia o·nik'e·ah	Inflammation of matrix of nail.	
onyxis o·nik'sis	Ingrowing nail.	

oophorectomy o′of·o·rek′to·me	Removal of an ovary or ovaries.
oophoritis o′of·o·ri′tis	Inflammation of an ovary.
oophorocystosis o·of′o·ro·sis·to′sis	Formation of an ovarian cyst.
oophoroma o·of′o·ro′mah	Malignant tumor of the ovary.
oophorostomy o·of′o·ros′to·me	Making an opening into an ovarian cyst for drainage.
opacity o·pas′i·te	State of being nontransparent.
opaque o·pak′	Impervious to light rays.
operable op′er·ah·b′l	Possible of being operated upon.
operation op′er·a′shun	Act performed with instrument or hand of surgeon.
operative op′er·a′tiv	Pertaining to an operation. Effective.
ophthalmia of·thal′me·ah	Severe inflammation of the eye.
ophthalmic of·thal′mik	Pertaining to the eye.
ophthalmodynia of·thal′mo·din′- e·ah	Pain in the eye.
ophthalmologist of′thal·mol′o·jist	An expert in the treatment of the eyes.

ophthalmology of'thal·mol'o·je	Study of the eyes.
ophthalmopathy of'thal·mop'ah·the	Disease of the eye.
ophthalmoplegia of·thal'mo·ple'-je·ah	Paralysis of the eye muscles.
ophthalmorrhagia of·thal'mo·ra'je·ah	Hemorrhage from the eye.
ophthalmoscope of·thal'mo·skop	Instrument used to inspect interior of eye.
opium o'pe·um	Narcotic used as a sedative, anodyne, and hypnotic.
oppilation op'i·la'shun	Constipation.
optic op'tik	Pertaining to the eye.
optician op·tish'an	Expert in craft and art of optics, able to fill ophthalmic prescriptions.
optometrist op·tom'e·trist	Expert in measuring the power of vision and prescribing corrective prisms or lenses.
optometry op·tom'e·tre	Measurement of vision and adaptation of lenses for aid thereof.
oral o'ral	Pertaining to the mouth.
orb orb	Sphere; eyeball.

orbit or'bit	Bony cavity which contains the eyeball.
orbital or'bi·tal	Pertaining to the orbit.
orchiectomy or'ke·ek'to·me	Excision of one or both testes.
orchitis or·ki'tis	Inflammation of a testis.
organ or'gan	Part of body that performs a special function.
organic or·gan'ik	Pertaining to an organ or organs.
organism or'gan·izm	Any organized body of living economy; an individual animal or plant.
orgasm or'gazm	Climax of sexual excitement.
orientation o're·en·ta'shun	Determination of one's position with regard to time and space.
orifice or'i·fis	Entrance or outlet of any body cavity.
origin or'i·jin	Source or beginning of anything.
Orinase Or'i·naz	Trademark for preparation of tolbutamide.
orthodontics or'tho·don'tiks	Dentistry dealing with prevention and correction of teeth irregularities and malocclusion.
orthopedic or'tho·pe'dik	Correction of skeletal deformities.

	orthopedist or′tho·pe′dist	Orthopedic surgeon.
	orthopercussion or′tho·per·kush′un	Percussion with distal phalanx of finger at right angles to surface.
	orthophoria or′tho·fo′re·ah	Normal or proper placement of organs, referring also to muscle balance of the eye.
	orthopnea or′thop·ne′ah	Inability to breathe except in an upright position.
	orthopsychiatry or′tho·si·ki′ah·tre	Branch of psychiatry which deals with mental and emotional development.
	orthosis or·tho′sis	Straightening of a distorted part.
	os os	Opening or mouth. Bone.
	oscillation os′i·la′shun	Fluctuation; vibration; variation.
	oscillometer os′i·lom′e·ter	Instrument for measuring oscillations, such as changes in blood pressure.
	osmoreceptor oz′mo·re·cep′tor	Nerve ending that responds to changes in the osmotic pressure of the blood.
	osmosis os·mo′sis	Passage of a solvent through a semipermeable membrane from a dilute solution to a more concentrated one.
	osmotic os·mot′ik	Pertaining to osmosis.

osseous os′e·us	Bony.
ossicle os′si·k′l	Small bone.
ossification os′i·fi·ka′shun	Process of bone formation.
osteitis os′te·i′tis	Inflammation of a bone.
osteoarthritis os′te·o·ar·thri′tis	Degenerative joint disease.
osteoblast os′te·o·blast	Bone-forming cell.
osteochondritis os′te·o·kon·dri′tis	Inflammation of bone and cartilage.
osteoclasis os·te·ok′lah·sis	Surgical breaking of a bone to correct deformity.
osteoclast os′te·o·klast	Instrument used in surgical fracture of bones. Large multinuclear cell.
osteocope os′te·o·kop	Pain in a bone or bones.
osteocyte os′te·o·site	Mature bone cell.
osteodynia os′te·o·din′e·ah	Pain in a bone.
osteogenesis os′te·o·jen′e·sis	The development of bone.
osteogenic os′te·o·jen′ik	Tissue concerned in growth or repair of bone.

osteoid os′te·oid	Resembling bone.
osteolysis os′te·ol′i·sis	Softening or dissolution of bone.
osteoma os′te·o′mah	Tumor composed of bone tissue or developing on a bone.
osteomalacia os′te·o·mah·la′she·ah	Condition marked by softening of bones.
osteomyelitis os′te·o·mi′e·li′tis	Inflammation of bone caused by pyogenic organism.
osteopathy os′te·op′ah·the	Disease of the bone.
osteoporosis os′te·o·po·ro′sis	Abnormal rarefaction of bone.
osteosclerosis os′te·o·skle·ro′sis	Hardening or abnormal denseness of bone.
osteotome os′te·o·tom	Knife or chisel for cutting bone.
osteotomy os′te·ot′o·me	Surgical cutting of bone.
ostium os′te·um	Door or opening into a tubular organ; pl. *ostia*.
otalgia o·tal′je·ah	Pain in the ear.
otitis o·ti′tis	Inflammation of the ear.
otocyst o′to·sist	Auditory sac of the embryo.

otodynia o′to·din′e·ah	Pain in the ear; earache.
otologist o·tol′o·jist	An ear specialist.
otology o·tol′o·je	The study of the ear.
otoplasty o′to·plas′te	Operative repair of the ear.
otorrhagia o′to·ra′je·ah	Profuse bleeding from the ear.
otorrhea o′to·re′ah	Discharge from the ear.
otosclerosis o′to·skle·ro′sis	Formation of spongy bone in capsule of ear labyrinth.
otoscope o′to·skop	Instrument for examining the ear.
ounce ouns	Measure of weight in avoirdupois and apothecaries' systems.
outpatient out′pa·shent	Patient who is treated at a hospital or clinic but does not occupy a bed.
ovarian o·va′re·an	Pertaining to an ovary or ovaries.
ovariotomy o′va·re·ot′o·me	Surgical removal of an ovary.
ovarium o·va′re·um	Sexual gland in female in which ova are formed.
ovary o′vah·re	Sexual gland in female.

	overbite o'ver·bite	Extent upper anterior teeth overlap lower.
	overweight o'ver·wate	Obesity.
	oviduct o'vi·dukt	A fallopian tube; duct passing from uterus to ovary.
	ovulation ov'u·la'shun	Discharge of mature unimpregnated ovum from the ovary.
	ovum o'vum	The female reproductive cell; pl. *ova*.
	oxidase ok'si·dase	Any enzyme which promotes an oxidation reaction.
	oxidation ok'si·da'shun	The act of being oxidized, or the state of being oxidized.
	oxide ok'sid	Any compound of oxygen with an element or radical.
	oxidize ok'si·dize	To combine or cause to combine with oxygen.
	oxygen ok'si·jen	Gaseous element existing free in the air.
	oxygenate ok'si·je·nat	Saturation with oxygen.
	ozone o'zon	Allotropic and more active form of oxygen.

P

	pabulum pab'u·lum	Food or aliment.

packyderma pak′e·der′mah	Abnormal thickening of the skin.	
palatal pal′ah·tal	Pertaining to palate.	
palate pal′at	Partition separating nasal and oral cavities.	
palatine pal′ah·tin	Pertaining to palate.	
palliative pal′e·a′tiv	Affording relief without cure.	
pallor pal′or	Paleness; absence of skin coloration.	
palmar pah′mar	Pertaining to the palm of the hand.	
palpable pal′pah·b′l	Perceptible by touch.	
palpate pal′pat	To examine by hand; to feel.	
palpation pal·pa′shun	Act of feeling with the hand.	
palpebra pal′pe·brah	The eyelid.	
palpebral pal′pe·bral	Pertaining to an eyelid.	
palpitation pal′pi·ta′shun	Abnormally rapid heart action felt by the patient.	
palsy pawl′ze	Paralysis.	
panchrest pan′krest	A panacea, or remedy, for every disease.	

	pancreas pan'kre·as	Large gland behind stomach, concerned in digestion, secretion of insulin, and production of glucagon.
	pancreatectomy pan'kre·ah·tek'- to·me	Excision of all or part of pancreas.
	pancreatitis pan'kre·ah·ti'tis	Inflammation of pancreas.
	panendoscope pan·en'do·skop	Cystoscope giving wide view of bladder.
	pang pang	Sudden, piercing pain.
	panhysterectomy pan'his·ter·ek'to- me	Complete extirpation of uterus and cervix.
	pannus pan'nus	Superficial vascularization of cornea.
	pansinusitis pan'si·nus·i'tis	Inflammation involving all paranasal sinuses.
	papilla pah·pil'lah	Small nipplelike elevation; pl. *papillae*.
	papillary pap'i·ler'e	Pertaining to a papilla or nipple.
	papillate pap'i·lat	Marked by nipplelike elevations.
	papilledema pap'i·le·de'mah	Edema of optic papilla.
	papilloma pap'i·lo'mah	Benign epithelial tumor.

papule pap'ul	Small circumscribed, solid elevation of the skin.
paracentesis par'ah·sen·te'sis	Surgical puncture of a cavity to withdraw fluid.
paracusis par'ah·ku'sis	Any abnormality or derangement of hearing.
paradidymis par'ah·did'i·mis	Body of tubules in anterior part of spermatic cord.
paradoxical par'ah·dok'se·kal	Seemingly contradictory to the normal rule.
paralysis pah·ral'i·sis	Loss or impairment of motor function.
paramedical par'ah·med'i·kal	In an adjunctive position, serving in the science or practice of medicine.
paramesial par'ah·me'se·al	Situated near the mesial line.
parametrium par'ah·me'tre·um	Outer lining of the uterus.
paranoia par'ah·noi'ah	Chronic, progressive mental disorder.
paranoic par'ah·no'ic	Individual exhibiting paranoia.
paranoid par'ah·noid	Resembling paranoia.
paraphilia par'ah·fil'e·ah	Aberrant sexual activity.
paraplegia par'ah·ple'je·ah	Paralysis of legs and lower part of body.

	pararenal par′ah·re′nal	Situated near the kidney.
	parasite par′ah·sit	Plant or animal which lives upon or within another living organism.
	parathyroid par′ah·thi′roid	Located beside the thyroid gland.
	parathyroidectomy par′ah·thi′roid·ek′-to·me	Excision of the parathyroid gland.
	paravertebral par′ah·ver′te·bral	Beside the vertebral column.
	paraxial par·ak′se·al	Beside an axis.
	parenchyma par·eng′ki·mah	The working part of an organ.
	parenteral par·en′ter·al	By subcutaneous, intramuscular, or intravenous injection.
	paresis pah·re′sis	Slight or incomplete paralysis.
	paresthesia par′es·the′ze·ah	Abnormal sensation such as burning or prickling.
	paries pa′re·ez	A wall of an organ or body cavity.
	parietal pah·ri′e·tal	Of or pertaining to walls of a cavity.
	paronychia par′o·nik′e·ah	Inflammation of tissue surrounding a fingernail.
	parotic pah·rot′ik	Situated or occurring near the ear.

	parotid pah·rot′id	Situated or occurring near the ear.
	parotitis par′o·ti′tis	Inflammation of parotid gland; mumps.
	paroxysm par′ok·sizm	Sudden recurrence of the symptoms of a disease.
	paroxysmal par′ok·siz′mal	Recurring in paroxysms.
	pars parz	Division or part of larger organ or structure; pl. *partes*.
	parturition par′tu·rish′un	Act or process of giving birth.
	partus par′tus	Labor or childbirth.
	passive pas′iv	Neither spontaneous nor active.
	patella pah·tel′lah	Triangular sesamoid bone; knee cap or knee pan.
	patent pa′tent	Open; unobstructed; apparent.
	pathogen path′o·jen	Any disease-producing microorganism or material.
	pathogenesis path′o·jen′e·sis	Development of morbid conditions or disease.
	pathogenic path·o·jen′ik	Producing disease.
	pathologic path′o·loj′ik	Indicative of or caused by a morbid condition.
	pathological path′o·loj′i·kal	Pertaining to pathology.

SHORTHAND DICTIONARY · 211

	pathologist pah·thol′o·jist	Expert in pathology.
	pathology pah·thol′o·je	Branch of medicine which treats of the essential nature of disease.
	patient pa′shent	Person who is ill or is undergoing treatment for disease.
	patulous pat′u·lus	Spreading widely apart; open; distended.
	pectoral pek′to·ral	Of or referring to the chest or breast.
	pectoralis pek′to·ra′lis	Pertaining to the breast or chest.
	pectoriloquy pek′to·ril′o·kwe	Transmission of vocal sounds through chest wall.
	pectus pek′tus	Breast; chest or thorax.
	pedal ped′al	Pertaining to the foot or feet.
	pediatrician pe′de·ah·trish′un	Expert in treatment of children and of their diseases.
	pediatrics pe′de·at′riks	Medical specialty which deals with children's diseases.
	pedicle ped′i·k′l	Stemlike part, such as a narrow strip which connects a tissue graft to donor site.
	pediculosis pe·dik′u·lo′sis	Infestation with lice.
	pedodontics pe·do·don′tiks	Dentistry dealing with teeth and mouth conditions of children.

pedologist pe·dol′o·gist	Specialist in study of life and development of children.
pedometer pe·dom′e·ter	Instrument for measuring infants.
pedopathy pe·dop′ah·the	Any disease of the foot.
peduncle pe·dung′k′l	Stemlike part.
pellicle pel′i·k′l	Thin skin or film which forms on surface of liquids.
pelvic pel′vik	Pertaining to bony arch (pelvis) at posterior extremity of trunk.
pelvis pel′vis	Pelvic girdle composed of two coxae, sacrum, and coccyx.
pemphigus pem′fi·gus	Skin disease with bullae which leave pigmented spots.
pendulous pen′du·lus	Hanging loosely; dependent.
penicillin pen′i·sil′lin	Antibiotic to fight bacteria.
penis pe′nis	Male organ of copulation.
pentobarbital pen′to·bar′bi·tal	A hypnotic and sedative.
Pentothal Pen′to·thal	Trademark for preparation of thiopental, intravenous anesthesia.
percept per′sept	The object perceived.

perception per·sep′shun	Recognition; response to sensory stimuli.
percussion per·kush′un	Striking a part with a finger to determine density of underlying structure.
perforated per′fo·rat′ed	Pierced with holes.
perforation per′fo·ra′shun	Act of boring or piercing through a part.
perfuse per·fuz′	To pour over or through.
perfusion per·fu′zhun	Pouring of fluid; introduction of fluid into tissues by injection.
perianal per′e·a′nal	Located around the anus.
periarticular per′e·ar·tik′u·lar	Situated around a joint.
peribronchial per′i·brong′ke·al	Surrounding the windpipe.
pericardicentesis per′i·kar′de·sen-te′sis	Surgical puncture of the pericardium.
pericardiectomy per′i·kar′de·ek′-to·me	Excision of the pericardium.
pericarditis per′i·kar·di′tis	Inflammation of sheath surrounding heart.
pericardium per′i·kar′de·um	Serous sac enclosing the heart.
perichondrium per′i·kon′dre·um	Fibrous connective tissue covering cartilage.

pericranium per′i·kra′ne·um	External periosteum of skull.	
periderm per′i·derm	Outer layer of fetal skin.	
perifolliculitis per′i·fo·lik′u·li′tis	Inflammation around hair follicles.	
perimeter per·im′e·ter	Line forming boundary of a plane.	
perinatal per′i·na′tal	Occurring shortly before and after birth.	
perineal per′i·ne′al	Pertaining to the perineum.	
perineocele per′i·ne′o·sel	Hernia lying between rectum and prostate or rectum and vagina.	
perineum per′i·ne′um	Region between anus and the external sexual organs.	
period pe′re·od	Interval for the regular recurrence of a phenomenon.	
periodontal per′e·o·don′tal	Situated around a tooth.	
periorbital per′e·or′bi·tal	Situated around the orbit or eye socket.	
periosteal per′e·os′te·al	Pertaining to the periosteum.	
periosteum per′e·os′te·um	Fibrous membrane surrounding bone.	
periostitis per′e·os·ti′tis	Inflammation of the periosteum.	

peripheral pe·rif′er·al	Situated at periphery or surface of body or organ.	
periphery pe·rif′er·e	Outer part or surface of an organ or part.	
perirenal per′e·re′nal	Situated around a kidney.	
perisinuous per′e·sin′u·us	Situated around a sinus.	
peristalsis per′e·stal′sis	The wavelike motion by which alimentary canal propels its contents.	
peritomy pe·rit′o·me	Surgical incision of tissue around cornea. Circumcision.	
peritoneal per′i·to·ne′al	Pertaining to membrane lining abdominal walls.	
peritonealize per′i·to·ne′al·iz	To cover with peritoneum.	
peritoneoplasty per′i·to′ne·o·plas′te	Operation of covering abraided areas with peritoneum.	
peritoneoscopy per′i·to′ne·os′·ko·pe	Inspection of peritoneal cavity by an instrument inserted through the abdominal wall.	
peritoneum per′i·to·ne′um	Serous membrane lining abdominal cavity and surrounding its viscera.	
peritonitis per′i·to·ni′tis	Inflammation of the peritoneum.	
periumbilical per′e·um·bil′i·kal	Situated around the umbilicus.	

perivascular per′i·vas′ku·lar	Situated around a vessel.
perivesical per′i·ves′i·kal	Occurring around the bladder.
permanganate per·man′gah·nat	Any salt of permanganic acid.
permeable per′me·ah·b′l	Affording passage; pervious.
pernicious per·nish′us	Tending to a fatal issue.
peroneal per′o·ne′al	Pertaining to the fibula or outer side of leg.
personality per′su·nal′i·te	That which characterizes a person.
perspiration per′spi·ra′shun	The secretion of sweat; sweat.
pertussis per·tus′is	Whooping cough.
perversion per·ver′shun	Turning aside from the normal course.
pervert per′vert	Person who indulges in unnatural acts.
pes pes	Terminal organ of leg or footlike part.
petechia pe·te′ke·ah	Pinpoint hemorrhages in the skin.
petit mal pe·te′ mahl′	Brief blackout of consciousness accompanied by minor rhythmic movements.

petrous pet′rus	Resembling a rock; hard; strong.	
pexis pek′sis	Fixation of matter by a tissue or by suture.	
phagocyte fag′o·sit	White blood cell that destroys foreign particles or cells.	
phagocytosis fag′o·si·to′sis	The engulfing of foreign or other particles by phagocytes.	
phagomania fag′o·ma′ne·ah	Insatiable craving for food.	
phalanges fa·lan′jez	Bones of the fingers or toes.	
phalanx fa′lanks	Any bone of a finger or toe.	
pharmaceutical fahr′mah·su′ti·kal	Pertaining to pharmacy or drugs.	
pharmacist fahr′mah·sist	Apothecary or druggist.	
pharmacy fahr′mah·se	Art of preparing, compounding, and dispensing medicines. An apothecary's shop.	
pharyngeal fah·rin′je·al	Pertaining to the pharynx.	
pharyngitis far′in·ji′tis	Inflammation of the pharynx.	
pharyngocele fah·ring′go·sel	Hernial protrusion of part of pharynx.	
pharyngodynia fah·ring′go-din′e·ah	Pain in the pharynx.	

	pharyngotomy far′ing·got′o·me	Surgical incision of the pharynx.
	pharynx far′inks	Musculomembranous sac between mouth, nares, and esophagus.
	phenacetin fe·nas′e·tin	Drug to reduce fever.
	phenobarbital fe′no·bar′be·tal	Hypnotic and sedative.
	phenol fe′nol	Poisonous, colorless, crystalline compound.
	phenomenon fe·nom′e·non	Sign or objective symptom; any remarkable change.
	phenylephrine fen′il·ef′rin	Vasoconstrictor used in sinusitis, rhinitis, and hay fever.
	pheochromocytoma fe′o·kro′mo·si·to′- mah	Small lobular, vascular tumor of adrenal medulla.
	phimosis fi·mo′sis	Tightness of foreskin so that it cannot be drawn back from over glans penis.
	phlebectomy fle·bek′to·me	Excision of a vein or part of a vein.
	phlebitis fle·bi′tis	Inflammation of a vein.
	phlebolith fleb′o·lith	A vein stone or calculus.
	phlebolithiasis fleb′o·li·thi′ah·sis	Formation of stones in the veins.
	phleborrhagia fleb′o·ra′je·ah	A venous hemorrhage.

phlebothrombosis fleb'o·throm·bo'sis	Clot in a vein with inflammation.
phlebotomy fle·bot'o·me	Opening of a vein for blood letting.
phlegm flem	Viscid, stringy mucus secreted by mucosa of air passages.
phlegmasia fleg·ma'ze·ah	Inflammation or fever.
phlyctenula flik·ten'u·lah	Small vesicle or pustule.
phobia fo'be·ah	Any persistent abnormal dread or fear.
phosphatase fos'fah·tas	Enzyme that catalyzes monophosphoric esters.
phosphate fos'fat	Any salt of phosphoric acid.
phosphorus fos'fo·rus	Nonmetallic, translucent element, inflammable and poisonous.
phrenasthenia fren'as·the'ne·ah	Feebleness of mind.
phrenic fren'ik	Pertaining to the mind. Pertaining to the diaphragm.
phreniclasia fren'i·kla'se·ah	Crushing of phrenic nerve with a clamp.
phrenocardia fren'o·kar'de·ah	Psychic condition characterized by cardiac region pain.
phrenoplegia fren'o·ple'je·ah	Loss or paralysis of mental faculties.

phthisical tiz′e·kal		Affected with phthisis.
phthisis ti′sis		Wasting away of body; pulmonary tuberculosis.
phyma fi′mah		Skin tumor or cutaneous tubercle.
physical fiz′e·kal		Pertaining to nature or to the body.
physician fi·zish′un		Authorized practitioner of medicine.
physics fiz′iks		Science of the phenomena and laws of nature.
physiologic fiz′e·o·loj′ik		Normal; not pathologic.
physiological fiz′e·o·loj′i·kal		Pertaining to normal; not diseased.
physiology fiz′e·ol′o·je		Science that treats of the functions of living organisms.
physiotherapy fiz′e·o·ther′ah·pe		Use of heat, massage, electricity in treatment of disease.
physique fi·sek′		Bodily structure and development.
pia mater pi′ah ma′ter		Innermost of three membranes covering brain and spinal cord.
pigment pig′ment		Any normal or abnormal coloring matter of the body.
pigmentation pig′men·ta′shun		Disposition of coloring matter of body; discoloration by pigment.

	pigmented pig′ment·ed	Stained by deposit of pigment.
	pilar pi′lar	Pertaining to the hair.
	pilocarpine pi′lo·kar′pin	Alkaloid; cholinergic agent.
	pimple pim′p′l	Papule or pustule.
	pinna pin′nah	The projecting part of ear lying outside of head.
	piriform pir′i·form	Pear shaped.
	pisiform pi′si·form	Pealike in size and shape.
	pithiatry pith·i′ah·tre	Medical treatment by persuasion or suggestion.
	pitting pit′ting	Formation of small depression.
	pituitary pi·tu′i·tar′e	Pertaining to mucus or phlegm or pituitary gland.
	pityriasis pit′i·ri′ah·sis	Group of skin diseases with branny scales.
	placebo plah·se′bo	An inactive substance given as medicine to please or gratify the patient.
	placenta plah·sen′tah	Organ within uterus establishing communication between mother and fetus.
	plantar plan′tar	Referring to the sole of the foot.

	planum pla′num	Flat surface of bone or other structure.
	plaque plak	Patch or flat area. A blood platelet.
	plasma plaz′mah	Fluid part of the blood or lymph.
	plasmacyte plaz′mah·sit	Plasma cell.
	plasmacytoma plaz′mah·si·to′mah	Neoplasm composed of plasma cells.
	plasmolysis plaz·mol′i·sis	Shrinkage of a cell due to withdrawal of water by osmosis.
	plaster plas′ter	Mixture to immobilize body parts or to make impressions.
	plastic plas′tik	Building up tissues; capable of being molded.
	platelet plat′let	Small circular, colorless disk concerned in coagulation of blood.
	plethora pleth′o·rah	Vascular turgescence, excess of blood, and fullness of pulse.
	pleura ploor′ah	Serous lining of the chest cavity and the lungs.
	pleural ploor′al	Pertaining to membrane covering lungs and lining of thoracic cavity.
	pleurisy ploor′i·se	Inflammation of the pleura, with exudation into its cavity and upon its surface.
	plexus plek′sus	Network of nerves or blood vessels.

	plica pli′kah	Ridge or fold of membrane.
	plication pli·ka′shun	Reducing size of a hollow organ or muscle by taking tucks in its walls.
	plugger plug′er	Dental instrument used for packing filling material into a tooth cavity.
	pneumatosis nu′mah·to′sis	Presence of gas in an abnormal situation in the body.
	pneumocardial nu′mo·kar′de·al	Pertaining to the lungs and heart.
	pneumocentesis nu′mo·sen·te′sis	Surgical puncture of a lung in order to drain fluid.
	pneumococcus nu′mo·kok′us	Organism causing lobar pneumonia; *Diplococcus pneumoniae.*
	pneumoconiosis nu′mo·ko′ne·o′sis	Chronic reaction in lungs to inhalation of dust.
	pneumoencephalo- gram nu′mo·en·sef′ah- lo·gram	Roentgenogram of brain.
	pneumonectomy nu′mo·nek′to·me	Surgical excision of lung tissue.
	pneumonia nu·mo′ne·ah	Inflammation of the lungs.
	pneumothorax nu′mo·tho′raks	Accumulation of air or gas in the pleural cavity.
	pneusis nu′sis	Respiration.

podalic po·dal′ik		Accomplished by means of the feet.
podiatry po·di′ah·tre		Diagnosis and treatment of disorders of the feet.
poison poi′zn		Any substance causing damage to body structure or function.
poliomyelitis po′le·o·mi′e·li′tis		Acute viral disease characterized by fever, headache, and stiffness of neck and back.
pollution po·lu′shun		Act of defiling or making impure.
polycythemia pol′e·si·the′me·ah		Excess in number of red corpuscles in blood.
polydipsia pol′e·dip′se·ah		Prolonged excessive thirst.
polyemia pol′e·e′me·ah		Excess in quantity of blood in body.
polygraph pol′e·graf		Instrument for recording the body's mechanical or electrical impulses that are indicative of emotional reactions.
polymorphonuclear pol′e·mor′fo·nu′- kle·ar		Having a deeply lobed or divided nucleus.
polymyxin pol′e·mik′sin		Generic term designating antibiotics from soil bacterium.
polyneuritis pol′e·nu·ri′tis		Inflammation of many nerves at once.
polyopia pol′e·o′pe·ah		Condition in which one object appears as two or more.

	polyorexia pol'e·o·rek'se·ah	Excessive hunger or appetite.
	polyp pol'ip	Morbid growth from mucous membrane.
	polyphagia pol'e·fa'je·ah	Excessive eating or craving for food.
	polypoid pol'e·poid	Resembling a polyp.
	polypus pol'i·pus	Smooth, pedunculated growth from mucous membrane; pl. *polypi*.
	polysaccharide pol'e·sak'ah·rid	A carbohydrate formed by the condensation of two or more monosaccharides.
	polyuria pol'e·u're·ah	Excessive urination in a given period.
	pons ponz	Any slip of tissue connecting two parts of an organ.
	Pontocaine Pon'to·kan	Trademark for preparation of tetracaine, a local anesthetic.
	popliteal pop·lit'e·al	Referring to the area behind the knee.
	pore pore	Small opening on a surface.
	postabortal post·ah·bor'tal	Occurring after abortion.
	posterior pos·te're·or	Situated behind or to the back of a part.
	posteroinferior pos'ter·o·in·fe'-re·or	Situated in back and below.

postganglionic post′gang·gle·on′ik	Situated behind, or after, a ganglion.
postmortem post·mor′tem	After death; examination of body after death.
postnasal post·na′zal	Occurring behind the nose.
postnatal post·na′tal	Occurring after birth.
postoperative post·op′er·a′tiv	Occurring after a surgical operation.
postpartum post·par′tum	Occurring after childbirth or delivery.
postprandial post·pran′de·al	Occurring after dinner or a meal.
posttraumatic post·traw·mat′ik	Occurring after injury.
postulate pos′tu·lat	Anything taken for granted or assumed.
posture pos′tur	Attitude or position assumed by the body.
potable po′tah·b′l	Fit to drink.
potassium po·tas′e·um	Metallic element of the alkali group.
potator po′tah·tor	A heavy drinker.
potency po′ten·se	Power; ability of male to perform sexual intercourse.
potential po·ten′shal	Capable of acting, but not yet active.

	potion po′shun	Draft; large dose of liquid medicine.
	pouch powch	Pocketlike space, cavity, or sac.
	pox poks	Eruptive disease; vulgar name for syphilis.
	practice prak′tis	Exercise of one's knowledge in the recognition and treatment of disease.
	practitioner prak·tish′un·er	One qualified and engaged in the practice of medicine.
	prandial pran′de·al	Pertaining to a meal, especially dinner.
	precardiac pre·kar′de·ak	Situated in front of the heart.
	precipitate pre·sip′i·tat	To cause substance in solution to settle down in solid particles.
	preclinical pre·klin′i·kal	Before symptoms make diagnosis possible.
	precordial pre·kor′de·al	Pertaining to the precordium.
	precordium pre·kor′de·um	Region over heart or stomach.
	precostal pre·kos′tal	In front of the ribs.
	preganglionic pre′gang·gle·on′ik	Situated in front of, or preceding, a ganglion.
	pregnancy preg′nan·se	Growth and development of fetus in the body.

pregnant preg′nant	With child; gravid.	
premature pre·mah·tur′	Occurring before proper time.	
premedication pre′med·i·ka′shun	Preliminary internal medication.	
premolar pre·mo′lar	Situated in front of molar teeth.	
prenatal pre·na′tal	Existing or occurring before birth.	
preoperative pre·op′er·a′tiv	Preceding an operation.	
prepuce pre′pus	Covering fold of skin.	
presbyopia pres′be·o′pe·ah	Impairment of vision in the aged.	
prescription pre·skrip′shun	Written direction for preparation and administration of a remedy.	
presentation pre′zen·ta′shun	Portion of fetus touched by examining finger through cervix.	
pressor pres′or	Producing a rise in blood pressure.	
pressoreceptor pres′o·re·sep′tor	Receptor sensitive to changes in blood pressure.	
pressure presh′ur	Stress or strain by compression, pull, or thrust.	
presystolic pre′sis·tal′ik	Pertaining to beginning of the systole.	

	prethyroideal pre′thi·roi′de·al	Situated in front of the thyroid gland.
	pretracheal pre·tra′ke·al	Situated in front of the trachea.
	preventive pre·ven′tiv	An agent used to avert the occurrence of something.
	prevesical pre·ves′i·kal	Situated in front of the bladder.
	primary pri′ma·re	First in order; principal.
	primordium pri·mor′de·um	Earliest discernible indication of an organ or part.
	Priscoline Pris′ko·len	Trademark for preparation of a drug producing vasodilation and cardiac stimulation.
	prism prizm	A transparent solid used to measure or correct imbalance of the ocular muscles.
	Privine Pri′ven	Trademark for a vasoconstrictor; agent causing constriction of blood vessels.
	probe prob	Slender instrument for exploration of wound or cavity.
	procaine pro′kan	Local anesthetic.
	process pros′es	Projecting part; prominence.
	proctagra prok′tag·rah	Pain in and around the anus.
	proctalgia prok·tal′je·ah	Neuralgia of lower rectum.

proctectomy prok·tek′to·me	Excision of the rectum.	
proctitis prok·ti′tis	Inflammation of the rectum.	
proctoclysis prok·tok′li·sis	Slow injection of large amounts of liquid into rectum.	
proctologist prok·tol′o·jist	Specialist in rectal diseases.	
proctopexy prok′to·pek′se	Surgical fixation of a prolapsed rectum.	
proctoscope prok′to·skop	Speculum with light for inspection of rectum.	
proctoscopy prok·tos′ko·pe	Inspection of rectum with a proctoscope.	
productive pro·duk′tiv	Producing or forming.	
progeny proj′e·ne	Offspring; descendants.	
prognosis prog·no′sis	Forecast of probable result of attack of disease or disorder.	
progression pro·gresh′un	Act of moving or walking forward.	
prolapse pro·laps′	Falling down or sinking of a part or viscus.	
proliferation pro·lif′er·a′shun	The reproduction and multiplication of similar forms, particularly tissue cells.	
prolific pro·lif′ik	Fruitful; productive.	

	prominence prom'i·nens	Projection or protrusion.
	promontory prom'on·to're	Projecting part or process.
	pronate pro'nat	To assume or place in a prone position.
	pronation pro·na'shun	The act of assuming the prone position.
	prophylactic pro'fi·lak'tik	Tending to ward off disease. An agent used for that purpose.
	prophylaxis pro'fi·lak'sis	Prevention of disease; preventive treatment.
	proprietary pro·pri'e·ta·re	Any chemical or drug produced under an exclusive right and protected against free competition.
	proprioceptive pro'pre·o·sep'tiv	Receiving stimulations within the tissues of the body.
	proptosis prop·to'sis	A forward displacement; projecting.
	prostate pros'tat	Gland surrounding neck of bladder of the male.
	prostatectomy pros'tah·tek'to·me	Surgical removal of prostate or part of it.
	prostatic pros·tat'ik	Pertaining to prostate gland.
	prosthesis pros'the·sis	Replacement of absent part by an artificial substitute.
	prostration pros·tra'shun	Extreme exhaustion or powerlessness.

protamine pro′tah·min	Any one of basic proteins, occurring in spermatozoa of fish.
protein pro′te·in	Organic nitrogenous compounds which form principal constituents of cell protoplasm.
proteinuria pro′te·in·u′re·ah	Presence of protein in urine.
proteolysis pro′te·ol′i·sis	Hydrolytic conversion of proteins into simpler substances by enzymes.
Proteus *Pro′te·us*	Gram-negative, motile, rod-shaped bacteria.
prothrombin pro·throm′bin	Component produced in liver, necessary for blood clotting.
protocol pro′to·kol	Original notes made on a case, experiment, or disease.
protoplasm pro′to·plazm	Essential substance of living cells.
protractor pro·trak′tor	Instrument for extracting foreign material from wounds.
protrusion pro·troo′zhun	State of being thrust forward or laterally.
protuberance pro·tu′ber·ans	A projecting part or swelling.
proximal prok′si·mal	Nearest to a point of reference.
prurigo proo·ri′go	Chronic skin disease marked by papules and itching.
pruritic proo·rit′ik	Characterized by itching.

	pruritus proo·ri′tus	Intense itching.
	pseudarthrosis su′dar·thro′sis	Deossification of a weight-bearing long bone.
	pseudocrisis su·dok′ri·sis	False crisis; a sudden temporary abatement of fever.
	pseudocyst su′do·sist	Abnormal space resembling a cyst.
	pseudoleukemia su′do·lu·ke′me·ah	Enlargement of lymph glands without leukemic blood findings.
	pseudoparalysis su′do·pah·ral′i·sis	False paralysis or loss of muscular power.
	psilosis si·lo′sis	Falling out of the hair.
	psoriasis so·ri′ah·sis	Chronic recurrent skin disease with scaling papules.
	psoriatic so′re·at′ik	Affected with or of the nature of psoriasis.
	psychasthenia si′kas·the′ne·ah	Feeling of unreality, anxiety, doubts, and inadequacy.
	psyche si′ke	Conscious and unconscious faculty for thought, judgment, and emotion.
	psychiatric si′ke·at′rik	Pertaining to psychiatry.
	psychiatrist si·ki′ah·trist	Specialist in mental illness.
	psychic si′kik	Pertaining to psyche or mind; mental.

psychoanalysis si′ko·ah·nal′i·sis	Method developed by Freud to explore and synthesize patterns of emotional thinking and development.
psychogenic si′ko·jen′ik	Having an emotional, rather than organic, origin.
psychologic si′ko·loj′ik	Pertaining to psychology.
psychology si·kol′o·je	Study of the mind and mental operations.
psychometrics si′ko·met′riks	Measurement of the duration and force of mental operations.
psychomotor si′ko·mo′tor	Pertaining to motor effects of psychic activity.
psychoneurosis si′ko·nu·ro′sis	Mental disorder which is of psychogenic origin.
psychopathic si′ko·path′ic	Pertaining to mental disease.
psychopathy si·kop′ah·the	Extreme mental disorder.
psychosexual si′ko·seks′u·al	Psychic or emotional aspects of the sex instinct.
psychosis si·ko′sis	Any deep, prolonged behavior disorder and break with reality.
psychosomatic si′ko·so·mat′ik	Pertaining to the mind-body relationship.
psychotherapy si·ko·ther′ah·pe	Treatment designed to produce a response by mental rather than by physical effects.
psychotic si·kot′ik	Characterized or caused by psychosis.

	ptosis to′sis	Prolapse or drooping of an organ or part.
	puberty pu′ber·te	Period of life when generative organs become capable of reproduction.
	pubes pu′bez	Hair growing over the pubic region.
	pubic pu′bik	Pertaining to the pubes.
	pubis pu′bis	The os pubis; pubic bone.
	pudendum pu·den′dum	The external genital organs.
	puerperium pu′er·peh′re·um	Period of confinement following childbirth.
	pulmonary pul′mo·ner′e	Pertaining to the lungs.
	pulmonic pul·mon′ik	Pertaining to the lungs.
	pulmonitis pul′mo·ni′tis	Inflammation of lungs; pneumonia.
	pulp pulp	Soft tissue within the chamber of a tooth.
	pulsation pul·sa′shun	Throb or rhythmical beat of the heart.
	pulse puls	Expansion and contraction of an artery which can be felt by the finger.
	punctate punk′tat	Marked with dots or pinpoint punctures.

puncture punk′tur	Wound made by pointed instrument.	
pungent pun′jent	Acrid; penetrating; producing a painful and sharp sensation.	
pupil pu′pil	Opening at center of iris of eye for transmission of light.	
pupillary pu′pi·ler·e	Pertaining to or affecting the pupil.	
purgative pur′gah·tiv	Cathartic; causing evacuations from the bowels.	
purpura pur′pu·rah	Skin condition characterized by submucous or intradermal hemorrhages.	
purulent pu′roo·lent	Consisting of or producing pus.	
pus pus	Liquid inflammation product made up of cells and a thin fluid.	
pustular pus′tu·lar	Pertaining to or of the nature of a pustule.	
pustule pus′tul	Small elevation of skin filled with pus.	
pustulosis pus′tu·lo′sis	Condition marked by outbreak of pustules.	
putrefaction pu′tre·fak′shun	Enzymic malodorous decomposition of organic matter.	
pyelectasis pi′e·lek′tah·sis	Abnormal expansion of the renal pelvis.	
pyelitis pi′e·li′tis	Inflammation of pelvis of kidney.	

pyelogram pi'e·lo·gram	Roentgenogram of kidney and ureter.
pyelography pi'e·log'rah·fe	Roentgenography of kidney and ureter.
pyelonephritis pi'e·lo·ne·fri'tis	Inflammation of kidney and its pelvis.
pyemia pi·e'me·ah	Pus in the blood.
pyloric pi·lor'ik	Pertaining to the pylorus.
pylorospasm pi·lo'ro·spazm	Spasm of the pylorus or of the pyloric portion of the stomach.
pylorostomy pi'lo·ros'to·me	Formation of opening through abdominal wall into pyloric end of stomach.
pylorus pi·lo'rus	Distal aperture of stomach to the duodenum.
pyoderma pi'o·der'mah	Any purulent skin disease.
pyogenic pi'o·jen'ik	Pus producing.
pyorrhea pi'o·re'ah	Discharge of pus.
pyosis pi·o'sis	Suppuration.
pyramidal pir·ram'i·dal	Shaped like a pyramid.
pyramis pir'ah·mis	Pointed or cone-shaped structure or part.

pyretic pi·ret′ik	Pertaining to or of the nature of fever.
pyrexia pi·rek′se·ah	Elevation of body temperature above normal; fever.
Pyribenzamine Pir′i·ben′zah·mene	Trademark for a preparation of antihistaminic.
pyrogen pi′ro·jen	A fever-producing substance.
pyromania pi′ro·ma′ne·ah	Obsessive preoccupation with fires.
pyuria pi·u′re·ah	Presence of pus in the urine.

Q

quackery
kwak′er·e — Misrepresentation of one's ability in diagnosis and treatment of disease.

quadrant
kwod′rant — One of four parts or quarters, as of the abdominal region or the eardrum.

quadriceps
kwod′reh·seps — Four headed.

quarantine
kwor′an·ten — Period of detention or isolation on account of suspected contagion.

quiescent
kwi·es′ent — At rest; motionless.

quinidine
kwin′eh·din — Used in treatment of cardiac arrhythmias.

quinine
kwin′in — Alkaloid antimalarial drug.

| | quintessence
kwin·tes′ens | Highly concentrated extract of any substance. |
| | quotidian
kwo·tid′e·an | Recurring daily. A form of intermittent malarial fever with daily recurrent paroxysms. |

R

	rabies ra′be·ez	Infectious disease due to virus and communicated to man by a bite of an infected animal.
	rachitic ra·kit′ik	Affected with rickets.
	rachitis ra·ki′tis	Rickets; inflammatory disease of vertebral column.
	radial ra′de·al	Pertaining to radius; radiating.
	radiate ra′de·at	To diverge or spread from a common point.
	radiation ra·de·a′shun	Act of diverging from a central point. Electromagnetic waves or particulate rays given off from some source.
	radical rad′i·kal	Directed to the cause; going to source of a morbid process.
	radioactive ra′de·o·ak′tiv	Having the property of emitting corpuscular or electromagnetic radiation.
	radiography ra′de·og′rah·fe	Recording or photographing by action of actinic rays on sensitized surface.

radioisotope ra′de·o·i′so·top	A radioactive isotope which is used for the effects of its radioactivity and also as a tracer.
radiologic ra′de·o·loj′ik	Pertaining to radiology.
radiologist ra′de·ol′o·jist	Physician with experience in diagnosis and treatment of disease with radiant energy.
radiometer ra′de·om′e·ter	Instrument for estimating roentgen-ray quantity.
radiopaque ra′de·o·pak′	Not permitting passage of X rays.
radiotherapy ra′de·o·ther′ah·pe	Treatment of disease by X ray.
radioulnar ra′de·o·ul′nar	Pertaining to the radius and ulna.
radium ra′de·um	An extremely radioactive metallic element.
radius ra′de·us	Line radiating from a center.
radix ra′diks	Lowermost part, or a structure by which hair, nail, or tooth is anchored in tissue.
rale rahl	Any abnormal respiratory sound heard in auscultation.
ramus ra′mus	Branch, as of a vein, artery, or nerve; pl. *rami*.
rancid ran′sid	Musty, rank taste or smell.

| | raptus
rap′tus | Sudden, violent attack. |
|---|---|---|
| | rarefaction
rar′e·fak′shun | Condition of being less dense. |
| | rash
rash | Temporary eruption on skin. |
| | ratio
ra′she·o | Expression of the quantity of one substance in relation to that of another. |
| | reaction
re·ak′shun | The response to a stimulus. |
| | reagent
re·a′jent | Substance employed to produce a chemical reaction. |
| | rebound
re′bownd | Reversed response on withdrawal of a stimulus. |
| | receptor
re·sep′tor | Nerve ending which transforms stimuli into nerve impulses. |
| | recess
re′ses | Small empty space or cavity. |
| | recession
re·sesh′un | Act of drawing away. In dentistry, retraction of gingival margin and underlying tissue away from the neck of a tooth. |
| | recipient
re·sip′e·ent | Person who receives the blood in a transfusion. |
| | recrudescence
re′kroo·des′ens | Recurrence of symptoms after period of improvement. |
| | recruitment
re·kroot′ment | Increase in a reflex when a stimulus is prolonged. |
| | rectal
rek′tal | Pertaining to the rectum. |

rectocele rek′to·sel	Hernial protrusion of part of rectum into vagina.	
rectosigmoid rek′to·sig′moid	Lower portion of sigmoid and upper portion of rectum.	
rectourethral rek′to·u·re′thral	Pertaining to rectum and urethra.	
rectovesical rek′to·ves′i·kal	Pertaining to rectum and bladder.	
rectum rek′tum	Terminal part of the large intestine.	
rectus rek′tus	Straight.	
recumbent re·kum′bent	Lying down.	
recuperation re·ku′per·a′shun	Recovery of health and strength.	
recurrence re·kur′ens	Return of symptoms after a remission.	
recurrent re·kur′ent	Running back or toward the source; returning after intermissions.	
reduce re·dus′	To restore to normal place or relation of parts. Decrease in weight.	
reducible re·du′si·b′l	Permitting of reduction; capable of being reduced.	
reduction re·duk′shun	Correction of a fracture, luxation, or hernia.	
referral re·fur′al	Process of directing a patient to appropriate specialist.	

	reflection re·flek′shun	Turning or bending back.	
	reflex re′fleks	Involuntary movement or action.	
	refraction re·frak′shun	Determination of refractive errors of the eye and their correction by glasses.	
	refractory re·frak′to·re	Resisting stimulation; not readily yielding to treatment.	
	refracture re·frak′chur	Operation of breaking a bone that had been broken and united with a deformity.	
	refrigerant re·frij′er·ant	A cooling remedy. Cooling, acidulous drinks and evaporating lotions.	
	regimen rej′eh·men	Strictly regulated scheme of diet or exercise.	
	region re′jun	Plane area with more or less definite boundaries.	
	regression re·gresh′un	Return to a former or earlier state.	
	regurgitant re·gur′ji·tant	Flowing back or in opposite direction from normal.	
	regurgitation re·gur′ji·ta′shun	Return of undigested food from stomach to mouth.	
	rehabilitation re′hah·bil′i·ta′shun	Restoration of normal form and function after injury or illness.	
	reinforcement re′in·fors′ment	Increasing of force or strength.	

reinnervation re′in·er·va′shun	Operation of grafting a live nerve to restore function of a paralyzed muscle.
relapse re·laps′	Return of a disease after apparent cessation.
relation re·la′shun	Condition or state of one object when considered in connection with another.
relaxant re·lak′sant	Lessening or reducing tension.
relief re·lef′	Mitigation or removal of pain or distress.
relieve re·lev′	Mitigate or remove pain or distress.
remedial re·me′de·al	Curative; acting as a remedy.
remedy rem′eh·de	Anything that cures, palliates, or prevents disease.
remission re·mish′un	Diminution or abatement of symptoms of a disease.
remittence re·mit′ens	Temporary abatement without cessation of symptoms.
remittent re·mit′ent	Having periods of abatement and of exacerbation.
remnant rem′nant	Something remaining; residue.
ren ren	One of two glandular bodies in lumbar region that secrete urine.
renal re′nal	Pertaining to the kidney.

SHORTHAND DICTIONARY

renicapsule ren′i·kap′sul	Adrenal gland.
reniform ren′i·form	Resembling a kidney.
renipuncture ren′i·punk′tur	Surgical puncture of the capsule of the kidney.
renography re·nog′rah·fe	Radiography of the kidney.
renopathy re·nop′ah·the	Kidney disease; nephropathy.
repression re·presh′un	Thrusting back from consciousness into unconscious sphere of ideas of a disagreeable nature.
reproduction re′pro·duk′shun	Production of offspring.
resection re·sek′shun	Excision of a considerable portion of an organ or structure.
reserpine res′er·pen	Antihypertensive and tranquilizer for management of anxiety and tension.
reserve re·zerv′	Something kept in store for future use.
reservoir rez′er·vwar	Place or cavity for storage.
resident rez′i·dent	Graduate and licensed physician resident in a hospital.
residual re·zid′u·al	Remaining or left behind.

residuum re·zid′u·um	Residue or remainder.
resilience re·zil′e·ens	Elasticity; property of returning to former shape or size.
resistance re·zis′tans	Resisting; withstanding.
resolution rez′o·lu′shun	Subsidence of a pathologic state.
resonance rez′o·nans	Sound which results from vibration of the normal chest.
resonant rez′o·nant	Giving a vibrant sound on percussion.
respiration res′pi·ra′shun	Act or function of breathing — inspiration and expiration.
respirator res′pi·ra′tor	Apparatus for giving artificial respiration.
respiratory re·spi′rah·to′re	Pertaining to respiration.
response re·spons′	Action or movement due to application of a stimulus.
restraint re·strant′	Forcible confinement of violently psychotic or irrational person.
resupination re′su·pi·na′shun	Act of turning upon the back or dorsum.
resuscitation re·sus′i·ta′shun	Prevention of asphyxial death by artificial respiration.
retainer re·tan′er	Appliance or device for retaining teeth in proper position.

retardation re′tar·da′shun	Delay; hindrance.
retching rech′ing	Involuntary effort to vomit.
retention re·ten′shun	Process of keeping in position.
reticular re·tik′u·lar	Netlike; formed by a network.
reticulocyte re·tik′u·lo·sit′	An immature red blood cell of reticular tissue.
reticulum re·tik′u·lum	Protoplasmic network in cells.
retina ret′i·nah	Innermost of three tunics of the eyeball.
retinaculum ret′i·nak′u·lum	Structure which retains an organ or tissue in place.
retinal ret′i·nal	Pertaining to the retina.
retinitis ret′i·ni′tis	Inflammation of the retina.
retinopathy ret′i·nop′ah·the	Any noninflammatory disease of the retina.
retinoscopy ret′i·nos′ko·pe	Determining refraction of the eye by lights and shadows.
retraction re·trak′shun	Act of drawing back.
retractor re·trak′tor	Instrument for drawing back edges of a wound. Any retractile muscle.

retrenchment re·trench′ment	Removal by plastic surgery of redundant tissue.
retrocardiac ret′ro·kar′de·ak	Behind the heart.
retrocession ret′ro·sesh′un	Going backward; backward displacement.
retroflexion ret′ro·flek′shun	Bending of an organ so that its top is turned backward.
retrograde ret′ro·grad	Going backward; catabolic.
retrogression ret′ro·gresh′un	Going backward; degenerating.
retrolental re′tro·len′tl	Behind the lens of the eye.
retromammary ret′ro·mam′ar·e	Behind the mammary gland.
retronasal ret′ro·na′zal	Behind the nose.
retroperitoneal re′tro·per′i·to-ne′·al	Situated behind the peritoneum.
retrosternal re′tro·ster′nal	Situated behind the sternum.
retroversion ret′ro·ver′zhun	Tipping of an entire organ backward.
retrusion re·troo′zhun	State of being located posterior to the normal position; malposition of a tooth.
reversal re·ver′sal	Turning or change in opposite direction.

reversion re·ver′zhun	Returning to a previous condition.	
rheumatic roo·mat′ik	Pertaining to inflammation of bone, joint, muscle, nerve, or tendon.	
rheumatism roo′mah·tizm	Inflammation of connective tissue structures of the body.	
rheumatoid roo′mah·toid	Resembling rheumatism.	
rhinitis ri·ni′tis	Inflammation of the mucous membrane of the nose.	
rhinoderma ri′no·der′mah	Chronic skin affection marked by hard, conical elevations.	
rhinodynia ri′no·din′e·ah	Pain in the nose.	
rhinolith ri′no·lith	Nasal concretion or stone.	
rhinologist ri·nol′o·jist	Specialist in the treatment of diseases of the nose.	
rhinoplasty ri′no·plas′te	Surgical repair of the nose.	
rhinorrhagia ri′no·ra′je·ah	Nosebleed.	
rhinorrhea ri′no·re′ah	Discharge of nasal mucus.	
rhinoscope ri′no·skop	Speculum used in nasal examinations.	
rhonchus rong′kus	Rattling in the throat; dry coarse rale.	

rhythm rith′m	Measured movement; recurrence of action at regular intervals.
rhytidectomy rit′i·dek′to·me	Excision of skin for elimination of wrinkles.
rib rib	One of paired bones extending from thoracic vertebrae to sternum.
rickets rik′ets	Condition caused by deficiency of vitamin D.
ridge rij	Projection or projecting structure.
rigidity re·jid′i·te	Abnormal stiffness or inflexibility.
ring ring	Any annular or circular organ or area.
ringworm ring′wurm	Disease of the skin.
roentgen rent′gen	International unit of X or gamma radiation.
roentgenogram rent·gen′o·gram	X-ray picture.
roentgenography rent′gen·og′rah·fe	Photography by means of roentgen rays.
roentgenologist rent′gen·ol′o·jist	Physician who devotes himself to diagnosis and treatment by roentgen rays.
rongeur raw·zhur′	Instrument for pulling, grasping, or compressing. (Also *forceps*.)

Rorschach Ror'shahk	Test of intelligence which also measures emotional elements of personality. Commonly known as the ink-blot test.
rosary ro'zah·re	Structure resembling a string of beads.
roseola ro·ze'o·lah	Any rose-colored rash; rubeola.
rotation ro·ta'shun	Process of turning around an axis.
roughage ruf'ij	Indigestible material such as fibers or cellulose in a diet.
rubefacient roo'be·fa'shent	Agent that causes reddening of the skin.
rubella roo·bel'ah	Acute virus disease with eruptions; German measles.
rubeola roo·be'o·lah	Measles; rubella.
rubeosis roo'be·o'sis	Redness; reddish discoloration of the skin.
rubor roo'bor	Redness of the skin due to inflammation.
ructus ruk'tus	Belching of wind; eructation.
rudimentary roo'di·men'tah·re	Imperfectly developed. Vestigial.
ruga roo'gah	Fold, ridge, or wrinkle.
rupture rup'chur	Forcible tearing or breaking of a part; hernia.

rushes rush′ez	Rapid waves of contractile activity in the intestine.	

S

sac sak	Any pouch; baglike organ or structure.
sacculation sak′u·la′shun	Little bag or sac.
sacculus sak′u·lus	Little bag or sac.
saccus sak′kus	Saclike space.
sacral sa′kral	Pertaining to the sacrum.
sacroiliac sa′kro·il′e·ak	Pertaining to the sacrum and ilium.
sacrum sa′krum	Triangular bone composed of five fused vertebrae.
sadism sad′izm	Sexual perversion.
sagittal saj′i·tal	Like an arrow; straight plane of the body.
salicylate sal′i·sil′at	Any salt of salicylic acid.
saline sa′leen	Salty; containing salt.
saliva sah·li′vah	Secretion from parotid, submaxillary, and sublingual glands of the mouth.

	salivation sal′i·va′shun	Excessive secretion of saliva.
	Salmonella Sal′mo·nel′ah	Rod-shaped, gram-negative microorganisms.
	salpingectomy sal′pin·jek′to·me	Removal of the uterine tube.
	salpingitis sal′pin·ji′tis	Inflammation of the uterine tube. Inflammation of the auditory tube.
	salpingocele sal·ping′go·sel	Hernial protrusion of a fallopian tube.
	salpingo-oophorectomy sal·ping′go- o′of·o·rek′to·me	Surgical removal of a uterine tube and an ovary.
	salpingo-oophoritis sal·ping′go- o′of·o·ri′tis	Inflammation of the uterine tubes and ovaries.
	salpingoplasty sal·ping′go·plas′te	Repairing of a uterine tube.
	salpingotomy sal′ping·got′o·me	Surgical incision of a uterine tube.
	salpinx sal′pinks	A tube, especially the auditory or uterine tube.
	salt sawlt	Sodium chloride; common salt.
	salubrious sah·lu′bre·us	Conducive to health; wholesome.
	salve sav	Thick ointment or cerate.

sanatorium san'ah·to're·um	Establishment for treatment of extremely ill persons.
sanatory san'ah·to're	Conducive to health.
sanguineous sang·gwin'e·us	Pertaining to blood.
sanguis sang'gwis	Fluid circulating through the heart, arteries, capillaries, and veins.
sanitarium san'i·ta're·um	Institution for promotion of health.
sanitary san'i·ta're	Promoting or pertaining to health.
sanity san'i·te	Soundness of mind.
sarcoblast sar'ko·blast	Primitive cell that develops into a muscle cell.
sarcoid sar'koid	Resembling the flesh; fleshy.
sarcoidosis sar'koi·do'sis	Disorder affecting organs with epithelioid cell tubercles.
sarcolemma sar'ko·lem'ah	Delicate sheath enveloping a muscle fiber.
sarcology sar·kol'o·je	Branch of anatomy which treats of the soft tissues of the body.
sarcolysis sar·kol'i·sis	Disintegration of the soft tissues.
sarcoma sar·ko'mah	Tumor made up of connective tissue, muscle, or bone.

sarcosis sar·ko'sis	Presence of multiple fleshy tumors.
satellite sat'e·lit	Vein that accompanies an artery.
saturation sat'u·ra'shun	Act of or condition of being saturated.
saucerization saw'ser·i·za'shun	Excavation of tissue of wound to form shallow depression.
scab skab	Crust of a superficial sore.
scabies ska'be·ez	Contagious skin disease due to the itch mite.
scale skal	Thin, compacted, platelike structure on surface of body, or shed from skin.
scalp skalp	Part of integument of head normally covered with hair.
scalpel skal'pel	Small, straight knife, usually with a convex edge.
scaly ska'le	Scalelike; characterized by scales.
scaphoid skaf'oid	Shaped like a boat; outer bone of first row of carpal bones.
scapula skap'u·lah	Shoulder blade; triangular bone in back of shoulder.
scapular skap'u·lar	Of or pertaining to the scapula.
scar skar	Mark remaining after healing of a wound.

	schizoid skiz′oid	Unsocial, introspective type of personality, characterized by inappropriate mood and disturbances in reality relationships.
	schizophasia skiz′o·fa′ze·ah	Disordered speech characteristic of schizophrenia.
	schizophrenia skiz′o·fre′ne·ah	Mental disorder marked by withdrawal from reality, inappropriate mood, and regressive tendencies.
	schizophrenic skiz′o·fren′ik	Pertaining to or characterized by schizophrenia.
	sciatic si·at′ik	Pertaining to the inferior dorsal part of the hip bone.
	sciatica si·at′i·kah	Intensely painful inflammation of the sciatic nerve.
	scirrhus skir′us	Hard cancer with marked predominance of connective tissue.
	scissors siz′erz	Cutting instrument with two opposed blades.
	sclera skle′rah	Firm, fibrous outer coat of eyeball.
	sclerectomy skle·rek′to·me	Excision of the sclera by scissors, by punch, or by trephining.
	scleredema skle′re·de′mah	Edematous hardening of the skin.
	scleritis skle·ri′tis	Inflammation of the sclera.

SHORTHAND DICTIONARY 257

	scleroderma skle′ro·der′mah	Systemic disease involving connective tissues of any part of the body.
	scleroid skle′roid	Having a hard texture.
	sclerosis skle·ro′sis	Hardening of a part from inflammation and in diseases of the interstitial substance.
	sclerotic skle·rot′ik	Hard, or hardening; affected with sclerosis.
	scolex sko′leks	Anterior end or head of a tapeworm.
	scoliosis sko′le·o′sis	Abnormal lateral curvature of the spine.
	scopolamine sko·pol′ah·min	Alkaloid; poisonous nerve depressant and mydriatic.
	scotoma sko·to′mah	Area of depressed vision within the visual field.
	scrotum skro′tum	Pouch containing the testes.
	scurvy skur′ve	Condition due to deficiency of vitamin C in diet.
	seasickness se′sik·nes	Nausea and malaise caused by motion of a ship at sea.
	sebaceous se·ba′shus	Pertaining to sebum or suet.
	seborrhea seb′o·re′ah	Excessive secretion of the sebaceous glands.

sebum se′bum	Secretion of sebaceous glands, composed of fat, keratahyalin granules, keratin, and cellular debris.	
Seconal Sek′o·nol	Trademark for preparation of secobarbital — sedative and hypnotic.	
secondary sek′un·der′e	Second or inferior in order of time, place, or importance.	
secrete se·kret′	To discharge or pour out cell products.	
secretion se·kre′shun	Process of elaborating a product as a result of gland activity.	
section sek′shun	Act of cutting; a cut surface.	
secundine se·kun′din	Placenta and membranes expelled after childbirth. The afterbirth.	
sedation se·da′shun	Producing a sedative or calming effect.	
sedative sed′ah·tiv	An agent to allay activity and excitement.	
sedentary sed′en·ter′e	Sitting habitually; of inactive habits.	
sediment sed′i·ment	A precipitate, especially one that is formed spontaneously.	
sedimentation sed′i·men·ta′shun	Act of causing deposit of sediment.	
segment seg′ment	Portion of a larger body or structure.	

	seizure se′zhur	Sudden attack or recurrence of a disease.
	sella sel′ah	Saddle-shaped depression; pl. *sellae*.
	semen se′men	Fluid spermatozoa produced by the male reproductive organs.
	semicanal sem′e·kah·nal′	Channel which is open on one side.
	semicomatose sem′e·ko′mah·tos	Condition of mild coma from which patient may be aroused.
	semiconscious sem′e·kon′shus	Half conscious; partially conscious.
	semilunar sem′e·lu′nar	Shaped like a half moon or crescent.
	semimembranous sem′e·mem′brah-nus	Made up in part of membrane or fascia.
	seminal sem′i·nal	Pertaining to the semen.
	seminormal sem′e·nor′mal	One-half the normal or standard strength.
	semipermeable sem′e·per′me-ah·b′l	Permitting passage of a solvent such as water, but preventing passage of a dissolved substance or solute.
	senescence se·nes′ens	State of growing old; beginning of old age.
	senile se′nile	Relating to old age.

sensation sen·sa′shun	Impression conveyed by an afferent nerve to the sensorium commune.
sense sens	Faculty by which conditions or properties of things are perceived.
sensibility sen′si·bil′i·te	Ability to feel or perceive.
sensitivity sen′si·tiv′i·te	State or quality of being able to respond quickly and acutely to stimulation.
sensitization sen′si·ti·za′shun	Process of rendering a cell sensitive to action of a complement.
sensorium sen·so′re·um	Sensory nerve center, located in the brain.
sensory sen′so·re	Pertaining to or subserving sensation.
sensualism sen′shu·al·izm	Condition of being dominated by bodily passions.
sepsis sep′sis	Poisoning due to the products of a putrefactive process.
septal sep′tal	Pertaining to the septum.
septicemia sep′ti·se′me·ah	Presence in the blood of bacterial toxins.
septum sep′tum	Partition; dividing wall between two cavities.
sequela se·kwe′lah	Condition following and caused by a disease.
sequestration se′kwes·tra′shun	Formation of a sequestrum; isolation of a patient.

sequestrectomy se′kwes·trek′to·me	Surgical removal of a sequestrum.
sequestrum se·kwes′trum	Piece of dead bone separated from sound bone.
serologic se′ro·loj′ik	Pertaining to antigen-antibody reactions in vitro.
serology se·rol′o·je	Study of antigen-antibody reactions in vitro.
seropurulent se′ro·pu′roo·lent	Consisting of both serum and pus.
serosa se·ro′sah	Membrane that lines the closed cavities of the body.
serosanguineous se′ro·sang·gwin′-e·us	Consisting of both blood and serum.
serous se′rus	Pertaining to or resembling serum; producing serum.
Serpasil Ser′pah·sil	Trademark for preparation of reserpine.
serpiginous ser·pij′i·nus	Creeping from one part to another.
serrated ser′at·ed	Having a toothlike edge; notched.
serum se′rum	Clear liquid which separates in the clotting of blood from the clot and the corpuscles.
sesamoid ses′ah·moid	Small bone developed in a tendon.
sessile ses′il	Attached by a broad base.

	sexual seks′u·al	Pertaining to or characteristic of sex.
	sexuality seks′u·al′i·te	Characteristic quality of male and female reproductive elements.
	shaft shaft	Long slender part such as portion of a long bone.
	sheath sheeth	Tubular structure enclosing or surrounding some organ.
	shingles shin′g′lz	Herpes zoster.
	shiver shiv′er	Slight chill or tremor.
	shock shok	Condition of acute peripheral circulatory failure due to injury.
	shoulder shol′der	Junction of the arm and trunk of the body.
	sibilant sib′i·lant	Of a shrill, whistling sound heard in auscultation.
	sibling sib′ling	One of two or more children of same parents; brother or sister.
	sicklemia sik·le′me·ah	Sickle cell anemia.
	sickness sik′nes	Condition marked by pronounced deviation from a normal, healthy state; illness.
	sigmoid sig′moid	Shaped like the letter S.
	sigmoidoscopy sig′moid·os′ko·pe	Inspection of the sigmoid flexure with a speculum.

sign sin	Indication of the existence of something; objective evidence of disease.
silicosis sil′i·ko′sis	Fibrosis of the lungs caused by inhalation of dust of stone, sand, or flint; grinders' disease.
simulation sim′u·la′shun	Malingering or feigning illness.
sinapism sin′ah·pizm	Mustard plaster.
sinew sin′u	Tendon of a muscle.
sinistrad sin·is′trad	Left or toward the left side.
sinus si′nus	Cavity within a bone; hollow space.
sinusitis si′nus·i′tis	Inflammation of a sinus.
sinusoid si′nus·oid	Resembling a sinus. Form of terminal blood channel.
skeletal skel′e·tal	Pertaining to the skeleton.
skeleton skel′e·ton	Hard framework of the body; bones of the body.
skiametry ski·am′e·tre	Method of investigating, diagnosing, and evaluating refractive errors of the eye by retinoscopy.
skiascopy ski·as′ko·pe	Investigation with a retinoscope.

Skiodan Ski′o·dan		Trademark for preparation of methiodal used in intravenous pyelography.
skull skul		Bony framework of the head and face. (Also *cranium*.)
sleeplessness slep′les·nes		Insomnia.
slough sluf		Dead tissue in or cast out from living tissue.
sloughing sluf′ing		Formation or separation of a slough.
smallpox smawl′poks		Variola; acute infectious disease caused by virus.
smear smer		Specimen for microscopic study.
sneeze snez		An involuntary, sudden, and violent expulsion of air through the nose and mouth.
snuffles snuf′f′lz		Catarrhal discharge from nasal mucous membrane in infants.
socket sok′et		Hollow or depression into which a corresponding part fits.
sodium so′de·um		Alkaline, metallic element; chief cation (element) of extracellular body fluids.
sodomy sod′o·me		Sexual contact between humans and animal species; mouth-genital contact.
softening sof′en·ing		Process of becoming soft.

Shorthand	Word	Definition
	soluble sol′u·b′l	Susceptible of being dissolved.
	solute so′lut	Substance dissolved in a solution.
	solution so·lu′shun	Liquid mix of two or more substances.
	solvent sol′vent	Dissolving; effecting a solution.
	soma so′mah	Body as distinguished from the mind.
	somatic so·mat′ik	Pertaining to the body as distinguished from the visera; physical.
	somnolence som′no·lens	Sleepiness; unnatural drowsiness.
	sonorous so·no′rus	Resonant; low-pitched sound heard in auscultation.
	sordes sor′dez	Foul, dark-brown matter which collects on lips and teeth in low fevers.
	sore sor	Ulcer or wound; lesion of the skin.
	souffle soof′f′l	Soft, blowing auscultatory sound.
	spasm spazm	Sudden, violent contraction of a muscle or group of muscles.
	spastic spas′tik	Pertaining to or characterized by spasms.
	spatium spa′she·um	Delimited area; space.

specialist spesh′al·ist		Practitioner devoted to a special class of diseases.
specialization spesh′al·i·za′shun		Medical practice limited to some special aspect of medicine or surgery.
specific spe·sif′ik		Pertaining to a species; that which distinguishes a thing.
specificity spes′i·fis′i·te		Quality or state of being specific.
specimen spes′i·men		Sample or part of a thing taken to show character of the whole.
spectacles spek′tah·k′lz		Pair of lenses in a frame to assist vision.
speculum spek′u·lum		Appliance for opening to view a passage or cavity of the body.
sperm sperm		Semen or testicular secretion.
spermatogenesis sper′mah·to·jen′-e·sis		Production of mature male germ cells.
spermatozoon sper′mah·to·zo′on		Mature male germ cell; pl. *spermatozoa*.
sphagitis sfa·ji′tis		Any throat inflammation.
sphenoid sfe′noid		Shaped like a wedge.
sphere sfer		Ball or globe.
sphincter sfingk′ter		Muscle surrounding and capable of closing an orifice of the body.

sphygmogram sfig′mo·gram	Record or tracing of arterial pulse.
sphygmoid sfig′moid	Resembling the pulse.
spica spi′kah	Bandage in which turns cross one another in a figure eight.
spicule spik′ul	Needle-shaped bone fragment or body.
spike spik	Sharp upward deflection in a curve, as in an oscillographic tracing.
spina spi′nah	Thornlike process or projection.
spinal spi′nal	Pertaining to the vertebral column.
spine spin	Spinal column; thornlike process or projection.
spinous spi′nus	Relating to a spine or spinelike process.
spirillum spi·ril′um	Relatively rigid, spiral-shaped bacterium.
splanchnic splank′nik	Referring to the viscera.
spleen splen	Large glandlike but ductless organ in the upper part of abdominal cavity.
splenectomy sple·nek′to·me	Excision of the spleen.
splenic splen′ik	Pertaining to the spleen.

splenitis sple·ni′tis	Inflammation of the spleen.	
splenomegaly sple′no·meg′ah·le	Enlargement of the spleen.	
splenonephric sple′no·nef′rik	Pertaining to the spleen and kidney.	
splenophrenic splen·o·fren′ik	Pertaining to the spleen and diaphragm.	
splint splint	Rigid or flexible appliance for the fixation of displaced parts.	
splinter splin′ter	Small fragment, as a piece of fractured bone.	
spondylitis spon′di·li′tis	Inflammation of the vertebrae.	
spondylolisthesis spon′di·lo·lis- the′sis	Forward displacement of one vertebra over another.	
sponge spunj	Absorbent pad of folded gauze or cotton.	
spontaneous spon·ta′ne·us	Voluntary; occurring without external influence.	
sputum spu′tum	Material expectorated through mouth.	
squama skwa′mah	Scale or platelike structure.	
squamous skwa′mus	Scaly or platelike.	
squeeze skwez	Subjection to pressure; compression.	

	stabile stab'il	Not moving; stationary.	
	stamina stam'i·nah	Vigor or endurance.	
	stammering stam'er·ing	Stuttering.	
	stapes sta'pez	Smallest of auditory ossicles. (Also *stirrup*.)	
	staphylococcus staf'i·lo·kok'us	Pathogenic bacteria which occur in clusters resembling grapes.	
	staphyloma staf'i·lo'mah	Protrusion of cornea or sclera, resulting from inflammation.	
	stasis sta'sis	Stoppage of normal flow of blood or other body fluids.	
	static stat'ik	At rest; in equilibrium; not in motion.	
	status sta'tus	State or condition.	
	staxis stak'sis	Hemorrhage.	
	stellate stel'at	Shaped like a star; arranged in a roset.	
	stenosis ste·no'sis	Constriction or narrowing of a duct or canal.	
	stereognosis ste're·og·no'sis	Faculty of recognizing the size and shape of objects by sense of touch.	
	sterile ster'il	Not fertile; barren; not producing young.	

	sterility ste·ril′i·te	Free from microorganisms; inability to produce offspring or induce conception.	
	sterilization ster′i·li·za′shun	Destruction of microorganisms by heat or chemical compounds; castration; vasectomy; salpingectomy.	
	sterilize ster′i·liz	To render free from microorganisms or incapable of reproduction.	
	sternal ster′nal	Pertaining to the sternum or breastbone.	
	sternoclavicular ster′no·klah·vik′- u·lar	Pertaining to the sternum and clavicle.	
	sternum ster′num	Unpaired plate of bone forming middle of anterior wall of the thorax.	
	steroid ste′roid	Compound such as sex hormones, bile acids, and sterols.	
	sterol ste′rol	Any saturated or unsaturated alcohol such as cholesterols.	
	stertorous ster′to·rus	Characterized by snoring; heavy breathing.	
	stethoscope steth′o·skop	Instrument for listening to sounds within the body.	
	stigma stig′mah	Spot or impression on the skin; mental or physical mark which aids in diagnosis of a condition.	
	stilbestrol stil·bes′trol	Diethylstilbestrol — for menopausal symptoms.	

	stillborn stil'born	Born dead.
	stimulant stim'u·lant	Producing stimulation; causing tension on muscle fiber.
	stimulus stim'u·lus	Agent, act, or influence that produces reaction in a receptor.
	stippling stip'pling	Spotted condition or appearance.
	stirrup stir'up	Stapes — innermost of the ossicles of the ear.
	stitch stich	Suture; use of needle and thread, catgut or wire to repair or close a wound.
	stockinet stok'i·net'	Cotton material to cover extremity preparatory to application of plaster or splints.
	stoma sto'mah	Any minute pore, orifice, or opening on a free surface.
	stomach stum'ak	Expansion of alimentary canal between esophagus and duodenum.
	stomachic sto·mak'ik	Pertaining to the stomach.
	stomatitis sto·mah·ti'tis	Inflammation of the oral mucosa.
	stone ston	Mass of hard and unyielding material; calculus.
	stool stool	Discharge of fecal matter from the bowels.
	strabismus strah·biz'mus	Squint.

strain stran	Overexercise; to use to an extreme and harmful degree.
strangulated strang′gu·lat′ed	Congested by reason of constriction.
strangulation strang′gu·la′shun	Choking or throttling respiration; arrest of circulation by compression.
strangury strang′gu·re	Difficult and painful discharge of urine.
stratum stra′tum	Layer; sheetlike mass of substance.
streptococcus strep′to·kok′us	Cells that divide in one direction only and grow in chains.
streptomycin strep′to·mi′sin	Antibiotic used for infections.
stria stri′ah	Streak or line or collection of nerve fibers in the brain; pl. *striae*.
striated stri′at·ed	Striped or streaked.
striation stri·a′shun	Quality of being marked by stripes or striae.
stricture strik′tur	Abnormal narrowing of a canal, duct, or passage.
stridor stri′dor	Harsh, high-pitched respiratory sound.
stridulous strid′u·lus	Making a shrill, harsh sound.
stroke strok	Sudden and severe attack as of apoplexy or paralysis.

stroma stro′mah	Supporting tissue framework of an organ.
structure struk′tur	Components and their manner of arrangement in constituting a whole.
struma stroo′mah	Scrofula; goiter.
stump stump	Distal end of the part of limb left following an amputation.
stupor stu′por	Lethargy; partial or almost complete unconsciousness.
stuporous stu′por·us	Affected with stupor.
stuttering stut′er·ing	Problem of speech involving disfluency, prolongation of sounds, and prolonged pauses.
sty sti	Inflammation of one or several of the sebaceous glands of the eyelid.
styptic stip′tik	Astringent and hemostatic remedy.
subacute sub′ah·kut′	Somewhat acute; between acute and chronic.
subconscious sub·kon′shus	Imperfectly or partially conscious.
subcostal sub·kos′tal	Situated below the ribs.
subcutaneous sub′ku·ta′ne·us	Beneath the skin.
subcuticular sub′ku·tik′u·lar	Situated beneath the epidermis.

subdermal sub·der′mal	Situated or occurring beneath the skin.
subdural sub·du′ral	Situated beneath the dura.
subendocardial sub′en·do·kar′de·al	Situated beneath the endocardium.
subjacent sub·ja′sent	Lying beneath or underneath.
subjective sub·jek′tiv	Perceived by affected individual only.
subliminal sub·lim′i·nal	Below the limen, or threshold, of sensation.
sublimis sub·li′mis	Elevated; superficial.
submandibular sub′man·dib′u·lar	Lying below the mandible.
submaxillary sub·mak′si·ler′e	Lying beneath the lower maxilla.
submucosa sub′mu·ko′sah	Layer of areolar tissue beneath mucous membrane.
submucous sub·mu′kus	Situated or performed beneath the mucous membrane.
subnormal sub·nor′mal	Below or less than normal.
substance sub′stans	Material constituting an organ or body.
substernal sub·ster′nal	Situated beneath the sternum.
subtle sut′l	Very fine; keen and acute.

subtotal sub·to′tal	Nearly but not quite total.	
subvaginal sub·vaj′i·nal	Situated under a sheath or below the vagina.	
succus suk′kus	Bodily secretion; juice.	
succussion su·kush′un	Act of shaking patient to detect fluid in cavities of the body.	
suckle suk′l	Derive or provide nourishment by breast feeding.	
sucrose su′kros	Sweetening agent.	
suction suk′shun	Act or process of aspirating.	
sudor su′dor	Sweat; perspiration.	
sudoriferous su′dor·if′er·us	Producing or secreting sweat.	
suffocation suf′o·ka′shun	Stoppage of respiration.	
suicide soo′i·side	Taking of one's own life.	
sulcus sul′kus	Depression in the surface of a tooth or bone.	
sulfadiazine sul′fah·di′ah·zene	Antibacterial agent.	
sulfaguanidine sul′fah·gwan′i·den	Antibacterial agent.	

	sulfanilamide sul′fah·nil′ah·mid	Antibacterial agent.
	sulfarsphenamine sulf′ar·sfen′ah·min	Compound used in treatment of syphilis.
	Sulfasuxidine Sul′fah·suk′si·den	Trademark for preparation of succinylsulfathiazole, an antibacterial agent.
	sulfate sul′fat	Any salt of sulfuric acid.
	sulfathalidine sul′fah·thal′i·dene	Trademark for preparations of phthalylsulfathiazole, an intestinal anti-infective.
	sulfathiazole sul′fah·thi′ah·zol	Antibacterial agent.
	sulfur sul′fur	Nonmetallic element; laxative and diaphoretic.
	summation sum·ma′shun	Accumulation of effects of multiple stimuli.
	sunburn sun′bern	Injury to skin due to excessive exposure to the sunlight, produced by ultraviolet rays.
	superficial su′per·fish′al	Pertaining to or situated near the surface.
	superior su·pe′re·or	Situated above; directed upward.
	superolateral su′per·o·lat′er·al	Above and at the side.
	supinate su′pi·nat	To assume or to place in a supine position.

	supination su′pi·na′shun	Act of assuming position of lying on the back. Turning hand with palm facing upward.
	supine su·pin′	Lying on the back or on the dorsum.
	suppository su·poz′i·to·re	Small, medicated mass to be introduced into vagina, rectum, or urethra.
	suppression su·presh′un	Sudden stoppage of a secretion, excretion, or discharge.
	suppuration sup′u·ra′shun	Formation of pus.
	suppurative sup′u·ra′tiv	Producing pus or associated with the formation of pus.
	supraclavicular su′prah·klah·vik′- u·lar	Situated above the clavicle.
	suprapubic su′prah·pu′bik	Situated or performed above the pubic arch.
	suprarenal su′prah·re′nal	Located above a kidney.
	suprarene su′prah·ren′	Adrenal gland.
	surgeon sur′jun	Practitioner of surgery.
	surgery sur′jer·e	Branch of medicine which treats diseases by manual and operative procedures.
	surgical sur′je·kal	Of or pertaining to surgery.

surrogate sur′o·gat	Something used as a substitute for another.	
susceptibility sus·sep′ti·bil′i·te	State of being readily affected or acted upon.	
susceptible sus·sep′ti·b′l	Capable of impression; readily acted on.	
suspirious sus·pi′re·us	Breathing heavily; sighing.	
suture su′tur	Stitch made to secure edges of a wound; fibrous joint uniting opposed surfaces.	
swab swahb	Device for moistening lips of helpless patient.	
swallowing swahl′o·ing	Taking in of a substance through mouth and pharynx into esophagus.	
sweat swet	Perspiration exuded by glands.	
swelling swel′ing	Abnormal enlargement or increase in volume of body part or area not due to cell growth.	
sycosis si·ko′sis	Disease marked by inflammation of hair follicles, especially of the beard.	
symbiosis sim′bi·o′sis	The living together or close association of two dissimilar organisms.	
symmetrical si·met′re·kal	Marked by equality in size and shape of parts.	
symmetry sim′e·tre	Equally proportioned.	

sympathectomy sim′pah·thek′-to·me	Transection of some portion of the sympathetic nervous pathways.
sympathetic sim′pah·thet′ik	Pertaining to or exhibiting sympathy; sympathetic nerve.
sympathy sim′pah·the	Influence produced in any organ by disease in another part.
symphysis sim′fi·sis	Line of union between bones originally distinct.
symptom simp′tum	Any evidence of a patient's condition or of disease.
symptomatic simp′to·mat′ik	Pertaining to or of the nature of a symptom.
synapse sin′aps	Junction between two neurons; anatomical relation of one nerve cell to another.
synapsis si·nap′sis	Pairing off and union of chromosomes from male and female.
synarthrosis sin′ar·thro′sis	Articulation in which the bones are immovably bound together.
synchondrosis sin′kon·dro′sis	A joint in which the surfaces are connected by a plate of cartilage.
synchronous sin′kro·nus	Taking place at the same time.
syncope sin′ko·pe	Fainting; temporary suspension of consciousness due to cerebral anemia.
syncytioma sin·sit′e·o′mah	Tumor in which uterine wall is infiltrated with wandering cells.

	syndactyly sin·dak′ti·le	Webbing between adjacent digits of the hand or foot.
	syndrome sin′drom	Set of symptoms occurring together.
	synergist sin′er·jist	Medicine that aids or cooperates with another; an adjuvant.
	synkinesis sin′ki·ne′sis	Associated movement; unintentional movement accompanying a volitional one.
	synovia si·no′ve·ah	Clear viscid fluid of a joint cavity.
	synovial si·no′ve·al	Referring to the clear fluid which is normally present in joint cavities.
	synovitis sin′o·vi′tis	Inflammation of a synovial membrane.
	synthesis sin′the·sis	Artificial building up of a chemical compound by union of its elements.
	synthetic sin·thet′ik	Artificial; pertaining to synthesis.
	syphilis sif′i·lis	Infectious venereal disease.
	syringe sir′inj	Instrument for injecting liquids into a vessel or cavity.
	syrup sir′up	Concentrated solution of a sugar used to flavor drugs.
	system sis′tem	Group of interrelated entities that contribute toward one vital function.

systematic sis′te·mat′ik	Pertaining or according to a system.	
systemic sis·tem′ik	Pertaining to or affecting the body as a whole; systematic.	
systole sis′to·le	Contraction phase of the cardiac cycle; the heart contraction.	
systolic sis·tol′ik	Pertaining to the contraction of the heart; produced by the systole.	

T

tabes ta′bez	Any wasting of the body; atrophy of the body.	
tablespoon ta′b′l·spoon	Household unit of capacity; approximately 4 fluid drams.	
tache tahsh	A vascular skin lesion; blemish.	
tachycardia tak′e·kar′de·ah	Abnormal rapidity of heartbeat; pulse rate above 100 per minute.	
tactile tak′til	Pertaining to the touch or to the sense of touch.	
talipes tal′i·pez	Clubfoot; a congenital deformity of the normal foot position.	
talus ta′lus	Bone of the ankle; part of the ankle joint; ankle bone.	
tamponade tam′pon·ad′e	The surgical use of a tampon.	
tantalum tan′tah·lum	Noncorrosive metal used for cranial plates and wire sutures.	

tantrum tan′trum		Violent display of bad temper.
tapeworm tap′werm		Parasitic intestinal cestode worm.
tarsal tahr′sal		Pertaining to the tarsus of the eyelid or to the instep.
tarsus tahr′sus		Region of articulation between the foot and leg. Framework of the eyelid.
tartar tahr′tahr		Dental calculus.
technique tek·nek′		Method of procedure and detail of any process or operation.
teething teth′ing		Eruption of teeth.
tegmen teg′men		Covering structure or roof.
telangiectasia tel·an′je·ek·ta′- ze·ah		Dilatation of capillary vessels and minute arteries.
telepathy te·lep′ah·the		Extrasensory perception of the mental activity of another person.
temperament tem′per·ah·ment		Physical character and mental cast of an individual.
temperature tem′per·ah·tur		Degree of sensible heat or cold.
template tem′plat		A pattern or mold. In dentistry, a curved or flat plate used as an aid in setting teeth for a denture.

tempora tem′po·rah		Region on either side of the head above the zygomatic arch.
temporal tem′po·ral		Pertaining to the lateral region of the head above the zygomatic arch.
temulence tem′u·lens		Drunkenness; intoxication.
tenacious te·na′shus		Holding fast; adhesive.
tenacity te·nas′i·te		Toughness; condition of being tough.
tenaculum te·nak′u·lum		Hooklike instrument for seizing and holding parts; pl. *tenacula*.
tenderness ten′der·nes		Abnormal sensitivity to touch or pressure.
tendinitis ten′di·ni′tis		Inflammation of tendons and of tendon-muscle attachments.
tendon ten′dun		Fibrous cord by which a muscle is attached to bone.
tenesmus te·nez′mus		Involuntary and painful straining at stool or in urinating.
tenonectomy ten′o·nek′to·me		Excision of part of a tendon to shorten it.
tenorrhaphy ten·or′ah·fe		Repair of a tendon by suture.
tension ten′shun		The condition of being stretched or strained.
tensor ten′sor		Any muscle that stretches or makes tense.

terminal ter′mi·nal	Forming or pertaining to an end.	
termination ter′mi·na′shun	Distal end; cessation.	
ternary ter′nah·re	Third in order; made up of three elements.	
Terramycin Ter′ah·mi′sin	Trademark for preparation of oxytetracycline, an antibiotic substance.	
tertiary ter′she·er·e	Third in order.	
tertipara ter·tip′ah·rah	Woman who has borne three children.	
tessellated tes′el·lat′ed	Composed of small squares; checkered.	
testicle tes′te·k′l	Male gonad.	
testis tes′tis	Male reproductive glands situated in the scrotum; pl. *testes*. (Also *testicle*.)	
testosterone tes·tos′ter·on	Hormone produced by testes in the male.	
tetanus tet′ah·nus	Acute infectious disease, caused by a toxin, characterized by spasm and convulsions.	
tetany tet′ah·ne	Syndrome marked by muscle twitchings, cramps, and convulsions.	
tetracycline tet′rah·si′klen	Broad spectrum antibiotic used against many organisms.	

	texture teks′tur	Any of the organized tissues or substances of the body.
	thalamus thal′ah·mus	Main relay center for sensory impulses to the cerebral cortex.
	theca the′kah	An enclosing case or sheath, especially of a tendon.
	thecal the′kal	Pertaining to a theca.
	thenar the′nar	Mound on the palm at the base of the thumb.
	therapeutic ther′ah·pu′tik	Pertaining to healing or to the treatment of disease.
	therapy ther′ah·pe	Treatment of disease.
	thermometer ther·mom′e·ter	Instrument for determining temperature.
	thiamine thi′ah·min	Component of the B complex of vitamins.
	thigh thi	Portion of lower extremity between the hip and knee.
	thiopental thi′o·pen′tal	Agent used intravenously or rectally to induce general anesthesia.
	thoracic tho·ras′ik	Pertaining to the chest.
	thoracocentesis tho′rah·ko·sen-te′sis	Surgical puncture of the chest wall.

thoracodynia tho′rah·ko·din′-e·ah	Pain in the chest.	
thoracolumbar tho′rah·ko·lum′-bar	Thoracic and lumbar parts of the spine.	
thoracoscope tho·ra′ko·skop	Endoscope for examining the pleural cavity.	
thoracoscopy tho′rah·kos′ko·pe	Diagnostic examination of the chest by instrument.	
thoracostomy tho′rah·kos′to·me	Operation to create a drainage opening into the thoracic cavity.	
thorax tho′raks	Part of the body between the neck and respiratory diaphragm.	
threshold thresh′old	Point at which a stimulus produces a sensation.	
thrill thril	Abnormal tremor or vibration felt on palpation.	
throat throte	Pharynx; fauces; anterior part of the neck.	
throe thro	Severe pain; paroxysm.	
thrombectomy throm·bek′to·me	Removal of a blood clot.	
thromboangiitis throm′bo·an′je·i′tis	Inflammation of the intima of a blood vessel with clot formation.	
thrombocythemia throm′bo·si·the′-me·ah	Fixed increase in the number of circulating blood platelets.	

	thrombocytopenia throm′bo·si′to·pe′- ne·ah	Decrease in number of blood platelets.
	thromboembolism throm′bo·em′bo- lizm	Obstruction of a blood vessel with a thrombus which has broken loose from its site of formation.
	thrombogenic throm′bo·jen′ik	Producing a clot or coagulum.
	thromboid throm′boid	Resembling a clot.
	thrombophlebitis throm′bo·fle·bi′tis	Inflammation of a vein wall causing formation of a thrombus.
	thrombosis throm·bo′sis	Formation, development, or presence of a thrombus.
	thrombus throm′bus	Stationary blood clot in a cavity of the heart or a blood vessel.
	thumb thum	First digit of the hand.
	thymol thi′mol	Antibacterial and antifungal agent.
	thymus thi′mus	Ductless glandlike body in the mediastinal cavity.
	thyroid thi′roid	Large ductless gland.
	thyroiditis thi′roid·i′tis	Inflammation of the thyroid gland.
	thyropenia thi′ro·pe′ne·ah	Deficiency of thyroid secretion.

thyrotoxicosis thi′ro·tok′si·ko′sis	Hyperthyroidism.
tibia tib′e·ah	Shinbone; large medial bone of leg below the knee.
tibial tib′e·al	Pertaining to the tibia.
tibiofibular tib′e·o·fib′u·lar	Pertaining to the tibia and fibula.
tic tik	Spasmodic muscular contraction of any part.
tick tik	Bloodsucking parasite.
tickling tik′ling	Light stimulation of body surface with reflex effect such as involuntary laughter.
timbre tim′ber	Peculiar quality of a tone or sound.
tincture tink′tur	Diluted solution of the active principle of a drug.
tinea tin′e·ah	Fungal infection of the skin; ringworm.
tingling ting′gling	Pricklike thrill caused by cold or striking a nerve.
tinkle ting′k′l	Ausculatory sound.
tinnitus tin′i·tus	Noise in the ears.
tissue tish′u	Group of similar cells and their related intercellular substance.

	titer ti′ter	Quantity of substance required to produce reaction with a given volume of another substance.
	toenail to′nal	Nail of one of the digits of the foot.
	toilet toi′let	Cleansing and dressing of a surgical or accidental wound or obstetrical patient.
	tolbutamide tol·bu′tah·mid	Oral hypoglycemic agent for treatment of diabetes.
	tolerance tol′er·ans	Ability to endure the continued or increasing use of a drug.
	Tolserol Tol′ser·ol	Trademark for preparation of mephenesin, a muscle relaxant.
	tomogram to′mo·gram	A roentgenogram of a selected layer of body tissue made by tomography.
	tone tone	Normal degree of vigor and tension; healthy state of a part.
	tongue tung	Movable, muscular organ on floor of the mouth.
	tonic ton′ik	Producing and restoring normal tone.
	tonometer to·nom′e·ter	Instrument to measure tension or pressure, as for the eyeball.
	tonsil ton′sil	Small rounded mass of lymphoid tissue.
	tonsillar ton′si·lar	Of or pertaining to a tonsil.

tonsillectomy ton′sil·ek′to·me	Excision of the tonsils.
tonsillitis ton′si·li′tis	Inflammation of the tonsils.
tonus to′nus	Slight degree of contraction present in muscles when inactive.
tooth tooth	One of the small bonelike structures in the jaws for masticating food.
topical top′e·kal	Pertaining to a particular spot; local.
torpid tor′pid	Not acting with normal vigor and facility.
torpor tor′por	Lack of response to normal stimulus; inactivity.
torsion tor′shun	Twisting; the state of being twisted.
torso tor′so	Trunk without head or extremities.
torticollis tor′ti·kol′is	Wryneck; unnatural position of the head.
tortuous tor′tu·us	Twisted; having many twists and turns.
torulus tor′u·lus	Small elevation; papilla.
torus to′rus	Bulging projection; swelling.
tourniquet toor′ni·ket	Instrument for compression of blood vessel to control bleeding.

	toxemia toks·e′me·ah	Presence of toxic products in the blood.
	toxic tok′sik	Pertaining to, due to, or of the nature of a poison.
	toxicity toks·is′i·te	State of being poisonous.
	toxicology tok′si·kol′o·je	Study of poisons.
	toxicosis tok′si·ko′sis	Any disease condition of toxic origin.
	toxin tok′sin	Poison.
	trabecula trah·bek′u·lah	Supporting fiber; fibrous membrane which forms a septum or partition.
	trabeculation trah·bek′u·la′shun	Formation of anchoring strands of connective tissue in a part.
	tracer tras′er	Dissecting instrument for isolating vessels and nerves.
	trachea tra′ke·ah	Windpipe; tube descending from larynx to bronchi.
	tracheal tra′ke·al	Pertaining to the trachea.
	trachelotomy tra′ke·lot′o·me	Surgical cutting of the uterine neck.
	tracheobronchial tra′ke·o·brong′ke·al	Pertaining to the trachea and bronchi.
	tracheocele tra′ke·o·sel	Hernial protrusion of the tracheal mucous membrane.

	tracheoplasty tra′ke·o·plas′te	Plastic surgery upon the trachea.
	tracheorrhagia tra′ke·o·ra′je·ah	Hemorrhage of the trachea.
	tracheostomy tra′ke·os′to·me	Surgical creation of an opening into the trachea through the neck in order to insert a tube to facilitate passage of air into the lungs.
	tracheotome tra′ke·o·tome	Instrument for incising the trachea.
	tracheotomy tra′ke·ot′o·me	Incision of the trachea through muscle of the neck.
	trachoma trah·ko′mah	Viral disease of conjunctiva and cornea.
	tracing tras′ing	Graphic record by an instrument capable of making a visual record of movements.
	tract trakt	A bundle or collection of nerve fibers serving some special purpose.
	traction trak′shun	Act of drawing or pulling.
	trait trat	Inherited bodily or mental characteristic.
	trance trans	Abnormal sleep from which the patient cannot be aroused easily. Hypnotic state.
	tranquilizer tran′kwi·liz′er	Agent which quiets and calms patient without affecting consciousness.

transection tran·sek′shun	Section made across a long axis; a cross section.
transference trans·fer′ens	Passage of symptom or affection from one part to another. Patient's feelings, whether positive or negative, toward the psychoanalyst.
transfix trans′fiks	To pierce through and through.
transfixion trans·fik′shun	Cutting through; a method of amputation.
transfusion trans·fu′zhun	Introduction of whole blood or other liquid directly into the bloodstream.
transillumination trans′i·lu′mi·na′-shun	Inspection of interior of a cavity by passing light through its walls.
transmission trans·mish′un	Transfer, as of a disease; communication of qualities to offspring.
transparent trans·par′ent	Permitting passage of light rays.
transplant trans′plant	Piece of tissue taken from body for grafting into another portion.
transplantation trans′plan·ta′shun	Grafting of tissues taken from same body or from another.
transurethral trans′u·re′thral	Performed through the urethra.
transverse trans·vers′	Crosswise; at right angles to long axis of a part.

transvestism trans·ves′tizm	Sexual deviation characterized by overwhelming desire to assume attire of and be accepted as a member of the opposite sex.
trauma traw′mah	Wound or injury.
treatment tret′ment	Management and care of a patient for purpose of combating disease.
tremor trem′or	Involuntary trembling or quivering.
treppe trep′eh	The phenomenon of gradual increase of muscular contraction following rapidly repeated stimulation.
triad tri′ad	Any trivalent element. Group of three entities or objects.
triangular tri·ang′gu·lar	Having three angles or corners.
tribromoethanol tri·bro′mo·eth′- ah·nol	General anesthetic, administered rectally.
trichinosis trik′i·no′sis	Disease condition due to infestation with trichinae.
trichitis tri·ki′tis	Inflammation of the hair bulbs.
trichloroethylene tri′klo·ro·eth′i·len	Inhalation analgesic and anesthetic.
trichology tri·kol′o·je	Study of the hair.

SHORTHAND DICTIONARY

trichomycosis trik′o·mi·ko′sis	Any disease of the hair caused by a fungus.
trichophobia trik′o·fo′be·ah	Morbid fear of hair.
trigone tri′gone	Triangular area.
trigonum tri·go′num	Three-cornered area.
trihexyphenidyl tri·hek′se·fen′i·dil	Antiparkinsonism agent. Used in parasympathetic blockade.
trimester tri·mes′ter	Stage or period of three months.
triquetrum tri·kwe′trum	Three cornered. Third carpal bone from radial side in proximal row.
trismus triz′mus	Lockjaw; early symptom of tetanus.
trocar tro′kar	Sharp-pointed instrument for piercing cavity wall in paracentesis.
trochanter tro·kan′ter	One of two bony processes below neck of the femur.
trochlea trok′le·ah	Inner articular process at the lower end of the humerus. Pulley-shaped part.
trochlear trok′le·ar	Resembling a pulley; pertaining to a trochlea.
trophic trof′ik	Of or pertaining to nutrition or nourishment.

	trophoblast trof′o·blast	A layer of extra-embryonic ectodermal tissue that attaches the ovum to the uterine wall and supplies nutrition to the embryo.	
	tropism tro′pizm	Involuntary response of an organism toward or away from a stimulus.	
	trunk trunk	Main part of body to which head and limbs are attached.	
	trusion troo′zhun	Malposition of a tooth.	
	truss trus	Device for retaining a reduced hernia in its place.	
	trypanosomiasis tri·pan′o·so·mi′- ah·sis	Disease caused by infection with various species of the genus *Trypanosoma*.	
	tryparsamide trip′ars·am′id	Chemical used in treatment of sleeping sickness and of neurosyphilis.	
	tubercle tu′ber·k′l	Nodule or small elevation of the skin. Characteristic lesion of tuberculosis.	
	tubercular tu·ber′ku·lar	Of, pertaining to, or resembling tubercules or nodules.	
	tuberculin tu·ber′ku·lin	Sterile liquid used in diagnosis of tuberculosis infection.	
	tuberculosis tu·ber′ku·lo′sis	Infectious disease marked by formation of tubercles in tissues.	
	tuberculous tu·ber′ku·lus	Affected with tuberculosis.	

tuberculum tu·ber′ku·lum	Nodule or small eminence.	
tuberosity tu′ber·os′i·te	Elevation or protuberance.	
tubocurarine tu′bo·ku·rah′rin	Muscle relaxant, antispasmodic, and convulsant.	
tubular tu′bu·lar	Shaped like a tube; pertaining to a tubule.	
tubule tu′bul	Any small tube or canal.	
tumefaction tu′me·fak′shun	Swelling; condition of being swollen.	
tumor tu′mor	Swelling or morbid enlargement.	
tunic tu′nik	Coat or membrane; covering.	
tunica tu′ni·kah	Membrane covering or lining a body part or organ.	
turbid tur′bid	Cloudy or muddy in appearance.	
turbidity tur·bid′i·te	Cloudiness; disturbance of sediment in a solution.	
turbinate tur′bi·nat	Top-shaped.	
turgescence tur·jes′ens	Distention or swelling of a part.	
turgid tur′jid	Swollen and congested.	
turgor tur′gor	State of being turgid; either normal or other fullness.	

	tussis tus′is	Cough.
	tussive tus′iv	Pertaining to or resulting from a cough.
	twinge twinj	Short, sharp pain.
	twitch twich	Brief contractile response of a skeletal muscle.
	tympanic tim·pan′ik	Pertaining to the tympanum. Includes three auditory ossicles — incus, malleus, and stapes.
	tympanites tim′pah·ni′tez	Gaseous distention of the abdominal cavity.
	tympanitis tim′pah·ni′tis	Inflammation of the tympanic membrane; *otitis media*.
	tympany tim′pah·ne	A tympanitic percussion note.
	typhoid ti′foid	An acute infectious disease caused by *Salmonella typhus*.
	typhus ti′fus	Any of a group of related infectious diseases caused by a species of *Rickettsia*.
	typical tip′i·kal	Possessing distinctive features or symptoms; conforming.

U

	uberous u′ber·us	Prolific.

ulcer ul′ser	A loss of substance on a cutaneous or mucous surface, causing gradual disintegration and necrosis of the tissues.
ulceration ul′ser·a′shun	Formation or development of an ulcer.
ulitis u·li′tis	Inflammation of the gums; gingivitis.
ulna ul′nah	Medial bone of the forearm.
ulnar ul′nar	Pertaining to the ulna.
ultraviolet ul′trah·vi′o·let	Beyond the violet end of the spectrum; said of rays or radiation between the violet and the roentgen rays.
umbilical um·bil′i·kal	Pertaining to the umbilicus.
umbilicus um′bi·li′kus	The navel; site of attachment of the umbilical cord in fetus.
unciform un′si·form	Hooked; shaped like a hook.
unconscious un·kon′shus	Insensible; incapable of responding to sensory stimuli.
undercut un′der·kut	Side cut made in the wall of a cavity to retain the filling in a tooth.
ungual ung′gwal	Relating to the nails.
Unguentine Ung′gwen·ten	Trademark for an ointment used as an antiseptic dressing for minor burns, cuts, bruises, and irritations.

	unguentum ung·gwen′tum	Ointment.
	unguinal ung′gwi·nal	Pertaining to a nail or to the nails.
	unguis ung′gwis	Nail of a finger or toe.
	unrest un·rest′	State of uneasiness or restlessness.
	urea u·re′ah	One of the products of metabolism which is excreted in the urine.
	uremia u·re′me·ah	Toxic condition due to failure of kidneys to excrete urinary constituents from the blood.
	uremic u·re′mik	Pertaining to or characterized by uremia.
	uresis u·re′sis	Passage of urine; urination.
	ureter u·re′ter	Tube which carries urine from the kidney to the bladder.
	ureteral u·re′ter·al	Pertaining to or used upon the ureter.
	ureteritis u′re·ter·i′tis	Inflammation of a ureter.
	ureterogram u·re′ter·o·gram	An X ray of the ureter.
	ureterolithiasis u·re′ter·o·li·thi′- ah·sis	Formation of a stone in the ureter.

	ureterolithotomy u·re′ter·o·li·thot′-o·me	Removal of a calculus from the ureter by incision.
	ureterotomy u′re·ter·ot′o·me	Surgical incision of a ureter.
	urethan u′re·than	Neoplastic suppressant.
	urethra u·re′thrah	Membranous canal through which urine is discharged from the bladder.
	urethral u·re′thral	Pertaining to the urethra.
	urethritis u′re·thri′tis	Inflammation of the urethra.
	urethrocele u·re′thro·sel	Prolapse of the female urethra through the meatus urinarius.
	urinalysis u′ri·nal′i·sis	Chemical or microscopical analysis of urine.
	urinary u′ri·ner′e	Pertaining to the urine; containing or secreting urine.
	urination u′ri·na′shun	Passage of urine.
	urine u′rin	Fluid secreted by kidneys, stored in bladder, and discharged through the urethra.
	uriniferous u′ri·nif′er·us	Conveying urine.
	urocyst u′ro·sist	Urinary bladder.
	urocystitis u′ro·sis·ti′tis	Inflammation of the urinary bladder.

	urodynia u′ro·din′e·ah	Pain accompanying urination.
	urography u·rog′rah·fe	Radiography of part of urinary tract.
	urolith u′ro·lith	Urinary calculus or stone.
	urology u·rol′o·je	Branch of medicine concerned with the urinary tract in both male and female, and with the genital organs in the male.
	uropenia u′ro·pe′ne·ah	Deficiency of urine or urinary secretion.
	urticaria ur′ti·ka′re·ah	Hives; vascular reaction of the skin with elevated patches and itching.
	uterine u′ter·in	Of or pertaining to the uterus.
	uterosacral u′ter·o·sa′kral	Pertaining to the uterus and sacrum.
	uterus u′ter·us	Womb; the hollow muscular organ which is the abode and place of nourishment of embryo and fetus.
	utriculus u·trik′u·lus	Small sac.
	uvea u′ve·ah	Iris; pigmented, vascular layer of the eye.
	uveitis u′ve·i′tis	Inflammation of the uvea.
	uvula u′vu·lah	Small, soft structure hanging from posterior center of the soft palate.

V

vaccination vak′si·na′shun		Injection of vaccine to produce immunity.
vaccine vak′sen		Suspension of attenuated or killed microorganisms for prevention or treatment of infectious diseases.
vacuole vak′u·ol		Minute space or cavity formed in the protoplasm of a cell.
vagina vah·ji′nah		Canal extending between the uterus and the external genitalia.
vaginal vaj′i·nal		Of the nature of a sheath; pertaining to the vagina.
vaginitis vaj′i·ni′tis		Inflammation of the vagina.
vagotomy va·got′o·me		Interruption of the impulses carried by the vagus nerve.
vagus va′gus		Tenth cranial nerve.
valgus val′gus		Bent outward; twisted. (The term is used only in conjunction with the noun it describes.)
valve valv		Fold in a canal or passage permitting fluid to move in one direction.
valvula val′vu·lah		Small valve.
valvular val′vu·lar		Pertaining to, affecting, or of the nature of, a valve.

vapor	Steam, gas, or exhalation.
va′por	
variable	Changing from time to time.
va′re·ah·b′l	Subject to change.
variation	Deviation in character of individual from those typical of the group.
va′re·a′shun	
varicella	Chickenpox.
var′i·sel′ah	
varicocele	Enlarged condition of veins of spermatic cord.
var′i·ko·sel	
varicose	Abnormally swollen; said of a vein.
var′i·kos	
varicosity	Varicose condition.
var′i·kos′i·te	
variola	Smallpox.
vah·ri′o·lah	
varix	Enlarged and twisted vein; pl. *varices*.
var′iks	
vas	Any canal for carrying a fluid. A vessel.
vas	
vascular	Pertaining to or composed of blood vessels.
vas′ku·lar	
vascularization	Development of new blood vessels in a part or tissue.
vas′ku·lar·i·za′shun	
vasectomy	Surgical removal of the ductus deferens or part of it.
vas·ek′to·me	
vasoconstriction	Constriction of the blood vessels.
vas′o·kon·strik′shun	

vasoconstrictor vas′o·kon·strik′tor	Agent causing constriction of the blood vessels.
vasodilatation vas′o·di·lah·ta′-shun	Dilatation of the blood vessels.
vasodilator vas′o·di·lat′or	Agent causing dilation of the blood vessels.
vasomotor vas·o·mo′tor	Agent which affects or regulates the caliber of the blood vessels.
vasotomy vas·ot′o·me	Incision into or cutting of the ductus deferens.
vault vawlt	Domelike or archlike structure.
vectorcardiogram vek′tor·kar′de·o·gram	A graphic record of the magnitude and direction of the electrical forces of the heart.
vehicle ve′hi·k′l	Medium through which an impulse is propagated.
vein van	Vessel through which blood passes from various organs back to the heart.
vellus vel′us	Fine hair over most of the body until puberty.
vena ve′nah	Vessel that conveys blood to or toward the heart; pl. *venae*.
venereal ve·ne′re·al	Due to or propagated by sexual intercourse.
venesection ven′e·sek′shun	Opening of a vein for purpose of withdrawing blood.

venipuncture ven′i·punk′tur	Puncture of a vein.	
venom ven′um	Poison secreted by insect, serpent, or other animal.	
venomoter ve′no·mo′tor	Causing veins to constrict or dilate.	
venostasis ve′no·sta′sis	Compressing veins of extremities to check return flow of the blood.	
venotomy ve·not′o·me	Surgical division or opening of a vein.	
venous ve′nus	Of or pertaining to the veins.	
venter ven′ter	Any belly-shaped part. The fleshy, contractile part of a muscle.	
ventilation ven′ti·la′shun	Act of supplying fresh air.	
ventral ven′tral	Pertaining or related to the belly; anterior aspect of the body.	
ventricle ven′tri·k′l	Small cavity, such as one in brain or heart.	
ventricular ven·trik′u·lar	Pertaining to a ventricle.	
ventriculitis ven·trik′u·li′tis	Inflammation of a ventricle.	
ventriculography ven·trik′u·log′-rah·fe	Roentgenography of the brain, utilizing air or an opaque medium injected into the cerebral ventricles.	

venule ven'ul	Little vein. (Also *venula*.)	
verbal ver'bal	Consisting of words; pertaining to speech.	
vermicular ver·mik'u·lar	Like a worm in shape or appearance.	
vermiform ver'mi·form	Wormshaped, as a vermiform process.	
vermifuge ver'mi·fuj	Agent which expels intestinal worms.	
verruca ver·rooh'kah	Epidermal tumor; wart.	
verrucose ver'oo·kose	Warty; covered with warts.	
version ver'zhun	Change of direction. In obstetrics, change of polarity of fetus.	
vertebra ver'te·brah	Any one of 33 bones of spinal column; pl. *vertebrae*.	
vertex ver'teks	Summit or top.	
vertical ver'ti·kal	Perpendicular to plane of the horizon.	
vertigo ver'ti·go	Sensation as if external world were revolving around the patient or patient revolving in space.	
vesical ves'i·kal	Pertaining to the bladder.	
vesicle ves'i·k'l	Small bladder or sac containing liquid.	

vesicocele ves′i·ko·sel		Hernial protrusion of the bladder.
vesicoclysis ves′i·kok′li·sis		Injection of fluid into the urinary bladder.
vesicotomy ves′i·kot′o·me		Surgical incision into the bladder; cystotomy.
vesicovaginal ves′i·ko·vaj′i·nal		Relating to the urinary bladder and the vagina.
vesicular ve·sik′u·lar		Composed of or relating to small saclike bodies.
vessel ves′el		Any channel for carrying a fluid.
vestibular ves·tib′u·lar		Pertaining to a vestibule.
vestibule ves′ti·bule		Space or cavity at the entrance to a canal.
vestigial ves·tij′e·al		Rudimentary; a remnant, trace, or relic.
veterinarian vet′er·i·nar′e·an		One who practices medicine with animals, especially domesticated animals.
veterinary vet′er·i·nar′e		Pertaining to domestic animals and their diseases.
via vi′ah		Way or passage.
viable vi′ah·b′l		Living; capable of living.
vial vi′al		Small glass bottle.

SHORTHAND DICTIONARY 309

vibration vi·bra′shun	Oscillation; rapid fluctuation to and fro.
vibrissa vi·bris′sah	Hairs within the nose.
vicarious vi·kar′e·us	Acting in place of another or of something else; occurring in an abnormal situation.
vice vice	Defect or blemish. Depravity.
vicious vish′us	Faulty or defective; malformed. Depraved or unruly.
vigil vij′il	Watchful wakefulness.
vigilance vij′i·lans	Morbid wakefulness; watchfulness.
vigor vig′or	A combination of attributes which expresses itself in rapid growth; high fertility.
villus vil′lus	Small vascular protrusion, especially from the free surface of a membrane.
vinculum ving′ku·lum	Band or bandlike structure.
Vinethene Vin′e·then	Trademark for vinyl ether.
vinyl vi′nil	Univalent group from vinyl alcohol.
violation vi′o·la′shun	Rape; act of violating or ravishing.

viomycin vi′o·mi′sin	An antibiotic substance, isolated from culture filtrates of a violet-colored soil microorganism.	
viral vi′ral	Pertaining to, caused by, or of the nature of virus.	
virgin vir′jin	Woman or girl who has not had sexual intercourse.	
virginity vir·jin′i·te	Maidenhood; condition of being a virgin.	
virile vir′il	Peculiar to men or the male sex; possessing masculine traits.	
virility vi·ril′i·te	Possession of normal primary sex characters in one of the male sex.	
virulent vir′u·lent	Exceedingly pathogenic, noxious, or deleterious.	
virus vi′rus	One of a group of pathogenic agents not always visible by ordinary microscopic examination.	
viscera vis′er·ah	Abdominal organs; a descriptive term; pl. of *viscus*.	
visceroptosis vis′er·op·to′sis	Downward displacement of the abdominal organs.	
viscid vis′id	Sticky or glutinous.	
viscous vis′kus	Glutinous; semifluid; sticky.	
viscus vis′kus	Any large interior organ in one of the body's three great cavities, especially the abdomen.	

visible	viz′i·b′l	Capable of being seen; perceptible by sight.
vision	vizh′un	Act or faculty of seeing; sight.
visualize	vizh′u·al·iz	To achieve a complete view of.
vita	vi′tah	Life.
vitality	vi·tal′i·te	Power to grow, develop, and perform living functions; vigor.
vitamin	vi′tah·min	One of the organic compounds present in natural foodstuffs, required for normal metabolic functioning.
vitellus	vi·tel′us	The yolk of an egg or of an ovum.
vitreous	vit′re·us	Semifluid, transparent substance lying between the retina and lens of the eye.
vitritis	vit·ri′tis	Glaucoma.
vocal	vo′kal	Pertaining to the voice.
voice	vois	Sound produced by speech organs and uttered by the mouth.
void	void	To cast out as waste matter.
vola	vo′lah	Hollow or concave surface, like the sole or palm.

volar vo′lar	Pertaining to the palm or sole; flexor surface of forearm or wrist.
voltage vol′tij	Electromotive force measured in volts.
volume vol′um	Measure of quantity of a substance.
voluntary vol′un·tar′e	Accomplished in accordance with the will.
vomer vo′mer	Flat bone that forms inferior and posterior part of the nasal septum.
vomit vom′it	To expel contents of the stomach through the mouth.
vomiting vom′it·ing	Forcible expulsion of contents of stomach through the mouth.
vomitus vom′i·tus	Matter vomited.
voracious vo·ra′shus	Having an insatiable appetite or desire for food.
vortex vor′teks	Whorled arrangement, design, or pattern.
vorticose vor′ti·kose	Having a whorled appearance.
vox voks	Voice.
voyeur voi·yer′	One who obtains sexual gratification from viewing sexual acts of others.
vulnerable vul′ner·ah·b′l	Susceptible to injury.

	vulva vul′vah	Region of external genital organs of a female.
	vulvitis vul·vi′tis	Inflammation of the vulva.

W

	wadding wod′ing	Carded cotton or wool used for surgical dressings; cotton batting.
	waddle wod′l	Clumsy, swaying walk or gait.
	waist waste	Narrowest portion of the trunk above the hips.
	wakefulness wake′ful·nes	Indisposition to sleep; sleeplessness.
	wandering wahn′der·ing	Moving about freely; too loosely attached.
	ward ward	Large hospital room accommodating several patients.
	wart wort	Epidermal tumor of viral origin; verruca.
	wash wosh	Lotion; solution applied to the skin or mucous membrane.
	waste waste	Useless matter eliminated from the body; to become thin.
	wean wean	Discontinue breast feeding of an infant.
	wedge wej	Instrument or material used by dentists to separate adjoining teeth.

weeping weep'ing	Lacrimation. Exudation or leakage of a fluid.
weight wate	Heaviness. The degree to which a body is drawn to the earth by gravity.
wen wen	Sebaceous cyst.
wet-nurse wet'nurs	Woman who nurses child of another at her own breast.
wheal hwele	Circumscribed elevation on skin, either redder or paler than the surrounding skin.
wheeze hweze	Whistling sound made in breathing.
whisper hwis'per	Soft, low, sibilant breathing sound; unvoiced passage of breath through glottis.
whistle hwis'el	Shrill musical sound produced by forcing of air into a cavity.
whoop hoop	Sonorous and convulsive inspiration of whooping cough.
whorl hworl	A spiral turn or twist, such as found in the cochlea of the ear, the arrangement of muscle fibers in the heart, and the ridges in a fingerprint.
will wil	Faculty by which the mind chooses its ends and carries out its purpose.
windburn wind'burn	Injury to skin due to excessive exposure to the wind.

	windchill wind′chil	Loss of heat from bodies subjected to the wind.
	window win′do	Circumscribed opening in a plane surface.
	windpipe wind′pipe	Trachea.
	winking wingk′ing	Quick closing and opening of the eyelids.
	wire wire	Long, circular, flexible structure of metal used in surgery and dentistry.
	withdrawal with·dro′al	Taking away or removal of anything; discontinuance of a drug or medicine.
	womb woom	Uterus.
	wound woond	Injury to the body caused by physical means.
	wrinkles ring′k′lz	Minute crevices or furrows in skin caused by frowning or old age.
	wrist rist	Region of articulation between the forearm and hand.
	wryneck ri′nek	Torticollis.

X

xanthine
zan′theen
An intermediate product in the transformation of adenine and guanine into uric acid. It possesses stimulant properties to muscle tissue, especially that of the heart.

xanthinuria
zan′thin·u′re·ah
Excess of xanthine in the urine.

xanthochromia
zan′tho·kro′me·ah
Any yellowish discoloration of the skin or of the spinal fluid.

xanthoma
zan·tho′mah
New growth of skin occurring as flat or slightly raised patches, yellowish in color, due to deposits of lipids.

xanthosis
zan·tho′sis
Yellowish discoloration or degeneration.

xenomenia
zen′o·me′ne·ah
Vicarious menstruation.

xeroderma
ze′ro·der′mah
Disease marked by roughness and dryness of the skin.

xeromycteria
ze′ro·mik·te′re·ah
Lack of moisture in the nasal passages.

xeronosus
zer·on′o·sus
Condition of dryness of the skin.

xerosis
ze·ro′sis
Abnormal dryness of the eye or skin.

xerostomia
ze′ro·sto′me·ah
Dry mouth; insufficient secretion of saliva.

xerotes
zer′o·teez
Dryness of the body.

| | xerotic
ze·rot′ik | Characterized by xerosis; dry. |

| | xiphoid
zi′foid | Sword-shaped; the xiphoid process. |

| | X ray
eks′ra | Electromagnetic radiation of short wavelength that affects photographic plates as light does. Roentgen ray. |

| | Xylocaine
Zi′lo·kan | Trademark for preparation of lidocaine, a local anesthetic. |

Y

| | yawn
yawn | Deep, involuntary inspiration of air with the mouth wide open. |

| | yaws
yawz | Infection marked by raspberry-like excrescences on face, hands, and feet. |

| | yeast
yeast | Species of *Saccharomyces*, rich in water-soluble vitamins. |

| | yogurt
yo′goort | A form of curdled milk produced by fermentation. |

| | yoke
yok | Connecting structure; a depression or ridge connecting two structures. |

| | yolk
yok | Nutrient part of the ovum. |

| | youth
yooth | Period between childhood and maturity. |

Z

	zaranthan zah·ran′than	Scirrhous condition of the breast.
	Zephiran Zef′i·ran	Trademark for preparation of benzalkonium, an antiseptic.
	zero ze′ro	Absence of quantity; 32 degrees below ice point on Fahrenheit scale; ice point of Celsius and Reamur scales.
	zinc zingk	A blue-white metal, many of whose salts are used in medicine as astringents or antiseptics.
	zona zo′nah	An encircling region or area. Belt or girdle; pl. *zonae*.
	zone zone	Encircling region or area. Any area with specific characteristics or boundary.
	zonule zon′ul	Small band.
	zoophobia zo′o·fo′be·ah	Morbid fear of animals.
	zoster zos′ter	Acute inflammatory disease, consisting of grouped vesicles along the course of a cutaneous nerve.
	zygoma zi·go′mah	Cheekbone; the nalar bone.
	zygote zi′got	Fertilized ovum; cell formed by union of two gametes.
	zymosis zi·mo′sis	Fermentation; infectious or contagious disease.

Reference

Section

COMBINING FORMS

Reference Section

COMBINING FORMS

The following combining forms occur most frequently in medical records and medical literature. The hyphen appended to a combining form indicates that it is the beginning element of a compound. If the hyphen precedes the combining form, the combining form is the ending element of a compound.

Combining Form	Meaning
a-	negative prefix: lack; without
ab-	away from
abdomin-	abdomen
ac-	to; toward
acet-	vinegar
acid-	sour
acou-	hear
acr-	peak; extremity
act-	do; drive; act
actin-	ray; radius
acu-	needle
ad-; -ad	to; toward; relating to
aden-	gland
adip-	fat
aer-	air
aesthe-	feel; perceive
af-	to; toward
ag-	to; toward
-agogue	leading; inducing
-agra	seizure; acute pain
-al	pertaining to
alb-	white
alg-	pain
all-	other; different
alve(ol)-	trough; channel; cavity
amb-	both; both sides
ambly-	dull; faint
amph(i)-	both; doubly; around
amyl-	starch
an-	negative prefix: lack; without
ana-	up; positive; again
ancyl-	crooked; looped
andr-	man; masculine
anemo-	wind
angi-	vessel
anis-	unequal; dissimilar
ankyl-	crooked; looped
ant(i)-	against; counter
ante-	before (time or place)
antr-	cavern
ap-	negative prefix: lack; without
-aph	sense of touch
ap(o)-	away from; detached
arachn-	spider
arch-	beginning; first; original
archo-	rectum; anus
arter(i)-	artery
arthr-	joint
articul-	joint
as-	negative prefix: lack; without
asthen-	weak
-asis	action
at-	negative prefix: lack; without
-atic	of
atel-	imperfect; incomplete

SHORTHAND DICTIONARY

Combining Form	Meaning	Combining Form	Meaning
atmo-	steam; vapor	carp-	wrist
atret-	imperforate; closed	cat(a)-	down; negative
audi-	hear	caud-	tail
aur-	ear	cav-	hollow
aut-	self	cec-	blind
aux-	increase	cel(e)-; -cele	tumor; hernia
ax(i), (on)-	axis	cell-	room; cell
ba-	go; walk; stand	cen-	common
bacill-	small staff; rod	cent-	hundred (metric system)
bacter-	small staff; rod	cente-	puncture; perforation
ball-	throw	-centesis	
bar-	weight; pressure	centr-	point; center
bary-	heavy; difficult	cephal-	head
bi-	(a) two; twice; (b) life	-cephal(ia), (ous), (us)	type or condition of head
bil(i)-	bile		
-biosis	way of	cept-	take; receive
-blast; blast-	cell; bud; child; formative element	cer-	wax
		cerebr-	cerebrum
blenn-	mucus	cervic-	neck
blep-	look; see	cheil-; chil-	lip
blephar-	eyelid	cheir-	hand
bol-	throw	-cide	killer; killing
brachi-	arm	chir-	hand
brachy-	short	chlor-	green
brady-	slow	chol-	bile
breph-	embryo; fetus	chondr-	cartilage
brevo-	short	chord-	string; cord
brom-	stench	chori-	protective fetal membrane
bronch-	windpipe		
bry-	full of life	chro-; chromat-	color
bucc-	cheek		
cac-	bad; abnormal	chron-	time
calc-	(a) stone; (b) heel	chy-	pour
calor-	heat	chyl-	juice; chyle
cancr-; chancr-	crab; cancer	-cid(e)	cut; kill
		cili-	eyelid
capit-	head	cine-; kine-	move
caps-	container	circum-	around
carbo(n)-	coal; charcoal	clas-	break
carcin-	crab; cancer	-clas(ia), (is), (ty)	breaking off or up
cardi-	heart		
-cardia	heart		

324 GREGG MEDICAL

Combining Form	Meaning	Combining Form	Meaning
clin-	bend; incline; make lie down	deci-	one-tenth (metric system)
clus-	shut	demi-	half
co-	together; with	dendr-	tree
cocc-	seed; pill	dent-	tooth
-cocc(us), (ic), (al)	bacteria	derm(at)-	skin
		-derm(a)	skin; covering
col-	together; with	desm-	band; ligament
colon-	lower intestine	deut(er)-	second; secondary
colp-	hollow; vagina	dextr-	right-hand; to the right
com-	together; with	di-	two
con-	together; with	di(a)-	through; apart
contra-	against; counter	didym-	twin
copra-	feces; excrement	digit-	finger; toe
cor-	(a) little image; (b) together; with	dipl-	double
		dis-	apart; away from
corpor-	body	disc-	disk
cortic-	bark; rind	dors-	back
cost-	rib	drom-	course
cox-	hip joint	-ducent	lead; conduct
crani-	skull	duct-	lead; conduct
creat-	meat; flesh	dur-	hard
-crescent	grow	dynam(i)-	power
cret-	distinguish; separate off	dys-	bad; difficult; improper
crin-	distinguish; separate off	e-	out from; beyond
crur-	shin; leg	ec-	out of
cry(m)-	cold	ect-	outside; situated on
crypt-	hid; conceal	-ectomy	cutting out
-cul(e), (a), (um), (us)	diminutive	electr-	amber
		em-	in, on
cult-	tend; cultivate	-emia	condition or disease of blood
cune-	wedge		
cut-	skin	end-; ent-	inside; within
cyan-	blue	enter-	intestine
cycl-	circle; cycle	ep(i)-	upon; after; in addition
cyst-	bladder	erg-	work; deed; energy
cyt-; -cyte	cell	erot-	love; sexual desire
dacry-	tear	erythr-	red
dactyle-	finger; toe; digit	-esis	process or action
-dactyl(ia), (y)	condition of fingers or toes	eso-	inside
		esthe-	feel; perceive
de-	down from	eu-	good; normal
dec-	ten (metric system)	-eurysis	operation of dilating

Combining Form	Meaning	Combining Form	Meaning
ex-	out of	gland-	acorn; gland
exo-	outside	-glia	glue
extra-	outside of; beyond	gli-	glue; gluey substance
faci-	face	gloss-	tongue
-facient	make	-glossia	condition of tongue
fasci-	band	glott-	tongue; language
febr-	fever	gluc-	sweet
-ferent	bear; carry	glutin-	glue
-ferous	bearing; producing	glyc(y)-	sweet
ferr-	iron	gnath-	jaw
fibr-	fibre	gno-	know; discern
-fication	making; causing	gon-	become; be produced; originate
fil-	thread		
fiss-	split	grad-; -grad	walk; take steps
flagell-	whip	-gram	write; record
flav-	yellow	gran-	grain; particle
-flect	bend; divert	graph-; -graph	write; record; something written
-flex	bend; divert		
flu(x)-	flow	grav-	heavy
for-	door; opening	gyn(ec)-	woman; wife
-form	shape	gyr-	ring; circle
fract-	break	haem(at)-	blood
front-	forehead; front	hapl-	simple; single
-fug(e)	flee; avoid	hapt-	touch
funct-	perform; serve; function	heb-	puberty; pubes
fund-	pour	hect-	hundred (metric system)
fus-	pour	helc-	sore; ulcer
galact-	milk	heli-	sun
gam-	marriage; reproductive union	hem(at)-	blood
		hemi-	half
gangli-	swelling; plexus	hepat(ic)-	liver
gaster-	stomach; abdomen	hept-	seven
-gastric	pertaining to stomach	hered-	heir
gelat-	freeze; congeal	heter-	other; different
gemin-	twin; double	hex(a)-	(a) six; (b) have; hold; be
gen-; -gen	become; product; originate	hidr-	sweat
		hier-	sacrum
-genic;	producing; generating	hipp-	horse
-genous		hist-	web; tissue
ger-	old age; aged	hod-	road; path
germ-	bud; early growth	hol-	whole; entire
gest-	bear; carry	hom(e)-	common; same

Combining Form	Meaning
horm-	impetus; impulse
hydr-	water
hyp(o)-	under; below
hyper-	above; beyond; extreme
hypn-	sleep
hypo-	under; below
hyster-	womb
-ia	state; condition
iatr-	physician
-iatrics	treatment of disease
-id	belong to; connected with
idi-	peculiar; separate
il-	negative prefix
ile-	ileum; portion of intestines
ili-	lower abdomen; ilius
im-	negative prefix
in-	(a) in; on; (b) negative prefix
infra-	beneath
insul-	island
inter-	among; between
intra-	inside; within
intro-	into; within
ir-	negative prefix
irid-	rainbow
is-	equal; same; alike
isch-	suppression
ischi-	hip; haunch
-ism	state; condition; practice
-itis	inflammation
jejun-	hungry
junct-	join
juxta-	near
kary-; cary-	nut; kernel; nucleus
kerat-; cerat-	horn
kil-	one thousand (metric system)
kine-; cine-	move
-kinesis	physical movement
labi-	lip

Combining Form	Meaning
lacrim-	tear
lact-	milk
lal-	talk; babble
lamin-	thin flat plate or layer
lapar-	flank; loin
laryng-	windpipe
lat-	bear; carry
later-	side
lep-	take; seize
-leps(ia), (is), (y)	seizure; violent attack
leuk-; leuc-	white
lien-	spleen
lig-	tie; bind
lingu-	tongue
lip-	fat
lith-; -lith	stone
loc-	place
log-	speak; express thought
-logy	science; study of
lumb-	loin
lute-	yellow
ly-	loose; dissolve
lymph-	water
-lysis	loosening; setting free
lyso-	loosen; dissolve
macr-	long; large
mal-	bad; abnormal
malac-	soft
mamm-	breast
mammill-	nipple
man-	hand
mani-; -mania	mental aberration
mast-; -mastia	breast; breast condition
medi-	middle
mega(l)-; -megalia	great; large
mel-	limb; member
melan-	black; dark
-melia	condition of limbs

Combining Form	Meaning	Combining Form	Meaning
men-	month	ocul-	eye
mening-	membrane	od(e)-; -ode	road; path
ment-	mind	odont-;	tooth
mer-; -mere	part; portion	-odent	
mes-	middle	-odontia	form or condition of teeth
met(a)-	after; beyond; accompanying	-odyn;	pain; distress
-meter	measurement; instrument	-odynia	
metr-	(a) measure; (b) womb	-oid	form
-metry	act of measuring	-ol; ole-	oil
micr-	small	olig-	few; small
mill-	one thousand (metric system)	-oma	tumor; swelling
		omphal-	navel
-mittent	send	onc-	tumor; mass; swelling
mne-	remember	onych-	claw; nail
mon-	single; only; sole	oo-	egg
morph-;	form; shape	oophor-	ovary
-morph		op-	see
mot-	move	-opia; -opy	eye defect
my-	muscle	ophthalm-	eye
-myces	fungus	or-	mouth
myc(et)-	fungus	orb-	circle; sphere
myel-	marrow	orchi(d)-	testicle
myring-	eardrum	organ-	implement; instrument
myx-	mucus; slime	orrh-	serum
narc-	numbness	orth-	straight; right; normal
nas-	nose	oscill-	backward and forward motion
ne-	new; young		
necr-	corpse	-osis	state; condition; action
nephr-	kidney	osm-	odor; smell
neur-; -neure	nerve; nerve cell	oss-	bone
-neuria	state of nervous system	ost(e)-	bone
noct-	night	ot-	ear
nom-	law, custom	-otic	of; affected with
non-	(a) negative; not; (b) nine	ov-	egg
nos-	disease	oxy-	sharp; sour; oxygen
nucle-	kernel	pachy(n)-	thick; dense
nutri-	nourish	pag-	fix; make fast
nyct-	night	-para;	bring forth; productive
ob-	against; toward	-parous	
oc-	against; toward	par(a)-	beside; beyond
oct-	eight	par(t)-	bear; give birth to

Combining Form	Meaning
path-; -path	sickness; that which one undergoes
path(is), (y),-(ic)	feeling; suffering; disease
pec-	fix; make fast
ped-	child
pedi-; -pede; -ped	foot
pell-	skin
-pellent	drive
pen-; -penia	need; lack
pend-	hang down
pent(a)-	five
peps-; pept-	digest
per-	through
peri-	around
pet-	seek; tend toward
-petal	directed; moving toward
pex-; -pexy	fix; make fast
pha-	say; speak
phac-; phak-	lentil; lens
phag-; -phag(e), (ia), (ic)	eat; destroy
pharmac-	drug
pharyng-	throat
phen-; phan-	show; be seen
pher-	bear; support
phil-	like; loving
phleb-	vein
phleg-; phlog-	burn; inflame
phob-; -phobia	fear; dread
phon-; -phon(e), (y)	sound
phor-; -phoria	bear; support
phos-; phot-	light
phrag-; phrax-	fence; wall off

Combining Form	Meaning
phren-; -phrenia	mind; midriff
phthi-	decay; waste away
phy-	beget; bring forth
phyl-	tribe; kind
-phyll	leaf
phylac-	guard
phys(a), (e)-	blow; inflate
pil-	hair
pituit-	phlegm; rheum
placent-	cake
plas-	mold; shape
-plas(ia), (is), (y)	change; development
plasty-; -plasty	broad; flat; forming
-pleg(ia), (y)	paralysis; stroke
plet-	fill
pleur-	rib; side
-plexy	stroke
pne-; -pnea	breathing
pneum(at)-	breath; air
pneumo(n)-	lung
pod-; -pod(e), (y)	foot
poie-	make; produce
pol-	axis of a sphere
poly-	much; many
pont-	bridge
por-	(a) passage; (b) callus
posit-	put; place
post-	after; behind (time or place)
pre-	before (time or place)
pro-	before (time or place)
proct-	anus; rectum
pros-	forward; anterior
prosop-	face
prot-	first
pseud-	false; spurious
psych-	mind; soul
pto-; -ptosis	fall

Combining Form	Meaning	Combining Form	Meaning
pub(er)-	adult	sept-	(a) fence; wall off; (b) seven
pulmo(n)-	lung		
puls-	drive	ser-	whey; watery substance
punct-	prick; puncture	sex-	six
pur-	pus	sial-	saliva
py-	pus	sin-	hollow; fold
pyel-	trough; basin	-sis	state; condition
pykn-	thick; compact	sit-	food
pyl-	door; orifice	skia-	shadow
pyle-	portal vein	solut-; -solvent	loose; dissolve; set free
pyr-	fire; heat		
pyret-	fever	som(e), (at)-; -some	body
quadr-	four		
quinque-	five	somn-	sleep
rachi-	spine	span-	scanty; scarce
radi-	ray	spas-	draw; pull
re-	back; again	spectr-	appearance
ren-	kidney	sperm(at)-	seed
ret-	net	spers-	scatter
retro-	backwards	sphen-	wedge
rhag-	break; burst	spher-	ball
rhaph-	suture	sphygm-	pulse
rhe-	flow	spin-	spine
rhex-	break; burst	spirat-	breath
rhin-	nose	splanchn-	viscera; entrails
rot-	wheel	splen-	spleen
-rrhag(e), (ia), (ic), (y)	bursting forth; excessive flow	spondyl-	vertebra; spinal column
		spor-	seed
-rrhaphy	suture of; sewing	squam-	scale
salping-	tube	sta-	stop; make stand
sanguin-	blood	stal-	send
sarc-	flesh	staphyl-	bunch of grapes
schis-	split	stear-; steat-	fat; tallow
schiz-	division; cleavage	sten-	narrow; compressed
scler-	hard	ster-	solid
scop-; -scope	look at; observe	sterc-	feces
-scopy	act of examining	stern-	breastbone
sect-	cut	steth-	chest; breast
semi-	half	sthen-	strength
sens-	feel; perceive	stol-	send
sep-	rot; decay	stom(at)-	mouth; orifice

Combining Form	Meaning	Combining Form	Meaning
-stomy	creating opening into	-tomy	operation of cutting
strep(h)-	twist	ton-	tension; tone
strict-	draw tight; compress	top-	place; location
struct-	pile up	tors-	twist
sub-	under; below	tox-	arrow poison
suf-	under; below	trache-	windpipe
sup-	under; below	trachel-	neck
super-	above; beyond; extreme	tract	draw; drag
supra-	above; over; upon	traumat-	wound
sy(n), (l), (m)-	with; together	trich-	hair
		trip-	rub
tac-	order; arrange	-tripsis	rubbing; friction
tach-	speed	trop-; -trop(e), (ic)	turn; react
tachy-	swift; rapid		
tact-	touch	troph-	nurture
-tasia	dilatation; stretching	tub-	oviduct; tube
tel-	end	tuber-	swelling; node
tele-	at a distance	tympan-	middle ear
tempor-	time; timely; temple	typh-	vapor; fever; stupor
teno(onto)-	tendon; tight stretched band	typhl-	blind
		tyro-	cheese
tens-	stretch	ultra-	beyond; excessive, extreme
ter-	three		
test-	testicle	uran-	roof of mouth; palate
tetra-	four	-uria	condition of urine
the-	put; place	ur(in)-	urine
thec-	case; repository	uter-	womb
thel-	nipple	vacc-	cow
therap-; -therapy	treatment	vagin-	sheath
		vas-	vessel
therm-; -thermy	heat	ven-	vein
		ventr-	belly; abdomen
thi-	sulfur	vert-; vers-	turn
thorac-	chest	vesic-	bladder
thromb-	lump; clot	vit-	life
thym-; -thymia	spirit; condition of mind	vuls-	pull; twitch
		xanth-	yellow; blond
thyr-	shield	xen-	strange; foreign
tme-	cut	xer-	dry
toc-	childbirth; labor	zo-	life
tom-; -tome	cut; instrument for cutting	zyg-	yoke; union
		zym-	ferment

Reference

DRUG QUICK REFERENCE

Section

DRUG QUICK REFERENCE

The drug products listed below account for two-thirds of all prescriptions written. The latest information on approximately 2,500 drug products is available in the current edition of *Physician's Desk Reference* (PDR).

Achrocidin
Achromycin
Achromycin V
Actifed
Actifed-C Expectorant
Afrin
Aldactazide
Aldomet
Aldoril
Alertonic
Ambenyl Expectorant
Amcill
*Ampicillin
Antivert
Aristocort
Arlidin
Artane
Atarax
Atromid-S
Azo Gantrisin

Benadryl
Bendectin
Bentyl Hydrochloride
    w/Phenobarbital
Benylin Expectorant
Biphetamine-T
Butazolidin
Butazolidin alka
Butisol Sodium

Carbrital
Chlor-Trimeton
*Chloral Hydrate
Combid
Compazine
Compocillin-VK
Cordran
Cortisporin
Coumadin
C-Quens
Crystodigin
Cytomel

Darvon

Darvon Compound
Darvon Compound-65
DBI-TD
Decadron
Declomycin
Demerol
Desbutal
Dexamyl
Dexedrine
Diabinese
*Digitoxin
*Digoxin
Dilantin
Dimetane
Dimetapp
Disophrol
Diupres
Diuril
Donnatal
Doriden
Dramamine
Drixoral
Dyazide

Elavil
Empirin Compound
    w/Codeine Phosphate
Enovid-E
Equagesic
Equanil
Erythrocin
*Erythromycin
Esidrix
Eskatrol

Feosol
Fiorinal
Furadantin

Gantanol
Gantrisin

Hydrodiuril
Hydropres
Hygroton

Ilosone
Indocin
Isordil
Isopto-Carpine

Kenalog

Lanoxin
Lasix
Librax
Librium
Lincocin
Lomotil

Maalox
Macrodantin
Mandelamine
Medrol
Mellaril
*Meprobamate
Miltown
Mycolog
Mycostatin
Mylanta
Mysteclin-F

Naldecon
Nembutal
NeoDecadron
Neosporin
*Nicotinic Acid
*Nitroglycerin
Noctec
Norgesic
Noringe
Norlestrin-21
Novahistine
Novahistine DH

Omnipen
Oracon
Orinase
Ornade
Ortho-Novum
Ortho-Novum 1/50-21

Ortho-Novum 1/80-21
Ovral
Ovulen-28
Ovulen-21

Parafon Forte
*Paregoric
Pediamycin
Penbritin
*Penicillin G,
    Potassium
Pentids
Pen-Vee K
Percodan
Periactin
Peritrate
Peritrate Sustained
    Action
Phenaphen w/Codeine
Phenergan
Phenergan Expectorant
Phenergan Expectorant
    w/Codeine
Phenergan VC Expecto-
    rant w/Codeine
*Phenobarbital
Placidyl
Polaramine
Polycillin

*Prednisone
Preludin
Premarin
Principen
Pro-Banthine
Proloid
Pyribenzamine

Quāālude
*Quinidine

Regroton
Renese
*Reserpine
Ritalin

Salutensin
Seconal Sodium
Ser-Ap-Es
Serax
Serpasil
Sinequan
Stelazine
Sudafed
Sumycin
Synalar
Synthroid

Talwin
Tandearil

Tedral
Teldrin
Temaril
Tenuate
Terramycin
*Tetracycline
Tetrex
Tetrex APC w/Bristamin
Tofranil
Thorazine
*Thyroid
Tigan
Tinactin
Triaminic
Triavil
Tuinal
Tuss-Ornade
Tylenol

Valisone
Valium
Vasodilan
V-Cillin-K
Vibramycin
Vioform-Hydro-
    cortisone
Vistaril

Zyloprim

*Generically-written drugs

Reference

જ
ABBREVIATIONS

Section

ABBREVIATIONS

Variations in the use of periods and capitalization with medical abbreviations are widespread.

Abbreviation	Meaning
A_1	Aortic first sound
A_2	Aortic second sound
$A_2 > P_2$	Aortic second sound equals pulmonic second sound
$A_2 > P_2$	Aortic second sound is greater than pulmonic second sound
$A_2 < P_2$	Aortic second sound is less than pulmonic second sound
A.A.	Achievement age; Alcoholics Anonymous
$\overline{AA}$, $\overline{aa}$	Of each
aa	Equal parts of each
abdom.	Abdomen
a.c.	Before meals (*ante cibum*)
ACC	Anodal closure contraction
Acc.	Accommodation
A.C.D.	Absolute cardiac dullness
ACE	Adrenocortical extract
ACTH	Adrenocorticotropic hormone
A.D.	Right ear (*auris dextra*)
ad; admov	Add; let there be added
ad lib	At pleasure; as much as needed
Adv.	Against
A-G	Albumin-globulin ratio
Alt. dieb.	Every other day
Alt. hor.	Every other hour
alt. noct.	Every other night
A.P.	Anterior pituitary; axiopupal; antero-posterior
a.p.	Before dinner (*ante prandium*)
Aq.	Water
Aq. dest.	Distilled water
ARD.	Acute respiratory disease
As.	Astigmatism; arsenic
A.S.	Left ear
A.V.	Atrioventricular; arteriovenous
Av.	Average; avoirdupois
AZT.	Aschheim-Zondek test
BBT.	Basal body temperature
b.d.	Twice a day
BFP.	Biologic false positive reaction
Bib.	Drink
b.i.d.	Twice a day (*bis in die*)

Abbreviation	Meaning
B.M.	Seawater bath; bowel movement
B.M.R.	Basal metabolic rate
B.P.	Blood pressure
b.p.	Boiling point
b.r.p.	Bathroom privileges
B.S.	Breath sounds; blood sugar
B.T.U., B.Th.U.	British thermal unit
BUN.	Blood urea nitrogen
B.V.	Vapor bath
C.	Centigrade; cathode; carbon
C	Precordial lead (electrocardiogram)
CA.	Chronological age
Ca.	Calcium; cathode; carcinoma
Cath.	Cathartic
c.b.c.	Complete blood count
C.C.	Chief complaint
cc.	Cubic centimeter
cf.	Compare; bring together
Cg.; Cgm.	Centigram
C.m.	Tomorrow morning
cm.	Centimeter
cm.^{3}	Cubic centimeter
c.mm.	Cubic millimeter
C.M.R.	Cerebral metabolic rate
c.m.s.	To be taken tomorrow morning
C.n.	Tomorrow night
C.N.S.	Central nervous system
c.n.s.	To be taken tomorrow night
Collut.	Mouthwash
Collyr.	Eyewash
Cont. rem.	Let the medicine be continued
Coq.	Boil
c.p.m.	Counts per minute
C.S.	Current strength
Cs.	Conscious; consciousness
C.S.F.	Cerebrospinal fluid
C.S.M.	Cerebrospinal meningitis
CST.	Convulsive shock therapy
cu. mm	Cubic millimeter
c.v.	Tomorrow evening (*cras vespere*)
C.V.A.	Costrovertebral angle
Cx.	Convex
D.	Dose; distal; dorsal; duration
D. & C.	Dilation and curettement

Abbreviation	Meaning
D-1 to D-12	Dorsal vertebra (1 to 12)
D.A.H.	Disordered action of heart
D.D.S.	Doctor of Dental Surgery
DDT	Chlorophenothane
Decub.	Lying down
de d. in d.	From day to day
Deg.	Degeneration; degree
dg.	Decigram
Dieb. alt.	On alternate days
Dieb. tert	Every third day
dil.	Dilute; dissolve
dim.	One half
Dir. prop.	With proper direction
DMF.	Accumulated dental caries
D.O.A.	Dead on arrival
D.O.B.	Date of birth
D.P.	Pulses (*dorsalis pedis*)
dr.	Dram
D.T.	Distance test
D.T.D.	Give of such a dose
D.T.P.	Distal tingling on percussion
DTR's	Deep tendon reflexes
D.V.M.	Doctor of Veterinary Medicine
E.C.T.	Electric convulsive therapy
E.D.	Effective dose
EEG	Electroencephalogram
EENT	Ears, eyes, nose, and throat
e.g.	For example (*exempli gratis*)
E.j.	Elbow jerk
EKG	Electrocardiogram
EKY	Electrokymogram
EMG	Electromyogram
emul.	Emulsion
E.N.T.	Ear, nose, and throat
E.O.M.	Extraocular movements
EPR	Electrophrenic respiration
E.R.	External resistance
ERG	Electroretinogram
ESP	Extrasensory perception
E.S.T.	Electroshock therapy
F.	Fahrenheit; field of vision; formula
F & R	Force and rhythm
FB	Fingerbreadth
FBS	Fasting blood sugar
F.D.	Focal distance; fatal dose
F.D.A.; F.D.P.; F.D.T.	Positions of the fetus
Feb. dur.	While the fever lasts
F.F.A.	Free fatty acids
F.H.	Family history
fl.; fld.	Fluid
F.L.A.; F.L.P.; F.L.T.	Positions of the fetus
F.M.	Make a mixture
F.U.O.	Fever of undetermined origin
G.; gm.	Gram
G.B.	Gallbladder
G.I.	Gastrointestinal; globin insulin
gl.	Gland
G.P.	General practitioner
gr.	Grain
G.S.W.	Gunshot wound
gt.; gtt.	Drop
g.u.	Genitourinary
H.	Hydrogen; hour
Hb.	Hemoglobin
HCT.	Hematocrit
H.D.	Hearing distance
H.d.	At bedtime
H.D.L.W.	Distance watch is heard by left ear
H.D.R.W.	Distance watch is heard by right ear
H.E.D.	Unit of roentgen-ray dosage
Hg.; Hgb	Hemoglobin
H_2O	Water
Hor. decub.	At bedtime
Hor. interm.	At the intermediate hours
hpf	High-power field
H.S.	House surgeon
h.s.	At bedtime
ht.	Height
IC	Inspiratory capacity
ID	Inside diameter; infective dose
Id.	Same
I.H.	Infectious hepatitis
I.M.	Intramuscularly
in.	Inch
in d.	Daily
IOP	Intraocular pressure
I.Q.	Intelligence quotient
I.R.	Internal resistance
I.S.	Intercostal space
I.V.	Intravenously
I.V.T.	Intravenous transfusion
k.	Constant
kg.	Kilogram
Kg.-m	Kilogram-meter
k.k.	Knee kicks (knee jerks)
K.U.B.	Kidney, ureter, and bladder
kv.	Kilovolt

Abbreviation	Meaning
kvp.	Kilovolt peak
kw.	Kilowatt
kw.-hr.	Kilowatt-hour
L.	Liter; lumbar
L. and A.	Light and accommodation
lb.	Pound
L.E.	Left eye
L.F.A.; L.F.P.; L.F.T.	Positions of the fetus
L.L.L.	Left lower lobe (lungs)
L.M.A.; L.M.P.; L.M.T.	Positions of the fetus
L.M.P.	Last menstrual period
L.O.A.; L.O.P.; L.O.T.	Positions of the fetus
L.P.	Lumbar puncture; linguopulpal
lpf.	Low power field
L.S.D.	Hallucinogenic
L.S.A.; L.S.P.; L.S.T.	Positions of the fetus
L.U.L.	Left upper lobe (lungs)
M.	Meter; mixture; muscle
m.	Meter
M.A.	Mental age
ma.	Milliampere
m.b.	Mix well
mc.	Millicurie
mcg.	Microgram
MCV	Mean corpuscular volume
M.D.	Doctor of Medicine
M.D.A.; M.D.P.; M.D.T.	Positions of the fetus
M.E.D.	Minimal effective dose
mEq.	Milliequivalent
M. et sig.	Mix and write a label
mg.	Milligram
M.I.D.	Minimum infective dose
ml.	Milliliter
M.M.	Mucous membranes
mM.	Millimole
mm.	Millimeter; muscles
Mol. wt.	Molecular weight
mp.	Melting point
mr.	Milliroentgen
M.S.L.	Midsternal line
M.V.	Veterinary physician
mv.	Millivolt
My.	Myopia
N.A.D.	No appreciable disease
nn.	Nerves
N.N.D.	New and nonofficial drugs
Noct. maneq.	At night and in the morning
N.T.P.	Normal temperature and pressure
Nv.	Naked vision
N.Y.D.	Not yet diagnosed
O.	Oxygen; eye
OB	Obstetrics
O.D.	Right eye; outside diameter
O.D.A.; O.D.P.; O.D.T.	Positions of the fetus
O.L.	Left eye
O.L.A.; O.L.P.; O.L.T.	Positions of the fetus
o.m.	Every morning
Omn. bih.	Every two hours
Omn. noct.	Every night
o.n.	Every night
OPD	Outpatient department
o.s.	Left eye
OTD	Organ tolerance radiation dose
O.U.	Both eyes
Ov.	Egg
oz.	Ounce
P.	Pulse; pupil
P_2	Pulmonic second sound
P & A	Percussion and auscultation
P.A.	Pulpo-axial
P. ae.	In equal parts
Part. aeq.	Equal parts
Part. vic.	In divided doses
P.C.	Avoirdupois weight
p.c.	After meals
pcpt.	Perception
Pcs.	Preconscious
P.E.	Physical examination
P.E.G.	Pneumoencephalography
P.H.	Past history
pH	Hydrogen ion concentration
P.L.	Light perception
P.M.I.	Point of maximal impulse
P.N.	Percussion note
P.O.	By mouth; orally
P. rat. aetat.	In proportion to age
p.r.n.	According as circumstances may require
p.s.	Per second
p.s.i.	Pounds per square inch

Abbreviation	Meaning	Abbreviation	Meaning
P.S.P.	Phenolsulfonphthalein	S.N.	According to nature
pt.	Pint	S.O.S.	If it is necessary
PTA; PTC	Blood coagulation factors	sp. gr.	Specific gravity
Px.	Pneumothorax	SQ	Subcutaneous
q.d.	Every day	S.R.	Sedimentation rate
q.h.	Every hour	ss.	One half
q.i.d.	Four times a day	s.s.	Soapsuds
q.l.	As much as desired	S.T.S.	Serologic test for syphilis
q.p.	At will	su.	Let him take
q.q.h.	Every four hours	s.v.	Alcoholic spirit
q.s.	Sufficient quantity	T.	Temperature; thoracic
q. suff.	As much as suffices	t.	Temporal
qt.	Quart	T.A.;	
q.v.	As much as you please	T.A.T.	Toxin-antitoxin
R.	Respiration; roentgen	TB	Tuberculosis
℞	Take	T.b.	Tubercle bacillus
rbc.	Red blood cell; red blood count	t.d.s.	Three times a day
		Te.	Tetanus
R.E.	Right eye	t.i.d.	Three times a day
R.E.G.	Radioencephalogram	TLC	Tender loving care; total lung capacity
Reg. umb.	Umbilical region		
Rep.	Repeat	tr.	Tincture
R.F.A.;		T.S.	Test solution
R.F.P.;		T.U.	Toxic unit
R.F.T.	Positions of the fetus	TV	Tuberculin volutin
R.L.L.	Right lower lobe (lungs)	U.	Unit
R.M.	Respiratory movement	U.S.P.;	
R.M.A.;		U.S.	
R.M.P.;		Phar.	United States Pharmacopoeia
R.M.T.	Positions of the fetus	Ut dict.	As directed
R.M.L.	Right middle lobe (lungs)	Utend.	To be used
R.N.	Registered Nurse	V.	Vision
R.O.A.;		v.	Vein; volt
R.O.P.;		Va.	Visual acuity
R.O.T.	Positions of the fetus	V. & T.	Volume and tension (pulse)
rpm	Revolutions per minute	V.C.	Acuity of color vision
R.Q.	Respiratory quotient	V.D.	Venereal disease
R.S.A.;		V.D.G.	Venereal disease—gonorrhea
R.S.P.;		V.D.S.	Venereal disease—syphilis
R.S.T.	Positions of the fetus	Ves.	Bladder
R.T.	Reading test	V.F.	Vocal fremitus
R.U.L.	Right upper lobe (lung)	V.f.	Field of vision
S.	Sacral; sulfur	V.M.	Voltmeter
s.c.	Subcutaneously	v.s.	Vibration seconds
S.D.A.;		vv.	Veins
S.D.P.;		V.W.	Vessel wall
S.D.T.	Positions of the fetus	wbc.	White blood cell; white blood cell count
S.E.	Standard error		
Sed.	Stool	W.R.	Wassermann reaction
Seq. luce.	The following day	Wt.	Weight
S.I.	Soluble insulin	X.	Unit of x-ray dosage
Si op. sit.	If it is necessary	z.	Symbol for atomic number
S.L.A.;		Z.Z.'Z."	Increasing degrees of contraction
S.L.P.;			
S.L.T.	Positions of the fetus		